JOB SEARCH AND CAREER BUILDING WORKBOOK

2016 EDITION:

MASTERING THE ART OF PERSONAL BRANDING ONLINE

2016 EDITION

BY JASON MCDONALD, PH.D.

© 2016, JM INTERNET GROUP

https://www.jm-seo.org/

Tel. 800-298-4065

For Hannah (Carnegie Mellon University, Class of 2017)

For Ava (Class of 2025)

For my bank account, so I can afford college and grad school for these two girls.

This page intentionally left blank

(Deal with it)

Table of Contents

0
INTRODUCTION

Welcome to the *Job Search and Career Building Workbook*!

Get ready to -

- Have some **fun**.
- Learn how to identify the **connection points** between the career of your dreams and the hard-headed demands of today's economy.
- Understand (and get in front of) the online **employee discovery paths** used by hiring managers.
- Influence Google, Bing, and Yahoo to optimize your **online personal brand** image.
- Master **social media marketing** via Facebook, LinkedIn, Twitter, & other key platforms for job search and career building.
- Create a step-by-step **Personal Branding Plan**.

Fully up-to-date for 2016, this Workbook teaches you a new way to go about **job hunting, personal branding,** and **career building** that leverages the New World Order of Google search and social media networking via LinkedIn, Twitter, Facebook, and other social media sites.

After all -

- It's a **New World** of Google searches, background checks, and online reputation management.
- It's a **New World** in which employers research potential hires via social media sites like Facebook, Twitter, Blogs, YouTube, Instagram, Google+, and, of course, LinkedIn.

- It's a **New World** in which old-school job search books and college career centers are nearly as obsolete as the paper Yellow Pages and physical libraries of the pre-Internet era.

» THE NEW WORLD OF JOB SEARCH AND CAREER BUILDING

In short, it's a **New World** when it comes to job search and career building!

How so? Let's step back, and discuss the New World of job search and career building circa 2016 / 2017.

First some questions:

> *When was the last time you visited your local bookstore? What about your local record shop? Or pulled out a paper map while driving around in your car?*
>
> *And if or when you are searching for a job, when was the last time you printed out your resume on physical paper, typed up an envelope, licked a postage stamp, and sauntered down to your local post office to mail it off via the USPS?*

My bet was it was a *long time ago, in a galaxy far, far away* (if you even remember).

Yes, bookstores still exist (*a few anyway*); yes, record stores still exist (*I believe Rasputin's is the last one here in the San Francisco Bay Area*); and yes, you can go to your local Auto Association or gas station and get a paper map (*at least I think so*).

And yes, the United States Postal Service still operates, although according to Amy Poehler in the movie, "Sisters," they have stopped making stamps.

IT'S A NEW (SOCIAL) WORLD

Most of you – whether you're a twenty-one-year-old job seeker, a thirty-four-year-old office worker ready to make her first major career move, a forty-one-year-old mom reentering the workforce, or a fifty-seven-year-old married white male building his resume as insurance against a lay off – most of you, I bet, use the Internet in your daily lives. Like several times a day: perhaps tens or even hundreds of times a day. It could be on your phone, on your PC or MAC, on your tablet, or even on your TV.

It's a New World, isn't it?

And yet –

When it comes to job search and career building, here's what we have to work with:

- Antiquated **job search books** that treat Google, LinkedIn, blogging, Facebook, Twitter, and other social sites as afterthoughts to job search rather than the core mechanisms by which jobs are discovered and gained in 2016.
- 1970s-based, **hippie job advice** of "following your dreams" rather than practical advice for today's tough job market to not only follow your career dreams but also research what job skills are sufficiently in demand to pay your rent or mortgage as well as provide a decent living.
- College or university **career centers** that (like the college library) haven't quite figured out their role in the Internet era, yet lumber on as the central strategy of career building at even the most prestigious universities in America.

Moreover, those of us actively seeking a job or already in the workforce may realize that we have to network both "in the office" as well as "online," but the "online" part can be pretty mysterious!

In addition, there is a cacophony of contradictory job advice on the blogosphere as well as a multitude of job listing sites like *Indeed*, *CareerBuilder*, or *Craigslist* that create an atmosphere of information overload.

Where can you find the best job listings?

How can you leverage social media to alert friends, family, and colleagues to your career goals, since it's often not "what you know" but "who you know" that gets you the job or promotion?

How can you network online?

How can you network online even to people whom you do not formally know?

How can you use LinkedIn for effective job-searching? What about Facebook, Twitter, or even Instagram?

How can you position your online identity so that potential employers see "the best possible you?"

How can you remove or at least push down negative information such as that drunken selfie you took at the frat party last year?

How can you build and nurture your online personal brand so that your online personal brand looks as awesome as your mom, girlfriend or boyfriend thinks you are?

Ok, maybe not your boyfriend or girlfriend, but at least your Mom?

How can you leverage the Internet to make jobs come to you, to get hiring managers to crawl to you on their knees begging you to come in for an interview, and convince financial executives to OK your outrageous Great Gatsby salary requests?

This, my friend, is what the *Job Search and Career Building Workbook* is all about: a way to make the Internet your new best friend when it comes to your job search or long term career goals.

» A New Way: The Job Search and Career Building Workbook

It's time for something **new**, something **different**, something that explains the New World of job search and career building, something that helps you leverage the Internet to find a job, get an interview, and build your career.

It's time for the *Job Search and Career Building Workbook*, a Workbook that:

- Helps you identify connection points between your **dream career** and the **market demands** of hiring managers today.
- Encourages you to brainstorm and write a **personal branding statement** so you know not only what specific type of job you want but what type of personal brand image you want to project online.
- Identifies the **employee discovery paths** used by hiring managers to find and sort through job candidates in your chosen field.

- Explains **SEO** (*Search Engine Optimization*), the art and science of getting your resume, your website, your blog to the top of Google, job search sites, and social media sites like LinkedIn.
- And, teaches you the art and science of **social media marketing** – how to use LinkedIn, Facebook, Twitter, and other platforms to position your personal brand in front of the people who can recommend, vet, or even hire you for the next great job.

It's time for the *Job Search and Career Building Workbook*, a practical guide that:

- Assigns you practical **TODOS** to get your job search off the ground.
- Gives you practical **worksheets** to help you step-by-step, milestone-by-milestone.
- And, points to **free Internet tools** to assist you in making keyword discovery, SEO, blogging, and social media as easy as possible for job search and career building.

▶▶ WHO IS THIS WORKBOOK FOR?

This book is for the following types of people:

- The person who is *just beginning his career* or *job search.*
- The person who is looking to *grow her career* with an eye towards the future.
- The person (such as a CEO, entrepreneur, or small business owner) for whom their *personal brand* is their business identity.
- And, the person who realizes that he or she knows enough to know *"it's all online"* and also knows enough to know he or she doesn't really know *"how the game is played."*

This Workbook is for:

- **High school** or **college graduates** just beginning their job search.

- **People already in the workforce** who are interested in making a job or career change and want to improve their online image.
- And, **folks** who realize that their **personal brand online** is the foundation of a successful long-term **career strategy** in today's Internet age.

Whether you're twenty-two, or forty-three, if you're looking for a job or building a career, this Workbook is for you.

≫ A Caveat: What this Book is Not

This book is *not,* however, the be-all and end-all of job search and career building guides.

First and foremost, it focuses almost exclusively on ***online*** opportunities. Unlike a traditional book such as *What Color is Your Parachute, Knock 'Em Dead,* or *Getting from College to Career*, it assumes you've already decided on an industry or career to pursue. It assumes you know what job you want (at least at a basic level). It assumes you've already written a great resume. It assumes you are doing the basics of checking job listing sites online (or that fun-filled career center on campus), networking with friends, family, and contacts "in the real world," and generally keeping your eyes and ears open to job search and career advancement opportunities.

(Check the companion *Job Search and Career-building Resource Book* for my list of recommended books on jobs and careers).

It is not a **substitute** to the above. It is a **complement**: it works in conjunction with guides such as *What Color is Your Parachute* or *Knock 'Em Dead*, the practical advice from career centers at colleges or universities, or (gasp!) the advice of friends, family, and colleagues as to how to get a job or build your career.

This Workbook, in summary, is not a complete guide to job searching and career building, nor is it a touchy-feely guide to figuring out your "dream job" or how to "do what you love."

It is, however, a complete guide to *online personal branding*, and to *online opportunities* to get a job or grow a career.

≫ Google Thyself (or LinkedIn Thyself, Facebook Thyself, etc.)

Before we dive in, let's step back for a moment and consider the big picture of your personal information on the Internet. We'll start with your last date, or your last job interview, or the last person who wanted to take your daughter out on a date if you're old and paranoid like I am.

Did you Google him (or her)? Did you check him or her out on Facebook? On LinkedIn, or Twitter?

Have you ever Googled yourself? Your Mom or Dad? Your ex (or current) boyfriend or girlfriend, husband or wife?

Have you ever checked out another person on Facebook, LinkedIn, or other social media site?

Have you ever perused someone's Facebook Profile, Twitter account, or Instagram activity and judged them as "dumb" and not worthy of a friendship or other form of outreach?

Researched the good, the bad, the ugly, and the embarrassing that constitutes their "digital footprint" online?

Done any (or all) of the above for yourself?

The answer is probably yes.

Employers Do It, Too

Do you think that potential *employers* are Googling potential *employees*? Checking them out on Facebook, LinkedIn, Twitter, and the gang? Pre-judging employees based on Google searches, Facebook or LinkedIn activity or other online activities to rule them "in" or "out" for a job interview or promotion? Not to mention using the Internet to find job candidates in the first place?

You betcha.

And, in terms of your own personal brand image, what do they find?

Is it positive, negative, embarrassing, or a little bit of both?

Even worse – is it non-existent?

(Don't worry – we're going to fix any of these issues).

Stop for a moment to look at the problem from an employer's perspective. When an employer hires an employee, it's a big risk. That employee might work out great, or he might be a disaster – anything from a thief to a lazy jerk to a social media loose cannon who posts inappropriate things about work to Twitter and causes problems for the company.

Employers, you see, **are paranoid**: they want to make very sure that the persons they hire are *trustworthy, loyal, helpful, friendly, courteous, kind, obedient, cheerful, thrifty, brave, clean* and *reverant* (to quote from the Boy Scout Law).

Hiring Managers Google Potential Employees and Also Use Social Media

According to a May, 2015, study from CareerBuilder, fifty-two percent of employers use social network sites to research job candidates, and in industries such as technology, that number climbs to seventy-six percent! (Source: CareerBuilder, http://jmlinks.com/8f, browsed: 1/20/2016).

EVERYONE GOOGLES EVERYONE

Here's the reality. Hiring managers, CEOs, and other small or large business employers will probably "Google you" or "LinkedIn you" or "Twitter you" before, during, and after a job interview. They'll use LinkedIn, Google, Instagram or other social sites to identify job candidates, and they'll probably use them to "background check" you. This is more likely in technology jobs, of course, and even more likely for more serious, sensitive jobs (like cybersecurity), and it's more common in places like the San Francisco Bay Area than it is in places like Biloxi, Mississippi.

No offense to Biloxi (great town, by the way).

But as goes San Francisco, so goes the nation. Also, as goes the technology sector so goes retail (46%), healthcare (49%), manufacturing (49%), professional and business services (54%), sales (61%), and financial services (64%).

(Those percentages are the percent of hiring managers who did online research via social networking sites on potential job candidates).

So, let's get back to you.

- Google yourself.
- Check yourself out on Facebook.
- Investigate your personal brand image on LinkedIn.
- Research yourself on Twitter.
- Ponder yourself on Pinterest.

You get the picture.

The State of Your Personal Brand Image Online

What do you find? Do you exist at all? What personal brand image do you project? Do you seem *friendly, trustworthy, skilled,* an *expert*? Or do you look *trashy, immature, ignorant, untrustworthy,* or even a security risk?

Your first **TODO** is to Google yourself (or LinkedIn, or Facebook yourself, etc.) and turn the tables: if you were a hiring manager would you:

- *Reach out to you for a first interview?*
- *Call you in for a second interview?*
- *Believe what you said on your resume, or in the interview?*
- *Hire you?*

Don't freak out by what you find (or what you don't). Don't freak out if you are totally invisible online, as you can recover.

This book is about **improving** your personal brand image online. The first step is to recognize just how important your online image is to your job search and career objectives. Related to this, you should audit your online personal brand, which might range from terrible to neutral to really fantastic; or, you might find that you are essentially "invisible" and "unfindable" online. The second step is to learn what personal branding is (in detail), and identify people to emulate and platforms like blogging, Facebook, and LinkedIn that can help you build a brand. In short, you need to learn the rules of the game. The third and fourth steps are to deploy your brand online (via content marketing and platforms like LinkedIn, Facebook, and Twitter), and to build a personal job / career networking system so that the employers and jobs come *begging* to you. You want a blog strong enough, a Facebook page powerful enough, and a LinkedIn profile interesting enough so that friends, colleagues, headhunters, employers, and even people you don't know see you as a strong job candidate and even extend offers for career advancement.

Let's get started!

» How Does This Workbook Work?

This Workbook starts with an overview to the New World of job search and career building. It then helps you to brainstorm and write a **Personal Branding Statement** or **PBS**. Next, it turns to discovery paths and possible job / career keywords including reputation management issues. It takes on content marketing, blogs, personal websites and the basics of SEO (Search Engine Optimization), which is how you make your content rank well on Google, Bing, and Yahoo. Then, it proceeds social media platform by platform (Facebook, LinkedIn, Twitter, etc.), explaining how they can be used for career building and personal branding. Finally, it sums up with metrics to measure your progress as well as the big picture of creating a **Personal Branding Plan**.

Along the way, I'll identify my favorite online tips and tools, while the companion *Job Search and Career-building Resource Book* will provide an even more comprehensive list of amazing, fun, and free online tools to make your job search and career process easier than ever. In addition, throughout the book I will point to *worksheets* (which my students call "Jason as therapist") to help you step-by-step through the major topics.

It's all very hands on. After all, this book can show you what you need to do to succeed in job hunting and career-building but you have to actually go out and do it.

The *Job Search and Career-building Workbook,* in short, is not only about **explaining** the New World online of career building. It is also about **teaching you how** to succeed in it: how to brainstorm, build, and maintain your personal brand image online. And, it's about **motivating** you to actually go out and do it.

Table of Contents

≫ REGISTER YOUR WORKBOOK

Unlike old-school print books, this Workbook is built to work *with* the Internet. Throughout, it has links to websites, resources, and tools that can help you with your career building objectives. Accordingly, if you register, you get access to a cornucopia of free goodies such as the companion *Job Search and Career-building Resource Book* (hundreds of free tools and free resources!), plus my **worksheets** to help you build out your personal branding plan.

Here's how to register your copy of this Workbook:

1. Go to https://jm-seo.org/workbooks
2. Click on *Job Search and Career-building*.
3. Use this password: **careers2016**
4. Next, simply follow the links for the tools, resource book, and worksheets referenced herein (as well as other free goodies)

≫ MEET THE AUTHOR

My name is Jason McDonald, and I have been active on the Internet since 1994 (*having invented the Internet along with Al Gore*) and taught SEO, AdWords, Social Media, and

Personal Branding since 2009 – online, at Stanford University Continuing Studies, at both AcademyX and the Bay Area Video Coalition in San Francisco, at workshops, and in corporate trainings across these United States. I love figuring out how things work, and I love teaching others!

This book grew out of a popular course I teach at Stanford Continuing Studies on "Personal Branding."

Online personal branding for job search and career building is an endeavor that I understand, and I want to empower you to understand it as well. Indeed, this book is a bit of a personal mission for me. Not only do I have two daughters (for whom I passionately desire the best of career paths, not to mention husbands), but I myself have struggled with my job search and career goals.

My Own Twisted Career Path

Originally, I was set to be a professor, majoring in Russian Studies and Economics at Harvard in 1985. I ultimately earned a Ph.D. in political science from the University of California, Berkeley, only to have that career fall out from under me (between the fall of the Soviet Union and the deep recession of 1992). Unemployment followed, and for a short while, I sold computers (for $1000 a month) and lived in a tiny studio in Oakland, California (that job ended when the company went bankrupt). I proceeded to work in print media (until leaving to start my own Internet media company), which was very profitable until the Great Recession of 2008 killed off that business. After some unemployment and soul-searching, I inventoried my skills and my desires, and soon, I was moved over to a career in teaching and consulting in Internet marketing – namely, SEO, social media marketing, and Google AdWords.

You see, I have had zigs and zags, unemployment and prosperity as nearly everyone does in today's tough economy.

Terrible Career Counseling

I had terrible career counseling in High School and College. I wish someone had sat me down as a High School senior or college freshman and worked with me on job search and career goals.

I wish someone had sat down with me and asked what was my "dream job" and how to create the infrastructure to make that job happen.

No one did - not in High School, not in college, and certainly not in Graduate School- and it took me more than twenty years to get to the career I have and love today: teaching, writing books on, and consulting on all facets of Internet marketing. (My next career move: *science fiction novelist* – stay tuned).

MY HOPE: BETTER CAREER COUNSELING

My hope for this book? To help people like you figure out their career options and make those dreams come true by leveraging the power of the Internet. I want you to have one foot on the ground (*practical realities*), with your head in the clouds (*your dreams*), and *your eye on success*: the step-by-step process of building an online brand powerful enough to help you with job search and career-building.

▶▶ SPREAD THE WORD: WRITE A REVIEW & GET A FREE eBOOK!

If you like this Workbook, please take a moment to write an honest review on Amazon.com. *If you hate the book, feel free to trash it in an online review. Either way, I appreciate your honest feedback.*

At any rate, here is my special offer for those lively enough to write a review of the book–

1. Write your **honest review** on Amazon.com.
2. **Contact** me via https://www.jm-seo.org/contact or call 800-298-4065 and let me know your review is up.
3. Include your **email address** and **website URL**, and any quick questions you have about it.
4. I will send you a **free** review copy of one of my other eBooks which cover AdWords, SEO, and Social Media Marketing.

This offer is limited to the first 100 reviewers, and only for reviewers who have purchased a paid copy of the book. You may be required to show proof of purchase and the birth certificate of your first born child, cat, or goldfish. If you don't have a child, cat, or goldfish, you may be required to prove telepathically that you bought the book. Lol.

>> QUESTIONS AND MORE INFORMATION

Curious about me? Find out more at https://www.jasonmcdonald.org/ or at my corporate website https://www.jm-seo.org/. Or just call 800-298-4065, say something flattering, and my secretary will put you through. *(Like I have a secretary! Just call if you have something to ask or say).*

I **encourage** my students to ask questions! If you have questions, submit them via https://www.jm-seo.org/contact/. There are two sorts of questions: ones that I know instantly, for which I'll zip you an email answer right away, and ones I do not know instantly, in which case, I will investigate and we'll figure out the answer together.

As a teacher, I learn most from my students. So please don't be shy!

>> COPYRIGHT AND DISCLAIMER

Uh! Legal stuff! Get ready for some fun:

This is a completely **unofficial** Workbook to online personal branding, job search, and career building. No one at Facebook, LinkedIn, Twitter, YouTube, Pinterest, Yelp, Google, Instagram, Snapchat or any other social media company has endorsed this Workbook, nor has anyone affiliated with any of those companies been involved in the production of this Workbook.

That's a *good thing*. This Workbook is **independent**. My aim is to "tell it as I see it," giving you no-nonsense information on how to succeed at social media marketing.

In addition, please note the following:

- All trademarks are the property of their respective owners. I have no relationship with nor endorsement from the mark holders. Any use of their marks is so I can provide information to you.

- Any reference to or citation of third party products or services whether for Facebook, LinkedIn, Twitter, Yelp, Google / Google+, Yahoo, Bing, Instagram, Pinterest, YouTube, or other businesses, search engines, or social media platforms, should not be construed as an endorsement of those products or services or related tools, nor as a warranty as to their effectiveness or compliance with the terms of service with any search engine or social media platform.

» ACKNOWLEDGEMENTS

No man is an island. I would like to thank my beloved wife, Noelle Decambra, for helping me hand-in-hand as the world's best moderator for our online classes, and as my personal cheerleader in the book industry. Gloria McNabb has done her usual tireless job as first assistant, including updating this edition as well the companion *Job Search and Career-building Workbook*. Thanks to Sonia Patwardhan, who helped with final edits, and gave very insightful suggestions to make this a stronger book.

And, again, a huge thank you to my students – online, in San Francisco, and at Stanford Continuing Studies. You challenge me, you inspire me, and you motivate me!

I would also like to thank my black Labrador retriever, Buddy, for countless walks and games of fetch, during which I refined my ideas about online career building and about life.

This book is dedicated to my daughters, Hannah (*Carnegie Mellon University, 2017*) and Ava (*future college graduate, 2025*). May your careers be as exciting and rewarding as mine (*but with less twists and turns, more money, and fewer difficult people*).

1
QUO VADIS?

This Workbook is a journey. A journey that you shall take, one for which I am only a guide. My mission is to help you **discover yourself** (at least in a job search or career-building sense), to **explain new opportunities** presented by the **Internet**, and to point out **techniques**, **tips**, and **tools** which will allow you to leverage the Internet to advance your career.

It is your journey. I can only pose the questions.

Quo vadis?

Quo vadis, of course, is Latin for "Where are you going?"

If you and I are lucky, we might get sixty or eighty or perhaps one hundred years on this earth. For many of us (certainly for me), we'll spend a lot of our time "at work," and that work can be a *means to an end* (e.g., money to support yourself or your family) or an *end in itself* (an expression of your hopes, desires, and dreams – what Max Weber, the German sociologist, called your *vocation*).

I don't want to be overly dramatic, but I want you to start this journey by asking you to ask yourself, "*Quo vadis?*" or "Where are you going?"

Extreme No.1: Dreamy-eyed Optimism

There are two extreme answers to this question. On the one hand, the dreamy-eyed writers of the 1960s and 1970s acted "as if" you could search your soul and find a career that was truly meaningful, in disregard of the ways of the world. Those were wonderful times, the 1960s and 1970s, times when America and the West were at their zenith, and times in which the harsh realities of the world of work were not so apparent.

It's no accident that the psychedelic music of the Beatles, the Doors, and other bands came from that time. *Quo vadis,* in those times was meant to be an emotional and spiritual question.

A job or career was meant to be first and foremost, *meaningful.*

In those days, you could "parachute" into your job; the economy was that good.

> *"Do what you love,"* it was said, *"and the rest will follow."*

Extreme No. 2: Stony-eyed Cynicism

Queue the "Great Recession" of 2008-2009, and the pendulum really began to swing back the other direction, the direction of cynical practicality. (This trend probably started as early as the 1980s). On the other hand, compared with a spiritual job quest, job seekers and career builders were advised to focus, first and foremost, on the needs of employers and on the skills desired by the marketplace.

> *"Get a job, any job."*

The spiritual quest of getting a job, short, was trampled under the *Quo vadis* of the practical need to support oneself and one's family financially.

The problem, here, is that a career with no meaning is an invitation for an emotional and spiritual breakdown. If, ultimately, you have no meaning in your job or career, you had better hope that something else – family, fame, religion, mountaineering, you name it – will provide sustenance for the soul. The trick is to find a balance between the "job of your dreams" and a job that "pays the rent."

Quo vadis? My Hope for You

I am a believer, however, that there is a Middle Path. A path somewhere between dreamy-eyed idealism and stony-eyed cynicism. There are careers out there that are meaningful, on the one hand, and financially rewarding on the other.

You just have to find them. And get them.

My hope in this Workbook is to help you to find your own Middle Path: a path, between the unreasonable optimism of the 1960s and 1970s and the harsh cynicism of the 1980s and 2000s.

Quo vadis?

What kind of career do you want? Or better put, what kind of career path can you create that, on the one hand, satisfies the human need for meaningful work and, on the other hand, satisfies the practical reality of putting food on your table?

It is your journey. I can only pose the questions.

Let's get started!

1

THE *INTERNET YOU*

The Internet most of us know today began in 1995 when restrictions on commercial usage were lifted by the US government. Many of you reading this book might not have even been born in 1995, and the rest might have just been toddlers or teenagers. It's hard to imagine a world in which job-searching and career-building were activities carried out face-to-face, over the telephone, via newspaper want ads, and with paper resumes. Believe me, just as the world of the 1950s sitcom "I Love Lucy" once existed, the pre-Internet world did, too!

Yes, people actually survived without Google, Facebook, or mobile phones!

And yes they actually searched for, and got, jobs and advanced their careers – all without email!

Yes, people actually mailed letters with stamps!

Internet 2.0: The Rise of Social Media

Everyone knows that by the year 2000 or even earlier, if you wanted to find a job or move to a better one, you did most of this searching (if not all of it) on the Internet. Sites like Craig's List, Indeed, CareerBuilder, and Monster all became the de facto way that employers advertised jobs, and job seekers looked for jobs. The want ads went the way of the Dodo bird.

The next wave, often called Internet 2.0, has been the wave of social media. What's new and still not fully understood is how the **rise of social media** has created new pitfalls and new opportunities for job seekers.

Social media sites like Twitter, Facebook, and LinkedIn as well as Google search vis-à-vis blogs or personal websites have radically altered the career landscape, yet few people have yet to take advantage of this new world order. LinkedIn, for example, was founded in 2002, while blog software programs like WordPress (begun in 2003), along with social media sites like Flickr and Facebook (both founded in 2004), began to transform the Internet at about the same time. From 2003 onward, in sum, the Social Media revolution changed the Internet from a place where big organizations – companies, non-profits, governmental entities, and job boards like Craigslist or Monster.com – were dominant to a place where ordinary individuals started to have an "Internet presence" in the form of LinkedIn profiles, posts to Twitter or Facebook, reviews on Yelp, and personal blogs on sites like WordPress.com and Blogger.com.

Social media along with easy personal websites or blogs meant that ordinary people began to have a visible presence on the Internet.

Social media has created new ways to search for a job and to position oneself as the ideal job candidate.

Social media has created new ways for people to network online with friends, friends of friends, contacts, and contacts of contacts to find a job or advance their career.

And, this trend is accelerating!

Suddenly, you, I, and the girl next door can have a blog, post to Facebook, create a profile on LinkedIn, and share news on Twitter. The New Social World Online has arrived and along with it a new **Internet You**. (*The mobile phone revolution has just accelerated this trend*).

The Good News: We're All Still Figuring This Out

While it might seem like social media has been around for a long time, the span of time from about 1999 (when Google was founded) or 2004 (when Facebook was founded) to 2016 is nearly nothing: 17 or 12 short years. In the span of human history, this is shorter than the blink of an eye. This means –

- Many people (employers, employees, competitors to you in the job search and career advancement struggle) remain in a state of **denial**, as if Google will go away, LinkedIn will just languish, Twitter will terminate, and Facebook will fade. *These folks are doing nothing.*

- Many others recognize the importance of search and social media to job search and career-building but don't know where to begin or what to do. *These folks are doing little or nothing like deer in the headlights.*
- A few smart people are realizing that they can leverage Google search vis-à-vis blogging and social media networks like LinkedIn, Twitter, and Facebook as well as Instagram, Pinterest, and others via social media marketing to vastly improve their online brand image AND to network with friends, family, and friends of friends to accelerate their careers. *These folks are reading this book (**that would be you**).*

The **good news**, in short, is that you can be a pioneer in this new way to search for a job and build your career. Moreover, because few people are really doing it or doing it well, you'll have a leg up in the job market. That, my friend, is what is called a *competitive advantage*.

Why You Care About The New *Internet You*

Why do you as a job seeker care about the Internet or social media?

Here's why you care: The Internet and social media have created an incredible *opportunity* (as well as *danger*) for you as a job-seeker or career-builder.

The *opportunity* is to create and nurture a powerful online personal brand image, an **Internet You**.

The **Internet You** is the sum total of everything available about you online: your blog posts, including articles or posts by others about you, your Facebook, Twitter, LinkedIn, Instagram, YouTube and other social media texts, pictures, videos, public records, and posts of all types— essentially everything about you available at the click of a mouse.

Why you care about this phenomenon is that the "**Internet You**" has arguably become as important, if not more important, than the "**Real World You**" to your career goals.

Opportunities and Dangers

Opportunity #1 is the **Internet You**, a publicity machine nurturing your amazing personal brand image online. Related to this profound opportunity is **Opportunity #2**, using social media sites like Facebook, LinkedIn, and Twitter to **network** with friends, family, and coworkers as well as friends of friends, friends of coworkers, and colleagues of colleagues. Social media, in short, takes the "schmoozing" and "networking" of looking for a job or a promotion to a whole new level. This "networking online" is an incredible complement to Opportunity #1.

But, where there are opportunities, there are **dangers**.

The big danger is "negative publicity." The *Internet You* might be nonexistent online, or (even worse) the *Internet You* might be downright embarrassing, showcasing negative acts or attitudes that will eliminate you from a job or career advancement, before you even know it exists.

Ironically, to a hiring manager, headhunter, or employer, the *Internet You that exists online may be more real than the actual physical you*! After all, a new employer hardly knows you, and in many cases even a boss, coworker, or promotion decision maker may not truly "know" you. What they read on your blog, see on your LinkedIn Profile or Twitter account may be more real than the physical You that they might meet in person.

> The *Internet You*, in short, has become as important **if not more important** to the job search and career-building process than the *Real World You*.

A hiring manager today, for example, can Google you, research you on LinkedIn, Facebook, and Twitter, before ever reaching out to you for a face-to-face interview. She might exclude you completely based on what she finds; or she might find information so compelling, that you not only get the job interview, but get the job as well. The *You* that meets her face-to-face in a job interview might be less important than the *Internet You* that exists online! And all of this goes ditto for friends, family, colleagues and other connections who can help or hurt you in your search for a job or a career promotion.

In this Chapter, we are going to ponder at a conceptual level, how the *Internet You* creates both *dangers* and *opportunities* for anyone who wants to get a job, or advance a career.

Let's get started!

To Do List:

>> Understand Cher, Lady Gaga, and the *Internet You*

>> Google Thyself (and Facebook and Twitter Thyself, too)

>> >> Deliverable: A Summary of the *Internet You*

>> UNDERSTAND CHER, LADY GAGA, AND THE *INTERNET YOU*

Let me tell you a story about my Mom. Through various twists and turns (largely because of their children), my Mom had an opportunity to meet the rock superstar known simply as "Cher." My Mom has a story about being with Cher in a limousine in Washington, D.C., and as they were driving along, they chatted mom-to-mom about their mutual joys and worries as moms. Cher, my Mom reminds me, is "just another mom" when it comes to her son, Chaz Bono. What's interesting is that as the limousine pulled up to the rally that they were attending, Cher stopped my Mom and informed her that she had to "become Cher."

She apparently took a deep breath, and "became" Cher before exiting the limo to her adoring fans. She changed from just another mom to "Cher the superstar" right before my Mom's eyes. My Mom literally witnessed the transformation from the "private" Cher to the "public" Cher – a transformation most of us will never see.

We Don't Really Know Cher

The point of this is to realize that you and I don't really "know" Cher. We know Cher's **public image** – an image from movies, from TV, from albums, and of course from the Internet. The "private Cher" isn't the same as the "public Cher," and the *Cher as a mom* certainly isn't the same as the *Cher on the Internet*.

CHER HAS A *PUBLIC YOU*

AND A *PRIVATE YOU*

(AND SO DO YOU)

Cher, like most pop stars, has a cultivated image for the viewing public, and that's quite different from her private reality as a regular person.

For those of you under thirty, let's use a different example: **Lady Gaga**, arguably the latest in a long line of music personalities who create, cultivate, and project a unique public persona in a very imaginative and provocative way. Known for her insane over-the-top outfits, Lady Gaga has cultivated an incredible public persona and has become a master of the use of Internet publicity. For example, Lady Gaga short-circuited Amazon's servers when she released her 2011 album, *Born this Way*, for 99¢ on Amazon, simply by sharing that fact on social media.

Here's the rub. Most of us do not know the "private" *Stefani Joanne Angelina Germanotta* (her real name) but rather know only the "public" Lady Gaga; we know only the *public image* that she has meticulously cultivated as an over-the-top advocate of self-empowerment.

> *Like Cher before her, Lady Gaga has a Public You and a Private You.*
>
> *And as with Cher before her, we really only know the "public image" of Lady Gaga.*

Step back from Lady Gaga's music for a moment, and ponder the phenomenon of a certain Ms. Germanotta who through luck and skill has become a household name. Ponder for a moment, her personal brand image: over the top rock star, insanely talented performer, singer of the national anthem at the Super Bowl, advocate for rape victims, and more.

> **Who is more real**: *Lady Gaga* or *Stefani Joanne Angelina Germanotta?*

To you or me, it's Lady Gaga, isn't it? Like Cher before her, Lady Gaga has succeeded in projecting something more powerful and probably different than her "real" personality; a *Public You.*

Andy Warhol

The intellectual who first seemed to notice that the *"Public You"* and the *"Private You"* were not the same thing was none other than the artist Andy Warhol. If you've ever heard the phrase "Fifteen minutes of fame," you've ingested an idea meme from this Pittsburgh-born, insanely great artist of Pop. Andy Warhol's art is all about the difference between *Public* and *Private Yous*, between the *illusion* that was *Elvis* and the *person* that was *Elvis Presley*.

> *The point of this short discussion about Cher, Lady Gaga, and Andy Warhol is to get you to realize that you – too – now have a* **Private You**, *a* **Public You**, *and an* **Internet You**.

Let me repeat that: You, too, have a *Private You*, a *Public You*, and an *Internet You*.

Whether you like it or not.

Let me repeat that, too: *whether you like it or not.*

The Private You, the Public You, and the Internet You

Now, it can be confusing to think of yourself as having multiple personalities or Yous. But it makes sense if you pause to think about it, and if you clearly separate the *Private You* from the *Public You* from the *Internet You*. They're interrelated but conceptually different.

Here's a summary:

> ***Private You.*** The *You* you are to yourself, your boyfriend, girlfriend or partner, perhaps to your parents (*or not*), perhaps to your children (*or not*), the *you* that is more than who you are in a business or career sense, the you with a personality, hopes, secrets, and dreams, which are much more than your career goals. In some situations, this *Private You* may be a *You* that you'd really prefer to keep private; a *You* you would prefer that coworkers or employers never meet, or perhaps do not meet until they have become comfortable with you, and you with them.

Public You. The *You* out in public, perhaps at work, in a job interview, at school or in other public situations. You wear different clothes when you go to a job interview, different language talking to your boss than your best friends, and differently when at work with supervisors and coworkers. Hopefully, the *Public You*, therefore, is a *you* that is always gracious, intelligent, polite and tolerant towards other people, cultures, ideas, etc. However, in some situations and for some people, the *Public You* can be quite disgraceful and something better forgotten. The *Public You* might also encompass your credit score, the *You* in public records such as records of bankruptcies or arrests, etc.

The point is that the *Public You* and the *Private You* are not the same thing.

The point is that the *Public You* may be helping (or hurting) your search for a better job or a career promotion.

The point is that many of us don't even realize we have a *Public You*, and we recklessly ignore it (or worse, damage it) and our job / career search.

The point is that you're beginning to see that how you act in public (at a job, in Church, in a store, with friends or coworkers) creates a public brand image that can either help, or hurt, your career.

The ***Internet You.*** The *You* you are on the Internet. For most of us, what's available about us online is the *Public You* that a hiring manager or employer, would encounter when doing research about you online. **The Internet You, in short, is the Public You when online**.

The Internet You is simply that image that you have created (whether you like it or not) on Twitter, Facebook, Instagram, on your blog, through posts by you, through posts or articles about you, through your credit score (oops), criminal record (oops, oops), etc.

The *Internet You*, in short, is what's visible about you online.

Examples of the Different Yous

I know it can seem *complicated* to understand these different "Yous," but it is very *important*. The irony is that most people do not realize that they are creating a public image every day in how they behave at work, how they speak with friends, family, or coworkers, in the ideas that they share, in the things that they condemn or endorse, in the clothes that they wear, in the tattoos that they have (or do not have), in the car that they drive, in the neatness (or lack thereof) of their office desk. In addition, they are doing this both "in the real world" at work and "in the virtual world" online.

Let's look at some examples of the different Yous.

IMPORTANT: In each case we are looking at You not from your own internal perspective but *from the external perspective of others.*

Private You. This would be how you appear to persons who know you well such as your spouse, your Mom, or your good friends. You might, for example, be a huge fan of the *Big Bang Theory* on Television, or you might be a profoundly religious person in the evangelical Christian faith, or you might be a radical Libertarian. You might be terribly afraid of spiders, or unable to swim, or you might be fantastic at playing the harmonica. Perhaps you drink too much, or smoke marijuana recreationally, user terrible curse words, or have really bad relations with your parents. Perhaps you struggle with depression, or perhaps you are an extrovert at a party but an introvert at work. *These aspects of your personality might be known only to your close friends or family, but not to your employers or coworkers.*

Public You. This would be how you appear to persons out in public. For example, if you go to Church, you might dress up or avoid using curse words. Or, if you are at a neighborhood cook out, you might not share your political belief in Libertarianism or your thoughts on American politics whether Democrat, Republican, Libertarian, or Communist. Or, if you are at work, you might wear better clothes, use more respectful language, or refrain from sharing how your religious beliefs contradict the lifestyles and behaviors of others. You might, for example, have a really terrible fight with your spouse yet go to work and act "as if" nothing has happened vis-à-vis your boss or coworkers. This goes double for your behavior at a job interview. *These aspects of your personality are visible to people in public.*

Internet You. This would be how you appear to others online. For example, friends who do not know you in a truly private sense might form opinions of you on Facebook based on what you share and what you comment on, as well as the beliefs you share. If, for example, you use curse words on Facebook or if you post pictures that are against meat-eating or for hunting, they will draw conclusions about your personality. Similarly, if you have an active blog, readers might draw conclusions about you as a person based on your blog posts, or if you have an active Instagram and you share pictures of yourself sky-diving, they might conclude that you are fearless. If they Google you, and find your blog on why American needs a Communist revolution or why America needs to go back to traditional values, they may form an opinion of you that will cross over to whether you are appropriate, or not, for a job or promotion offer. *These aspects of your personality are visible to others online.*

In summary, you'll realize that there are different "Yous" across different social spaces, and you'll realize that you are constantly building your personal brand – the *Private You*, the *Public You*, and the *Internet You* – 24 hours a day, 7 days a weak, and whether you are conscious of it or not. You may be building a **positive** brand image (you can play the harmonica, you understand double entry bookkeeping) or you may be building a **negative** brand image (you use curse words, you don't know how to spell, you are politically intolerant).

Regardless, however, of whether you like it or not, you are building a personal brand image through every action you take online.

Personal Branding

At this point, some of you may be freaking out. You may be remembering an Instagram photo that wasn't that flattering, a comment to a blog that was politically incorrect, or (God forbid) a criminal proceeding that was posted to a public records site on the Web.

You may be realizing that sharing the mug shot of you getting arrested for underage drinking to Instagram, Twitter, Facebook, and Snapchat was not your smartest career move. Or you may be doing a quick inventory of every embarrassing photo you ever posted of yourself to Facebook or Instagram.

You may have paused for a moment to Google yourself, and not exactly liked what you found.

Many of us haven't realized that in today's Internet society the cameras are always on, the recorders are always recording, and we've left a digital footprint which we may not be proud of. Don't freak out – we're going to address this problem. For now, just take a deep breath and let me explain.

You've now realized that there is an *Internet You* available to potential employers or hiring managers. There may be a lot of information about you online, or very little. Conceptually, however, the point is that nearly all of us have some type of *Internet You*.

You Manufacture You

Now, let's return to Cher and Lady Gaga. They can help us out. How? By showing us that they "manufacture" their Public Yous.

> *Cher doesn't leave her public image to chance, and nor does Lady Gaga. Behind the scenes, they (and their publicists) consciously conceptualize and promote the public persona they wish to "be." (And probably try to squelch the public persona they'd rather keep secret).*

Cher and Lady Gaga can help us out by showing us that they pro-actively construct their online images or public personas.

Prior to the Internet, famous personalities like Paul Newman, Pope John Paul II, or Cher, clearly had a *Private You* and a *Public You*. Some persons, especially Hollywood celebrities as well as politicians, famous authors, famous scientists and others, pro-actively cultivated their "public image," and often used this "public image" for material gain. This remains true in today's Internet age; an age in which stars such as Lady Gaga or Justin Bieber also pro-actively nurture a particular public persona that advances their career goals.

> *Did someone just say Donald Trump? Boy does he have a powerful Internet You, Public You, or Personal Brand image! (You may like it, you may hate it, but you can't deny it).*

What's happened since the New Internet World emerged is that you and I suddenly also have this dynamic. We have a *Private You*, a *Public You*, and an *Internet You*. And, as we search for a job, or build our careers, our mission is to manage and nurture our *Public You* and especially our *Internet You*, to project a positive personal brand image.

> *Like Lady Gaga, Cher, and even Donald Trump your mission is to a) define the Public You you wish to project, b) to tirelessly promote this image, and c) to squelch or at least push off the front stage, the Public You which you may not be so excited about.*

> *Like Lady Gaga, Cher, and even Donald Trump, we also want to tirelessly promote and build network connections that can promote us in our career goals.*

> *The marketing term for this is personal branding.*

In the next chapter, we'll explore *personal branding* in more detail, but for now, let it suffice to define the concept as follows:

> **Personal Branding** *is the art and science of defining, creating, and nurturing a positive brand image in public and on the Internet that advances one's job seeking and career goals. It also includes efforts to obfuscate negative information, should that exist. And it includes efforts to network in such a way as to advance one's career.*

Your Public and Private Should be in Rough Harmony

Did I just imply you should try to squelch negative information about yourself online?

Now, let's return to Cher for a moment before you get too cynical. The *public Cher* and the *private Cher* are not in total contradiction to each other. While Cher might not win an award for most wholesome artist of the year, she is nonetheless, relatively wholesome as Hollywood celebrities go, and her public support of her son, Chaz Bono, seems to coincide with private support as well.

Cher isn't being dishonest to have a public Cher and a private Cher, but the two are certainly not the same thing.

In most cases, the Private You, the Public You, and the Internet You should be in some sort of harmony, or at least not in total conflict.

Now that is not to say that disasters don't strike. With respect to highly public individuals, terrible tragedies do occur. As in the example of people as disparate as Tiger Woods, Donald Trump, or Bill Clinton, the *Private You* and the *Public You* can be quite incongruous. These public figures do their best to present an advantageous *Public You*, even if at times, a more negative image might emerge from their darker *Private You*.

Or, perhaps in the persona of a Donald Trump or a Bill Clinton, perhaps the *Public You* is accurate but just not very appealing. (I'm not taking sides).

I am not advocating that you suppress really terrible information about yourself, and I am certainly not advocating that you lie about yourself, or hide a criminal record or something like that.

I am simply advocating that you "put your best foot forward" in terms of your Public You and *Internet You*, and – to the extent necessary – attempt to highlight the positive and obfuscate the negative.

Secrecy vs. Privacy: The Private You vs. the Secret You

In fact, I would venture to make a distinction between a *Private You* and a *Secret You* online. Here's a conceptual example of the difference between *privacy* and *secrecy*: *going to the bathroom*. A husband and wife, for example, should have no secrets between them, such as extramarital affairs. Something is secret when it is so damaging upon release, that it reveals a terrible moral or ethical shortcoming like an affair or a crime. Privacy is something altogether different. The husband and wife both know that each person "goes to the bathroom," and they know "what goes on in there," but it's not a secret, it's just private.

Similarly, I would recommend that if you have any serious secrets to hide such as criminal conduct, then you have a much more serious problem than most of us online in the job-search or career-building endeavor. That's a *Secret You* online, and something that should be rectified to the full extent of the law.

The *Private You*, in contrast, might reveal your passion for My Little Pony, your tendency to get just a little too crazy at parties (without hurting anyone), or even some unfortunate but paid-for misdemeanors from your youth. These are things that you wish to keep private from your employer; if they were to be discovered, however, they might embarrass you but would not cost you your job. Embarrassing, in short, is not illegal.

(Have a little fun, and watch Katy Perry's "Last Friday Night" on YouTube at http://jmlinks.com/9x, including Rebecca Black's cameo. You can watch Rebecca's viral video (which she may wish to forget), here: http://jmlinks.com/9y.)

Cher may not always look as amazing as she does on stage, and Lady Gaga might not be as politically correct as she appears in her songs. Katy Perry and Rebecca Black hopefully don't have any skeletons in their closet worse, than the two terrible videos above. Nevertheless, we hope that their *Public* and *Private Yous* are in decent harmony, don't we? And I hope the same is the true for you, too.

Personal Branding and the *Internet You*

The point to realize is that, as you build your job search or career building strategy, the You that the hiring manager or outside business partner sees is usually not the *Private You* but the *Public You*, and especially the *Internet You*. Your own Personal Branding strategy thus becomes a conscious effort to manage your *Public You / Internet You* in a positive direction to advance your career goals. Keep the *Private You* private, at least with respect to embarrassing information.

Here's a summary of the Yous:

The You	Where It Exists
PRIVATE YOU	The You you are at home, with friends or family. Your hobbies, fears, skills that don't necessarily relate to work like playing a harmonica or enjoying Telenovelas.
PUBLIC YOU	The You you are at work, at church, at school, etc. Hopefully, you are on your best behavior, and this forms your personal brand image vis-à-vis bosses and coworkers. This may also include public records such as bankruptcies, credit scores, or even criminal records.
THE INTERNET YOU	A specific part of the Public You, namely the You you have created and is available online on your blog, your Facebook, your LinkedIn, your Twitter, etc. This You can be accessible via online searches and forms your personal brand image, especially to new employers or key decision-makers who do not yet know you. Hopefully you are on your best behavior online.
THE SECRET YOU	This would be the You that may contain information that is very negative, such as a criminal record or drug problem. There is a distinction here between "secret" and "private." Hopefully you do not have a Secret You.

▶▶ GOOGLE THYSELF (AND FACEBOOK THYSELF AND TWITTER THYSELF)

Here's the rub for many of us - *the Internet is like an elephant; it never forgets.* If you unfortunately posted some politically incorrect remark onto Twitter, it's not easily forgotten; if you shared online an embarrassing selfie of yourself at a Frat party to Instagram, it's not easily erased; if you were dumb enough to post a public review to Yelp for that DUI attorney that got you out of jail, it might not be easily taken down. Not to mention if you've ever been arrested or have a low credit score; lots of information is now available at just the click of a mouse, and employers even use paid services to dig deeper into public records on any prospective hires.

> *You, I, Hillary Clinton, Cher, and everyone else now leave a constant "digital footprint," that can impact our online personal brand image in a positive or negative direction.*

The Good News: Most of Us (Fortunately) Have a Weak or Nonexistent *Internet You*

Most of us, fortunately, haven't done that many stupid things in life, and most of us haven't been so stupid as to share them online. Few of us have been arrested, most of us have decent credit scores, and our own Rebecca Black "Friday videos" remain (fortunately) hidden on our iPhones. However, before we dive into Personal Branding in the next chapter, it's a worthwhile exercise to inventory those items in your past that you are not particularly proud of, items that might speak negatively against a new job or career advancement. And it's important to "Google thyself" and discover what a savvy hiring manager or the person in charge of headhunting you or the person who could advance you in your career might find online about you.

GOOGLE YOURSELF: WHAT DO YOU FIND?

Your first **TODO** is, therefore, to Google thyself:

- Go to https://www.google.com/, type in your name or your name plus characteristics about you (e.g., the school you graduated from, the company you work for, your special skill such as CPA or WordPress expert, or the city you live in). What do you find?
- Go to Facebook, LinkedIn, Twitter, and use their own search engines. Input your name and any additional keywords such as your city, employer, or skills or attributes you might have. What do you find about yourself?
- Similarly, go to Google and use the special *site:* command plus your name (and any modifiers as per above), and see what you find on Twitter, Facebook, Instagram, etc. An example is to go to Google and type in *site:twitter.com "Jason McDonald"* to capture information on Twitter about "Jason McDonald." Here's a screenshot:

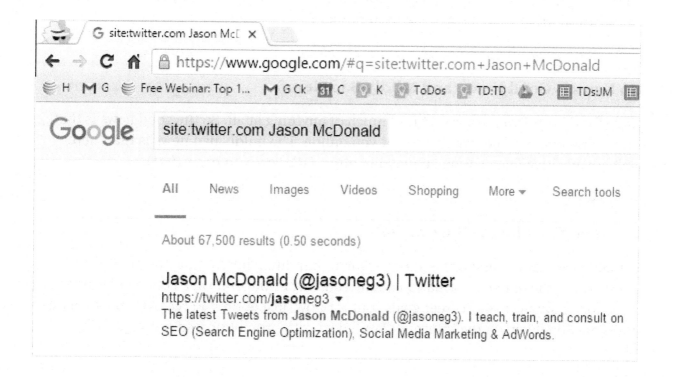

Important: there is no space between the colon and the website as in *site:twitter.com* not *site:{SPACE}twitter.com*.

Does anything about you show up at all? Is it positive or negative? Where is it located on the Internet – Twitter, Facebook, a Website, a blog, etc.?

Next, quickly go to the major Social Media sites such as Twitter, Facebook, and LinkedIn, and again type in your name plus a few qualifying characteristics.

Can you easily find yourself? If so, what do you find? Is it positive or negative?

If you were a hiring manager researching you, what would you think? What you take the next step of calling you in for a job interview, hiring you, or giving you a promotion? Why or why not?

If you find negative items, make a list of them in a spreadsheet and note where they are found on the Internet (a blog, a Facebook post, a Twitter post, a government website, etc.). How hard did you have to dig to find them?

No News is Good News (and Mildly Bad News)

Now, for many of you, you won't find much of anything at all. So the good news is that there is no negative information about you online. The mildly bad news is that there isn't any positive information about you online. (*We're going to fix that*).

Personal Branding to the Rescue

Personal reputation management or personal branding, therefore, is the art and science of nurturing the online information about You, a.k.a. your *Internet You*, in a positive direction to support your career goals. But for now, just audit and record what's already out there about you on the Internet. (We'll deal with promotion and networking later).

▶▶ DELIVERABLE: A SUMMARY OF THE *INTERNET YOU*

Your chapter **DELIVERABLE** has arrived. Go to https://www.jm-seo.org/workbooks (click on Job Search and Career-building, enter the code 'careers2016' to register if you have not already done so), and click on the link to the "Summary of the *Internet You*" worksheet. By researching yourself online, you will establish baseline of your current *Internet You*, be that good, bad, ugly, or nonexistent.

THIS PAGE INTENTIONALLY LEFT BLANK

(PONDER IT)

3
YOU ARE A BRAND

You are a brand.

Even if you do not realize it and *even if you do not like it.*

*Your **personal brand** is the Public You: the You that's perceived by hiring managers and employers, combining the Internet You with every other facet of your public persona.*

In this chapter, we are going to do a deep dive into *personal branding*, but first let's get a high level overview to **brands** and **brandING** (the process of building a brand). A **brand** is that warm, fuzzy **feeling** (or that cold, negative feeling) you get about a company, product or service. Think, for example, about Apple. What comes to mind?

Sleek, well-designed products. Easy-to-use functions on iPhone and iPads. Privacy protection that is second-to-none.

That's a *corporate* brand. There are *personal* brands as well. Think, for example, about *Ellen DeGeneres*. What comes to mind?

Funny comedian, nice person, good dancer, and gay rights activist.

That's the Ellen DeGeneres brand. Now think about Donald Trump or Al Capone or Tiger Woods.

Some brands have "issues." Some brands have positives, and negatives. However, it depends on whom you ask as to which brand is "positive" and which "negative." The brand is in conversation with the consumer, so to speak.

Indeed, in all cases, there is a lot of **brandING** going on, as Apple builds its brand image, Ellen nurtures hers, and Tiger Woods tries to repair his.

Leave those celebrity brands aside for a moment, let's return to you.

You, too, are a brand.

Your friends and family have a "mental picture" of your personality as do your teachers, coworkers, and/or supervisors – in both a professional and a personality sense. (*To prove this to yourself, think of people whom you know such as teachers, coworkers, employers, and sketch out a "mental map" of their personality including how you would describe them as a prospective employer*).

You see, everyone has a brand image, however. And not all of them are positive, are they? Some are far, far more positive than others.

Some personal brands, or Public Yous, don't say much at all: these people are fuzzy at best, and you'd find it difficult to summarize what they stand for.

Some people are very skilled at networking and "getting the word out" about their career, and others, not so much.

Everyone has a personal brand. (The concept is credited to Tom Peters in a famous article, "The Brand Called You," at http://jmlinks.com/jk). The rise of the Internet has meant that everyone is beginning to have an **online** personal brand, whether they like it, or not. Indeed, a potential employer, after all, will also create a "mental picture" of **you as a brand** before, during, and after your employment.

You are a brand, *whether you like it or not.*

Your brand impacts your career, *whether you like it or not.*

*The sooner you become pro-active about your personal **brandING**, the better off you'll be.*

In this chapter, we will first discuss the static concept of a *brand*, by looking at famous people with famous personal brands. We will then dive into the dynamic concept of *branding (brandING)*, how to define, nurture, and promote your personal brand online. Your deliverable is a completed *Personal Branding Statement and Content Marketing Sketch*.

Let's get started!

TODO LIST:

>> Research and Reverse Engineer Powerful Personal Brands Online

>> Brainstorm Your Desired Personal Brand Image

>> Sketch Out Your Content Marketing Machine

>> >> Deliverable: a Personal Branding Statement and Content Marketing Sketch

>> RESEARCH AND REVERSE ENGINEER POWERFUL PERSONAL BRANDS ONLINE

The Internet, like so many things in our culture, started at the top and filtered down. What was originally a military project for communication among defense research facilities and university centers became today's pervasive Internet of cat videos, sales at Walmart, and pictures of you doing stupid things on Instagram. It started at the top, and filtered down.

Online personal branding is following the same path. Personal branding started at the top – with people who were "already famous" – and the process is now filtering down to average people like you and me. First, Presidents like John F. Kennedy and Richard Nixon needed personal brands (and personal brand repair), next pop stars like Madonna and Kurt Cobain; sports stars like Tim Tebow and Ray Lewis… and now it's you and me.

Nearly everyone has some type of personal brand image online; just Google yourself, research your posts on Facebook, or look at what you've tweeted.

Imitation is the Highest Form of Flattery

They say that imitation is the highest form of flattery, and so one of the best steps towards building your own personal brand is to identify the online brand images of people whom you admire (or *even those whom you do not*). The next step will be to reverse engineer their brand*ING* strategy.

How to Identify Personal Brands Online

One easy way to identify persons with strong online personal brands is to just brainstorm famous TV personalities that you like and admire. Do you like sports? Politics? Cooking? TV or movies? Pop music? Professional wrestling? It's up to you what you like, but strong online personal brands exist in almost every human endeavor.

> *Choose an endeavor, and brainstorm some famous people whom you find with strong online brands.*

Take comedian, Ellen DeGeneres, for example. I personally love her positive humor and her friendly personality.

> *Do I know Ellen? Nope, just as I do not know Cher. I only know her online brand image and her television brand image.*
>
> *I bet you don't know Ellen, either, but I bet you'd agree with me that her personal brand image is of a fun, positive comedian.*
>
> *That's not an accident.*

Now, think about how Ellen nurtures and promotes her brand image. She has a television show, a blog, a Facebook page, a YouTube channel, and an Instagram account... you get the picture: Ellen is both on TV and online, in movies and in books. She has a promotion machine, and – to be a bit cynical – she probably manipulates it to encourage our view that her life is "totally together" and that she is "totally positive."

Is that true? Who knows? How many "perfect" celebrities have fallen apart in a big surprise? You get my point: we only know the *Public Ellen* or *Internet Ellen*, but not the *Private Ellen*. And really for this book, we only care about the *Public Ellen*.

Throughout, Ellen constantly promotes a positive, friendly personality – even when attacked. As an advocate for Gay rights and marriage equality, for example, she was criticized and responded not in a *negative* way, but in a *positive* way – which is, in accordance with her personal brand image. (You can watch her YouTube response to criticisms at http://jmlinks.com/8y).

REVERSE ENGINEER BRANDS YOU LIKE

To "reverse engineer" Ellen's personal brand image (or that of another famous person), use these steps:

1. **Identify** a person whose online brand image interests you (e.g., comedian, professional chef, star athlete, health guru, author, etc.).

2. **Find them** on the Internet on sites such as their personal website or blog, Facebook page, YouTube channel, Twitter account, etc. Bookmark these or note the URL's.

3. **Write a Personal Branding Statement about that person.** For example: "Ellen DeGeneres is a female TV and stand-up comedian and actress, who is famous for her positive sense of humor and dancing skills. Besides TV and movies, she has an active Internet presence on sites like Twitter, YouTube, and Facebook. She is married to Portia de Rossi, and has become known as an activist for marriage equality."

4. **Think critically about what you like, and dislike**, about her personal branding and about the media and methods used to promote it (e.g., how she uses YouTube, Facebook, TV, etc.).

Admiration is Not Endorsement

It is important to realize that you do NOT have to agree with a personal brand, for you to admire and reverse engineer it in a marketing sense. You may not, for example, agree with Ellen on Gay rights, but you can still admire her skills as a creator of a powerful personal brand. Similarly, you may not agree with Donald Trump on politics, but you may still admire and reverse engineer how he has nurtured and promoted his personal brand. The goal is to become skilled at reverse engineering the online brand images of famous people, so that you can imitate what you like and ignore what you do not.

I have a list of people with powerful online brand images at http://jmlinks.com/8z. Please browse this list, and a) Write a **personal branding statement** for persons who interest you, and b) Begin to reverse engineer how they nurture and promote their personal brand online.

Reverse Engineer Online Personal Brand Images

Beyond the rich and famous, it's helpful to go a down a notch and try to identify people more like you and I am, i.e., not as famous as Ellen DeGeneres or Tim Tebow, but still sophisticated enough to have a strong Internet brand image.

You're looking for people like you, or people who you would like to become more like (with the caveat that we are talking about their professional Internet Yous and not their Private Yous).

Here are the steps to identify people who may be close to your own desired personal brand image:

1. **Identify some keywords** that describe your personal brand image in a work, business, or professional sense. (*We'll go through these keywords later, but for now, just identify some keywords such as "awesome personal injury attorney," "hypnotherapist to reduce stress," or "orthopedic surgeon specializing in knee surgeries.")* Try to choose keywords that are common enough that hopefully some celebrity-types will exist who "match" your target keywords.

2. **Go to Google** and search for some of those phrases.

3. **Identify people** who have personal websites and blogs that are close to your keywords. Hopefully, they also have strong profiles on one or more social media networks such as YouTube, Twitter, Facebook, Instagram, etc.

4. **Browse their websites**, especially their home pages, their "about us" pages, and their blogs if those exist.

5. Write down your best guess as to their **personal branding statement**.

6. **Note** other sites used such as Facebook, Twitter, LinkedIn, or Instagram, which they use to **promote their brand**.

7. Pay attention to not just their personal brand image but also the way in which they **create content** such as blog posts, videos, pictures, etc., and **promote content**, to nurture and grow their image online.

An Example: Hypnotherapy

I'll give you an example from my own personal goals. I am very interested in hypnosis, and sometimes, I fantasize about becoming a stage hypnotherapist (*after becoming a successful self-help author*) …

Hence, I would brainstorm keywords such as "hypnosis," "hypnotherapist" and even "Los Angeles" (*thinking that's where the truly open-minded people live in America*). A Google search might be, "Los Angeles Hypnotherapists."

After doing that, I ended up at Dr. Nancy Irwin's website at http://jmlinks.com/9a. She has a very professional personal website and blog. She also has an active social media strategy on YouTube, Twitter, and so forth. If you click on her "about" page, you'll see a description of who she is, and what she offers in terms of hypnotherapy. In other words, you can reverse engineer both her personal branding statement, as well as, see ways that she promotes herself online, from her personal website or blog to Twitter. (Remember this is her professional *Public You*, and we have no idea about her *Private You*).

> In short, your mission is to identify personal brands online that you want to emulate such as Nancy Irwin.
>
> So now, you'll have two lists: one of very prominent people like Ellen DeGeneres, and another of modest, average people like Nancy Irwin who, nonetheless have pretty strong online personal brand images.

In the **deliverable** for this chapter, you'll list personal brands you admire online and sketch out what you like, and dislike, about their personal brand image as well as what you can figure out about how they **create content** to support this image and **promote that content**. By identifying people who are close to your desired brand image, you'll be able to see not only how they define themselves in an online branding sense but also how they promote themselves on social media.

This is important; you are reverse engineering these steps:

1. **Personal Branding Statement (PBS)**. What is their "value" to other people? Write down a quick summary of what they produce that other people want (i.e., their **PBS**), as in hypnotherapy, CPA services, or even dog training skills.
2. **Content Platforms**. Which platforms do they use for their content? This could be a personal website or blog, a strong Facebook page, an Instagram account, a LinkedIn profile, etc.

3. **Content Production**. What type of content do they produce? Is it blog posts? YouTube videos? Infographics? eBooks?
4. **Content / Brand Promotion**. How do they promote their online personal brand image? Do they have an email newsletter? Do they come up high on Google searches via SEO? Do they use sharing on Facebook to get their users to share their content with others?

Don't worry if you don't understand all the components. You're just getting started. For now, just identify a list of three to five persons online, who have robust personal brand images. You'll use these as "place markers" to compare / contrast with your own desired personal brand image and branding strategy.

▶▶ BRAINSTORM YOUR DESIRED PERSONAL BRAND IMAGE

Now, since you've identified and reverse engineered some persons online, it's time to begin to brainstorm your vision of who you are, and who you want to become as a *Public You* and *Internet You*. Remember, we are not born into our professional or career identities but rather, we make these over time. We are not *born* experts, but rather we *become* experts!

> *Defining your Personal Brand is an almost spiritual, or religious exercise. I recommend you find a quiet, thoughtful place to do this. It could be taking a pad and pencil out into the woods, or it could be going to your neighborhood Starbucks, where you type into your laptop undisturbed.*

Your first **TODO**, therefore, is to write a draft of your **Personal Branding Statement (PBS)**. For the worksheet, go to https://www.jm-seo.org/workbooks (click on Job Search and Career-building, enter the code 'careers2016' to register if you have not already done so), and click on the link to the "Personal Branding Statement" worksheet.

As you **brainstorm your PBS**, here are some more important concepts to remember:

- **Your PBS Should Be Present AND Future Oriented.** It does not have to be who you are today; it can be who you want to be tomorrow. In fact, it's good to be oriented towards the future, as you are engaged not in a static personal brand but in the process of online personal brand-***building*** for the future.

- **Your PBS should focus on the *Public You / Internet You* and not the *Private You*.** It is the "*You*" you want to be *online*, not the "*You*" you are as a total human being! Identify the job you want, and the skills you have that are relevant for that career. Again, a future orientation is actually good; who you want to be in the future and not who you are today.
- **Your PBS should be honest**: Your online personal brand image should be in harmony with your true self, putting your best foot forward for potential employers and those who can help your career. (*We hope that Ellen DeGeneres truly is a positive person in real life, and that Nancy Irwin actually does know something about hypnotherapy*).
- **Your PBS Should Be Realistic about the Job Market.** We live in the real world, where the job market is tough. Keep an eye, therefore, on what is demanded in the marketplace. You are looking for "connection points" between what a potential employer might want and what you have to offer. This is especially true for young people and for people with few skills or short work histories.
- **Your PBS Should be Concise.** A good Personal Branding Statement is about a paragraph in length. Imagine you are meeting a potential employer at a trade show party, and she asks you, "Hey, tell me about yourself."

Here's mine:

> *Jason McDonald is an Internet marketing expert, bringing skills in SEO (Search Engine Optimization), AdWords, and social media marketing on sites like Yelp, Facebook, and LinkedIn to his students and clients to help them succeed in their own online marketing efforts. Jason assists business owners and marketers in his online and Bay Area training classes to learn these skills and succeed at do-it-yourself marketing. He also works with consulting clients to achieve their marketing goals via a more one-on-one marketing methodology. His style is participatory and hands on, and his personality brings enthusiasm and humor to what is often perceived as a technical or dry area of marketing.*

I often find it helpful to write your PBS in the Third Person, as that reminds you to look at your statement from the perspective of a hiring manager, employer, or company that might hire you as an outside freelancer or consultant. Your PBS should answer the questions they might ask you at a job fair or trade show gathering. These questions include:

- **What can you do for me** (the hiring manager)?
- What are your special **skills, education,** or **qualifications** that can help me (the hiring manager) obtain what I want to achieve?
- What type of **job / career / gig** (that I have) do you want to get?
- What are your **personality attributes** as in are you a detail-oriented, friendly, efficient, independent worker, etc.?

Remember, "less is more." Do not ramble on and on. Don't feel the need to substantiate or prove your skills; these are done in other locations on your website, or even in a job interview.

WRITE A CONCISE PBS

Being concise and writing just one, short paragraph will force you to define yourself in a very specific way. Once you've written a draft, try reading it out loud to friends, family, teachers, colleagues, or coworkers.

Ask them to pretend to be an employer and you are a prospective hire, meeting for the first time at a job fair or trade show gathering.

Read your PBS to them out loud.

Do they understand "what you have to offer?" Do they understand "what you can do for them?" Does it convey your brand image, in terms of your personality such as introvert or extrovert, friendly or efficient, etc.?

Are you being true to yourself? We all have to make a living, but are you describing your skills and the job or career you want, in such a way that it is in harmony with your lifelong goals? Honesty is the best policy, not just with your employer but with yourself.

▶ SKETCH OUT YOUR CONTENT MARKETING MACHINE

Let's go back for a second to Ellen DeGeneres. She is obviously a very talented comedian and actress, but she is also a talented marketer and has a formidable marketing machine at her disposal. How so?

- Ellen **produces a lot of content**: TV shows, movies, blog posts, YouTube videos, monologues, interviews on the shows of other people, images, etc. Ellen is a top content-producer!
- Ellen **has quite a few channels** to **promote** and **distribute** her content: a TV show, a YouTube channel, a Twitter account with more than 54 million followers, and an Instagram account with more than 25 million followers. Ellen is a powerful self-promoter!

You also need to sketch out a **content marketing machine**. Content is the "fuel" for your online personal brand image. Content is what you will put up on your blog, share on Twitter, update or post on LinkedIn, produce on YouTube (and share elsewhere), etc.

You'll need a lot of content!

I have devoted an entire chapter just to content marketing! It's important!

However, for now, revisit your Personal Branding Statement, and brainstorm logical types of content that you'll need to fuel your online brand image. Don't produce it just yet, but start to brainstorm the types of content you'll want *en masse*. If you're a *writer*, for example, it's quite logical that you'll need a lively and robust *blog*. If you're going after a career in *photography*, you'll need a lively supply of interesting *photos*. And if you are an experienced corporate *marketer*, you'll need things like a *SlideShare* account with sample marketing presentations, a YouTube channel with videos of your trade show booths and demo's, and/or a portfolio of ad campaigns you've set up on Google AdWords and Facebook.

A hiring manager isn't going to take your word for it; she's going to research you online, and you'll need content on the Web and social media to validate yourself as a helpful expert.

The same procedure applies to a professional headhunter identifying prospects on LinkedIn, or a promotion manager at your own company two levels up, or a competitor scout that wants to steal you away.

Also, your online content will not only substantiate that you are a "helpful expert," but also will actually promote you – by building connections with people you know, people who know people you know, and people who don't know you at all.

IDENTIFY CONTENT TO PRODUCE

Your content, in short, should be viewed from the perspective of a hiring manager or employer. It should make it easy (or easier) to find you online, and when you're found, should make you seem if not awesome or fantastic, at least competent. For extra credit, it should be so lively and useful, that people will spontaneously want to read it, and even go so far as to share it with others via social media like LinkedIn, Facebook, or Twitter.

Your second **TODO**, therefore, is to supplement your "Personal Branding Statement" with a "Content Marketing Sketch." For the worksheet, go to https://www.jm-seo.org/workbooks (click on Job Search and Career-building, enter the code 'careers2016' to register if you have not already done so), and click on the link to the "Personal Branding Statement" worksheet. Next, fill in the second worksheet entitled "Content Marketing Sketch" worksheet.

» DELIVERABLE: A PERSONAL BRANDING STATEMENT AND CONTENT MARKETING SKETCH

In its entirety, the deliverable for this chapter, therefore, has two interrelated elements: your **Personal Branding Statement** and **Content Marketing Sketch**. For the worksheets, follow the instructions above. Sit down in a quiet place and fill them out.

Don't worry if you're not completely settled in either your PBS or content marketing sketch, as these will evolve over time. The tasks at this point are to get a rough draft down on paper, to begin to see how the PBS you want to create relates to the content you need to produce to substantiate your personal brand, and to master the promotional tools you need to use to make yourself famous.

Well, at least more famous than you are now, or famous in your industry or company or target circle of employers, hiring managers, and professional recruiters.

Isn't this exciting?

This page is intentionally blank.

(Why is that?)

3

BE FOUND

LOOK COOL

Imagine a **hiring manager** at a big company, a **business owner** looking for a new employee at a small company, or someone involved in the **recruiting** and **hiring** process at a medium business, non-profit, or government agency. He's looking to hire someone because he has a **need**: he has a "job to fill." His need must find a match in the **skill set** of a prospective hire, plus he'll want a match between the **corporate culture** of his firm and the **personality** of the new hire. In addition, a hiring manager like the one I am describing, is undoubtedly **risk-averse**: he doesn't want to hire a psycho killer, or even a person who doesn't get along well with others, or who has embarrassing facts in their past.

The hiring criteria, therefore, are:

- The **skills** of the new hire need to match the **needs** of the job, or at least be close enough to meet the requirements after on-the-job training.
- The **personality** of the new hire needs to match the **corporate culture** of the firm. She needs to be able to "get along" with coworkers and managers.
- The new hire shouldn't have any terrible **skeletons in her closet**, nothing so dangerous or embarrassing that it could spell trouble for the business or organization.

In addition, there's the issue of **compensation**, the pay rate and benefits package available vs. whether this is an entry-level, a mid-level, or a management level position. The "cooler" you look, the "higher" the offer of pay and other compensation.

Also, if a friend or colleague recommends you as the best job candidate, all the better.

In this Chapter, we're going to look at the world of job search and career advancement from the perspective of the employer or hiring manager, with an eye as to how Google, Facebook, LinkedIn and Internet job search sites like CareerBuilder, Craigslist, or Monster, might be used as discovery and research tools.

Let's get started!

TODO LIST:

>> Be Found: Brainstorm Relevant Discovery Paths

>> Keywords: Think Like Your Targets

>> >> Deliverable: A Job / Career Keyword Worksheet

>> Monitor Your Online Reputation

>> >> Deliverable: An Online Personal Reputation Audit

>> Be Cool: Be A "Helpful Expert"

>> BE FOUND: BRAINSTORM RELEVANT DISCOVERY PATHS

Before we plunge into Facebook, LinkedIn, CareerBuilder and the gang, it's worthwhile to sit back and ponder the big questions of job search and career-building. We've discussed already why you should brainstorm a "match" between the career you want and the demands of the job market. At this point, we're drilling into how the world looks to the hiring manager or employer. (I'll just say *hiring manager* from here on in).

Identifying Job Candidates

First of all, how does a hiring manager "search" for a job candidate? How might she research potential candidates, after she has a "short list" of whom she wants to call in for an interview and/or a list of strong candidates to be given an offer? In marketing terms, we're identifying the **discovery paths** that might be used.

The first path, of course, is the **real world**. The hiring manager might ask friends, family, colleagues, and coworkers to help her identify job candidates and to research their skillset and personality after the fact. Your job references – the persons whom she can call or email to verify your skills and personality, for example, fall into this category of the real world. We all should have strong job references, and we all should cultivate the real world during our job search and efforts at career-building!

> *To find a job or advance your career, schmooze ("network") with everyone you know and solicit their help vis-à-vis contacts that they know but you do not. To get a job or a promotion, make sure you not only have strong references but that, in the long term, you make professional friends and avoid making enemies.*

However, this is a book about Internet search and social media. Let's face it, the hiring manager will quickly exhaust her list of real-world personal contacts and turn to the Internet. She's also likely to be skeptical of job references, as everyone knows that they are cultivated and even coached as to what to say about a job candidate. The reality today is that the Internet has become either a primary or secondary way to identify job candidates. *The sooner you wrap your head around this, the more successful you will be at job search and career building.*

The Five Discovery Paths

Fortunately, there are only five paths of discovery on the Internet. Only five. Every way that someone identifies a job candidate or researches someone for career advancement can be categorized into one of the following five **discovery paths**:

> **Search.** The search path occurs when the hiring manager or recruiter is "searching" for a job candidate. For example, she needs to hire a person skilled in WordPress web design. She likely types into Google, "WordPress Web Designers," goes to LinkedIn and types in the same, or visits a career site like CareerBuilder.com to search resumes by keywords like "Web design," or "WordPress." Let's say she's looking for an entry-level customer service representative. It's the same process, only that the keywords change to words such as "customer service," "good with people," or "basic phone skills." (Remember: this "search" might happen on Google, LinkedIn, CareerBuilder, or Monster, or it can be as simple as querying contacts she knows in the real world. Nevertheless, she is pro-actively searching for candidates).

Review / Recommend / Trust. The review / recommend /trust path is based on "trust indicators." In it, the hiring manager already has a short list of job candidates and/or is ready to research people to whom to give offers for a career advancement. She "has the person," but is looking to their "online reputation" to validate her choice. Here, she might use the search methodology but rather than searching on keywords, she's going to search for your name and/or your name plus a hot-button word, if there are a lot of people with your same name. For people who have a relatively common name like I do, "Jason McDonald," the relevant search phrases are something like *Jason McDonald SEO* or *Jason McDonald Social Media* or *Jason McDonald San Francisco*. (In marketing terms, these are called "branded" or "reputational queries.") This research might be on Google, LinkedIn, Facebook, or even in a background check database but the process is driven by your name and hot-button words. The point here is to a) Verify positive attributes about you (that you really do know WordPress), and/or b) To find / validate negative attributes such as whether you have a criminal record or have participated in potentially embarrassing or damaging activity on Internet sites like Facebook, Twitter, or YouTube.

eWOM (Electronic Word-of-Mouth) / Share / Viral. Here, she's using the social nature of the Internet and social media sites. The hiring manager, for example, might email or message her contacts on LinkedIn about you as a candidate, or she might reach out to her contacts explaining that she's looking to hire a new customer service rep. In the reverse direction, *you* might reach out to *your* contacts (or *contacts* of *your contacts*) via a site like LinkedIn to inform them that you are looking for a new job, or seeking to advance your career. Do they know anyone who's hiring? Or do they know anyone at company "x," where you'd like to get hired? This path is all about *electronic word-of-mouth* or *eWOM*.

BRAINSTORM HOW THEY MIGHT FIND YOU

Interrupt. The interrupt path is the bad boy of job search. It's when you cold call hiring managers, or spam email them. It's when you shamelessly find a reason to call or email a hiring manager "out of the blue." Seen from the other direction, it's when a recruiter or "head hunter" solicits you via email or LinkedIn to see whether you're interested in a new job. By being findable, you'll get more inquiries from headhunters, and by having a "reason," you'll find it easier to get hiring managers to accept your unsolicited inquiries. (More on this later).

Browse. The browse path is a little similar to the interrupt path. In it, a hiring manager might browse resumes on a career site, read a trade magazine, or even see a post by you on Twitter. You might be the "helpful expert" on a topic of interest (e.g., new ways to use WordPress for eCommerce, or new ways to use social media for customer service). In addition to the hiring manager, people in your target companies might read your blog, follow you on LinkedIn or Twitter, or love your photo-sharing on Instagram. These influencers or key decision-makers might then wonder if "you're available," reach out to you, and then recommend you to the hiring manager as a great catch. With enough luck, *browse* might turn into *contact*, and *contact* into *hire*.

Your goal as a job candidate, is to project a powerful, friendly, and helpful personal brand image in all of the discovery paths, so that you are **easy-to find**, perceived as a trustworthy, **helpful expert** when researched as an individual, and **shareable** as a job candidate among friends and contacts, who can help you get a job interview or advance your career. This is true in the real world, and it is also true in the world of the Internet.

Here are some examples:

Search. When a hiring manager searches Monster.com, CareerBuilder.com, or LinkedIn, for someone with WordPress skills, you want your profile to show up prominently and look very attractive. Your **TODO** is to engineer yourself to be easy-to-find on your target skills via a strong profile.

Review / Recommend / Trust. Once someone lands on your LinkedIn profile, for example, you want an attractive photo, an easy-to-understand professional headline, and enough connections, endorsements, and recommendations to look not just trustworthy, but awesome. You want a strong personal website or blog. Your **TODO** is to engineer your LinkedIn profile and/or personal website to accomplish this feat.

BECOME EASY-TO-FIND

eWOM / Share / Viral. You're looking for a job, or you're looking to advance your career. You know *Aileen*, and *Aileen* knows *Jerry*, the hiring manager at your target company: ACME Computing, Inc. You want Aileen to mention this to Jerry, or when Jerry is looking for candidates for Aileen to mention you. Your **TODO** is to alert your Internet contact network that you're "in the market" for a new job, so that they are aware of this fact (if asked) or can pro-actively help you along (if they're willing).

Interrupt. Here, you are going to be pro-active. For example, you'll do some research on a target company and email or reach out via social media like LinkedIn or Twitter to target decision-makers at target companies. You might not reach out to the hiring manager directly, but you may reach out to a contact of theirs or a decision-maker. Your **TODO** is to identify contacts of merit, and brainstorm the "excuses" you need to reach out to them, without getting sent to their spam filters. That "email out of the blue," isn't really going to be so "out of the blue," because the "reason" for your call or email will be something that piques their interest.

Browse. If you're farther along in your career, or you're in a more technical job category, you want to be perceived as a **thought leader**. You want the industry cognoscenti to read your blog posts, watch your YouTube videos, and/or see your Tweets. Your **TODO** is to set up your content resources so that people not only find them, but also that they read or watch them, and even take the next step of reaching out to you with an offer of a career advancement.

≫ KEYWORDS: THINK LIKE YOUR TARGETS

Words are incredibly important to the human experience. Indeed, if we didn't have words and language, we'd probably still be roaming the savannas of Africa hunting and gathering, or *still watching MTV like we did in the 1980s. Or still sending letters out with stamps. Or still paying with cash.*

You get the point: words are powerful things. "Let there be light, and there was light."

At this point in your quest to improve your job search and career-building capabilities, let's stop for a moment and ponder words, or specifically **keywords** and how important they are to the process of getting a job and/or advancing your career.

Hiring managers, recruiters, and upper management search the Internet, ask their contacts either face-to-face or via Internet techniques like email or social media posts, they research your online reputation, and check your references by using **keywords**.

Let's take an example: An auto repair shop that is looking to hire an entry-level auto mechanic, preferably with skills on European brands such as BMW, Volvo, and Mercedes. Here's a likely path they might take to the find a prospective hire.

First, they might post an ad on Craigslist.com, entitled "Auto Mechanic" or "Auto Tech." In fact, let's take a look at an actual ad posted to Craigslist in the Bay Area. Here's a screenshot (I've highlighted the keywords):

AUTOMOTIVE***AUTO TECH ***IMMEDIATE OPENING***MECHANIC (south san francisco) ☒   print

Position(s) available working at a busy, well established (37 years) independent, family-owned auto repair in So. San Francisco. We are looking for auto mechanic / technician to be part of our team - qualified person will have 8+ years experience in diagnosing and repairing vehicles, have their own tools and the ability to work on a variety of makes and models. ASE certification is a plus.

compensation: **Health benefits - Vacation tim**
employment type: **full-time**

We work on American (old and new), Japanese and some European -- Mercedes, BMW, Audi, VW, Subaru, Volvo . (You do not have to be experienced in ALL, but you must be able to work on more than just European vehicles) We are a smog test and repair station (smog license not necessary, but a plus).

Our working hours are Monday-Friday 8 am - 5 pm.

Salary based on experience and ability to diagnose and produce.

If you are a team player who possess a positive attitude, are both thorough and efficient and demonstrates pride of work, please fax resume and a short hand written description about your qualifications -- ASE certifications, smog license, and any other skills you possess, tell us why you feel you're the right person for this position.

The screenshot might a be a little hard to read, so let's list some of the **keywords** for this simple ad:

Automotive

Tech

Mechanic

Auto Repair

ASE certification

American

Japanese

European

Mercedes

BMW

Audi

VW

Subaru

Volvo

SMOG Test and Repair

SMOG license

team player

Positive attitude

Now, back up to the preceding section, and ponder what this ad tells you about the "mindset" of the hiring manager. In this example, she's looking for an auto mechanic with skills at repairing a pretty wide variety of cars, preferably with ASE certification and a SMOG license.

Do you see the **keywords**? They're essentially embedded in the ad itself: words like *auto mechanic, BMW,* or *ASE certification.* Do you see the attributes or helper words? These are words like *team player* or *positive attitude.*

Let's take a look at a different ad, this time one for an entry-level marketing writer:

Again, I've highlight the keywords, which are:

> *writer*
>
> *marketing*
>
> *communications*
>
> *technology*
>
> *entry-level*
>
> *Web 3.0*

Again, the hiring manager has essentially embedded the keywords in the ad itself. One of the more interesting words is *rock star*, which (if you think about it) probably translates to a person with a "can do" attitude and a "go getter" personality. It also indicates that the corporate culture is probably very informal – more like a startup than a Fortune 500 corporation. There are, you see, many clues just in that one word itself!

Todo: Brainstorm Your Keywords

It's a good exercise to go to a job site like Craigslist, CareerBuilder, or Monster, and browse the ads with an eye to keywords. In fact, your **TODO** is to do just that, plus sit down by yourself or with some friends, family, or colleagues, and start to write down on a piece of paper, or a WORD / Google document, a list of potential keywords that describe the job you want, whether it's your first job or the next job in your career. Don't worry at this point about organization, about volumes, or values, or anything technical, just create a list of keywords that "describe" the job you want from the perspective of the hiring manager.

CREATE A KEYWORD LIST

Pay attention to different types of keywords, such as **skill keywords** (*WordPress, Web Design, can work on BMWs, etc.*), **job level** keywords (*entry-level, advanced, intermediate*), and **personality** keywords (*team-player, positive attitude, detail-oriented*).

Tools: Tools to Assist in Keyword Discovery

Fortunately, there are some good tools and methods that can assist you in this exercise. Here are some of the best:

- **Job Categories**. Go to a site such as Craigslist or CareerBuilder, and write down the categories as indicated on the site. Use the site navigation / search and look for "preset" categories or "autosuggestions" as you type. Craigslist, for example, has a nice hierarchy of jobs. Look for related skills, adjacent skills, or skills you might not have thought of. Thoroughly browse available job listings with an eye to keywords that match "what you want," with "what they are looking for." **Add them to your list**.
- **Autocomplete Engines**. Go to a site such as Indeed.com or CareerBuilder, and start typing keywords you've already brainstormed. Pay attention to the autocomplete suggestions. Look for related skills, adjacent skills, or skills you might not have thought of. Thoroughly browse available job listings with an eye to keywords that match "what you want," with "what they are looking for." **Add them to your list**.
- **Use LinkedIn**. Sign in to LinkedIn, and use the LinkedIn search box to type in your keywords. Pay attention to the results returned and **add relevant keywords to your list**.
- **Use Google's autocomplete and related searches**. Go to Google.com, and type in your keywords plus the word "job". Pay attention to Google's autocomplete feature. Hit enter, and scroll to the bottom, look for "related searches" at the bottom of the page. A good search is "job description." **Add relevant keywords to your list**.

My **Job Search & Career-building Dashboard** and **Job Search & Career-building Resource Book** each have a section on keyword-generating tools. Use the *Google AdWords Keyword Planner*, for example, to brainstorm synonyms and related job titles and words. (Remember: To access the **Dashboard**, just go to https://www.jm-seo.org/dashboard/careers/).

> *As you brainstorm your keywords, remember to look for "connection points" between the job you want and the needs of the employer; you need to match your preferences with the demands of the marketplace.*

Write all your keywords down on a WORD document / Google doc (or even a white board in your home office). Don't worry about organization at this point – you want to capture the "universe" of possible words that describe your dream job, or at least the next job on your career-building journey. After you have brainstormed your keywords, you'll have a pretty messy but complete list of the target keywords *by which a hiring manager might search.*

Next, step back and look at the keywords. Identify "keyword groups" that describe a job and/or skillset which describes a potential position that matches what you have with what they want. Your **TODO** is to take your keywords and write at least one, but up to five, different job descriptions that describe the job(s) that you want. Break these into skills, job level, and attitude keywords.

▶▶ DELIVERABLE: A JOB / CAREER KEYWORD WORKSHEET

We've come to the first deliverable for this chapter: a job / career keyword worksheet. Part 1 of this Worksheet will map out the keywords that hiring managers use to search that also match up to the type of job / career your desire. Part 2 will sketch out one to five keyword-heavy job descriptions that describe, in the words of a hiring manager, the ideal candidate for each position. Go to https://www.jm-seo.org/workbooks (click on Job Search and Career-building, enter the code 'careers2016' to register if you have not already done so), and click on the link to the "Job / Career Keyword Worksheet."

▶ MONITOR YOUR ONLINE REPUTATION

In Chapter 1, you "Googled" yourself as well as checked yourself out on the major social networks (Twitter, LinkedIn, Facebook, Instagram, etc.), and, if necessary, ran a background check and credit report. This is to establish a baseline of the *Internet You*, the *You* that a hiring manager might find if he researched your online brand identity. What would he find, if anything? What would be positive, and what would be negative, in terms of your job or career goals?

Now, it's time to set up a **Personal Reputation Monitoring** system. You want to systematically monitor the *Internet You* and your online reputation. There are two elements here:

1. **Search**. If a hiring manager pro-actively searches for your keywords on Google, on LinkedIn, on a career site like CareerBuilder or Monster for resumes, do you come up for your target keywords? If so, how high towards the top? If not, you'll have a **TODO** of beginning to plan out how to remedy this (More in Chapter 6 on Search Engine Optimization).
2. **Research**. If a hiring manager is researching your online reputation and you as an individual to see if you would be a good hire or a candidate for a promotion, what will he find? You want to know what's out there on the Internet about you specifically, and over time, take steps to make that online personal brand image as positive and powerful as possible.

In subsequent chapters, we'll explore how to influence your online reputation in a positive manner, but at this point, we just want to set up a personal reputation monitoring system. Here are the three basic **TODOs**:

TODO Search – (they're looking for a job candidate)

- Identify the **media** that are most likely to be searched by a hiring manager to potentially find candidates like you based on keywords. It might be LinkedIn or Google, or hiring sites like Monster or CareerBuilder. It might be industry-specific job boards or places where candidates have profiles or can post their resumes. Your first step is to list out the media, which a hiring manager (or recruiter / headhunter), might use if she were proactively looking for you.
- Next, using the keywords you have identified in your Keyword Worksheet, map out **relevant search queries** that she might use. (These are called "educational queries" or just "search queries").

- Next, **create a spreadsheet** or gridline that has the keyword query, the media, and whether you show up or not in search, and if so, in what position. Don't be surprised if you are completely invisible – that's pretty common!

TODO Research – (they've found one, and are researching his or her reputation)

- Identify the media that are most likely to be used by a hiring research who knows your name (*when / if you are a prospective hire*), and wants to research your online reputation. It's almost certainly Google, but may also be sites like LinkedIn, Facebook, Twitter, and even background databases or credit reporting agencies.
- Next, using your name plus attributes that might go alongside your name (e.g., your keywords as in "Jason McDonald SEO" or "Mary Smith WordPress" or "Aileen McDonald Tulsa Oklahoma"), map out relevant search queries. (These are called "branded" or "reputational" search queries).
- Next, create a spreadsheet or gridline that has the branded search query, the media, and whether you show up or not in search, and if so, what type of information is present. *Is it positive, negative, or neutral*? Briefly describe what you find.

Tools to Monitor Your Reputation

The **Job Search and Career-building Dashboard** has a section of reputation monitoring tools. (Remember: To access the Dashboard, just go to https://www.jm-seo.org/dashboard/careers/). Here are some of my favorites and how to use them:

- **Google Alerts**. Make sure you have a Gmail and/or Google account, and are signed in to Google. Next, go to https://www.google.com/alerts. You can learn more about them at http://jmlinks.com/8u.
- **Saved Google Searches**. Simply go to Google and Google your own name plus your keyword(s). You can then "bookmark" these searches in your browser. You can learn how to bookmark in Google Chrome at http://jmlinks.com/8v. To see an example for "Jason McDonald SEO," go to http://jmlinks.com/8w.
- **SocialMention.com** (http://jmlinks.com/8x) – enter your name and/or your name plus keywords to monitor recent mentions across social media.

»» DELIVERABLE: AN ONLINE REPUTATION AUDIT

We've come to the second **deliverable** for this chapter: The *Online Personal Reputation Audit Worksheet*. This worksheet maps out how visible you are in terms of *search*, and how positive or negative your online reputation is in terms of **research**. Go to https://www.jm-seo.org/workbooks (click on Job Search and Career-building, enter the code 'careers2016' to register if you have not already done so), and click on the link to the "Online Personal Reputation Audit Worksheet."

You'll want to fill this out at least monthly when you are pro-actively searching for a job, and at least quarterly if you are in career-building mode. It's OK, if at first you are completely invisible. However, over time you want to become more visible in search and more positive when research is done into your online reputation.

In Chapter 6 on personal websites and SEO, we'll discuss ways to improve your online reputation, but in a nutshell:

- **Prevent Negative Information**. Making enemies in real life, or online, is never a good idea. Try your best to get along with other people in your professional life. The best way to prevent negative information about you online is NOT to motivate "haters" to post that information in the first place!
- **Crowd Out Negative Information with Positive Information**. As we get into Content Marketing, especially but not only blogging, you'll want to start pushing out content onto the Internet, that puts your best personal brand image forward (and crowds out less flattering materials).

These two mechanisms of **preventing negative information** and **crowding out negative information with positive information** are the two primary tools of online reputation management.

≫ Be Cool: Be a "Helpful Expert"

As we conclude this chapter, let's return to our hiring manager. What does she want? What is she looking for? How does what you have to offer meet her needs, whether it's for a new hire or for someone to promote?

BE A HELPFUL EXPERT

In a nutshell, in most cases, she's looking for what I would call a **helpful expert**. This might be at an entry-level, a mid-level, or an advanced level expert, but nonetheless she's looking for someone who has:

- **the required skillset** – the ability to do the job required, in a proficient if not outstanding manner; and
- **a good attitude and personality** – someone who, if not cheerful, at least has a "good attitude" and is "easy to work with."

Everything else in this Workbook really boils down to this: creating and nurturing a personal brand image that presents you as a **helpful expert** in your chosen field.

5
PARTY ON

Most books on **job search** and **career-building** either focus on the high level of the "spirituality" of searching for a job or focus on the low level of "technical details" such as which job search sites to use, how to network on LinkedIn, and the age-old debate over whether a paper resume can exceed one page in length.

It's either a 1960s hippie journey to a "job worth doing" or a cold-and-heartless struggle to "put food on the table" a la George Orwell's 1984.

I want to offer you a different, more relevant "mental model" of how to look for a job and advance your career in today's Internet age: **a party with a purpose**.

You see, you're **throwing a party** in a sense, when you look for a job or seek to advance your career. How so? Well, in a nutshell, here's how:

You're "inviting" potential employers to take a look at you, you're letting them "feast" on your blog, your YouTube channel, your latest share of industry news, etc. you're "convincing them" that you are a trustworthy, helpful expert (i.e., that your "party" is not only fun but useful), and you have an ulterior motive: to saunter off together with a potential employer for a "private interview" and ultimately to "get the job" or "get a promotion."

It's a party with a purpose!

Yes, you want to get a job you love! Yes, you want to find employers who will pay you well! Yes, you want to throw a "party" that attracts the kinds of employers you want, provides them with what they want (great food and entertainment). And yes, you want this party to end up in a consummated deal: a career you love, and a job that pays you well.

In this Chapter, we are going to explore what's more formally called "content marketing," and we'll use this metaphor of a **party** to help you understand what you're doing on the Internet as you build the "brand called you."

Let's get started!

Todo List:

» You're Throwing a Party (About You)

» Recognize the Job Search and Career-building Illusion

» Revisit the Relevant Discovery Paths

» Identify Goals and KPIs

» Set Up a Content Marketing Machine

»» Deliverable: A Content Marketing Plan

»» Appendix: Top Content Marketing Resources

» You're Throwing a Party (About You)

Have you ever **attended** a party? You know, received an invitation, showed up, said hello and various meets and greets to other guests, ate the *yummy yummy* food, drank the liquor (or the diet soda), hobnobbed with other guests, ate some more food, danced the night away, thanked the hosts, and left?

> *Attending* a party is all about *showing up*, *enjoying* the entertainment and food, and *leaving*.

Have you ever **used** Twitter, Facebook, or Instagram? How about Pinterest, Snapchat, or YouTube? You know, logged in, checked out some funny accounts, read some posts, posted back and forth with friends and family, checked your updates, and then logged out? Have you ever **used** Google to find something? Perhaps have you used either social media or Google to find something you wanted to "buy" like a home cleaning service, a party jump house for the kids, or even a new Gucci purse?

That's *attending* a party. That's *using* search and/or social media.

> *Using* search or social media is all about *logging in, enjoying* what's new and exciting, and *logging out.*

In this scenario, you're the "buyer" looking for something to "buy" from the "seller."

> *But there's a flip side to the job search and career-building process: being the "seller" and producing the "party," a party so amazing that the "buyer" not only gets excited but she actually "makes the purchase."*

Let's look at this more concretely. Imagine that you are the person "throwing the party" and the hiring manager is the person "showing up""

> *For example, you will be "producing" a LinkedIn profile (the "party"), one that will so excite a hiring manager or recruiter ("the party attendee") that they will reach out to you with a job interview request.*

> *For example, you will be "producing" a blog post that is so insightful that a key influencer or key employee ("the party attendee") at one of your target companies will recommend to the hiring manager that she give you a call.*

> *For example, you will be "producing" an Instagram feed so provocative that a key employee ("the party attendee") at a commercial photography company will be moved to pull your resume to the top of the heap.*

Throwing a party, you see, is something entirely different from **attending** a party. Similarly, **marketing yourself for your career** via search and social media is something entirely different from **using** search or social media.

You are the "**party thrower**."

The employer or hiring manager is the "**party attendee**."

Your Internet **content** - such as your blog, your YouTube channel, your Instagram feed, or your LinkedIn profile and posts – is the **food**, **entertainment**, and **fun** that keeps the party going.

This chapter explores the basics of Internet *content marketing*: of **throwing** the "search and social media party" vs. just **showing up**.

That word *marketing* is very important. We're exploring how to use search and social media to enhance your personal brand online, grow your visibility to more employers and those who can advance our career, or even (*gasp!*) use search and social media to get job interviews and land amazing jobs.

PARTY ON: BECOME A

GREAT PARTY-THROWER

Internet marketing is the art and science of throwing "great parties" on Google, Bing, Twitter, Facebook, LinkedIn, YouTube, Pinterest and the like in such a way that potential employers not only show up to enjoy your "online party about you" but also are primed to take the next steps of asking you in for an interview and even giving you that job or promotion.

Let's explore this analogy further. How is Internet *marketing* and Internet *career-building* like *throwing a party*?

Here are three ways:

Invitations. A great party needs great guests, and the first step to getting guests is to identify an attendee list, and send out invitations. Who will be invited? How will we invite them – will it be by phone call, email, postal mail, etc.? For your Internet career marketing, you'll need to identify your target employer(s) and brainstorm how to get them to "show up" on your blog or social media sites, via tactics like sending out emails, being found on search engines like Google or Bing, having an amazing blog that gets shared on LinkedIn, cross-posting your Facebook to your Twitter, or your LinkedIn to your blog, advertising, or even using "real world" face-to-face invitations like "Hey, follow me on Twitter to stay informed about important industry happenings."

And – just like at a real-world party – friends can invite friends. So, you want to use **promotional tactics** to get contacts of employers to "show up" at your party and then "invite" potential employers to your online party about you.

Internet marketing requires having a promotion strategy.

Entertainment. Will your party have a band, a magician, a comedian, or just music? What is your entertainment strategy? What kind of food will you serve: Mexican, Chinese, Indian, Tapas, or something else? Similarly, for your Internet marketing: why will potential employers "hang out" on your blog, check you out on LinkedIn, "like" your Facebook page or "subscribe" to your YouTube channel? Will it be to learn something? Will it be because it's fun or funny? Will it be because you are a "person to watch?"

Internet marketing for job search and career-building requires –

- *having a **content marketing strategy**, a way to systematically produce informative, useful content (blog posts, infographics, images, videos) that showcases your expertise, talent, and personality...*
- *having a **promotion strategy** so that hiring managers, employers, and key employees who can advance your career actually to visit your blog, watch your YouTube video, enjoy your LinkedIn shares of key industry news...*
- *having a clear **call to action** so that these key influencers **to take the next step** of reaching out to you with an email, phone call, or even job interview or job offer...*

Hosting. As the host of your party, you'll "hang out" at the party, but while the guests (a.k.a. potential employers) are busy enjoying themselves, you'll be busy, meeting and greeting, making sure everything is running smoothly, and doing other behind-the-scenes tasks. Similarly, in your Internet marketing for job search and career-building, you'll be busy coordinating content, interacting with guests and even policing the party to "kick out" rude or obnoxious guests.

Internet marketing requires behind-the-scenes management, often on a day-to-day basis, to ensure that everything is running smoothly, up to and including dealing with "rude" guests.

INTERNET MARKETING IS

THROWING A PARTY

Let's assume, for example, you're going to throw your wife an amazing 40th birthday party (or if you're young your girlfriend an amazing 21st birthday party). Before that party, you'll probably start attending other parties with a critical eye – noting what you like, and what you don't like, what you want to imitate, and even reaching out to the magicians, bands, and bartenders to find out what they cost and possibly hire them for your own party.

You'll "inventory" other parties and make a list of likes and dislikes, ideas and do-not-dos, and use that information to systematically plan your own party.

As an Internet marketer, therefore, you should "attend" the parties of other personal brands online. Identify personal brands you like online, "follow" or "like" them, and keep a critical eye on what they're doing. **Inventory** your likes and dislikes, and **reverse engineer** what other savvy career marketers are up to. And in your industry, do the same: follow companies in your own industry, again with the goal of "reverse engineering" their Internet marketing strategy, successes, and failures. Companies, after all, can be experts at marketing and to market a product isn't that different from marketing yourself.

For your first **TODO**, return to my list of people with powerful online brand images at http://jmlinks.com/8z. Please browse this list, and a) identify persons who interest you as potential "models" of strong online personal brands, and b) begin to reverse engineer how they nurture and promote their personal brand online in terms of a search strategy and a strategy on social media sites like LinkedIn, Facebook, YouTube, or Twitter. What is their Personal Branding Statement, and how are they promoting this online?

It's really important to have a specific list of three to five people, whom you want to follow and emulate. Imitation, after all, is the highest form of flattery. Download the **Personal Brand Examples worksheet**. For the worksheet, go to https://www.jm-seo.org/workbooks (click on Job Search and Career-building, enter the code 'careers2016' to register if you have not already done so), and click on the link to the "Personal Brand Examples" worksheet.

In addition, go to Google and search for "famous" or "relatively famous" people who are likely to be "like" the brand you want to become. If, for example, you are a photography student and want to land a job as a corporate photographer, do Google searches for "corporate photographers" and identify some strong personal brands that inspire you. If, for example, you want to get a job as a C+ programmer in the consumer electronics sector, Google "C+ programmers" and identify some strong personal brands. Bookmark or write down the personal websites of a few of these people.

Another good way to identify strong personal brands to emulate is to first go to Amazon, second search for books based on your keywords, and then Google those authors. Almost every author will have a personal website, Facebook page, Twitter account, etc. LinkedIn searches are yet another way to build your list. Your mission is to create a short list of strong personal brands online that will serve as sources for party inspiration.

» RECOGNIZE THE JOB SEARCH / CAREER BUILDING ILLUSION

Successful Internet marketing, like all forms of marketing, has a heavy dose of **illusion**, just like successful parties have a heavy dose of illusion.

How so?

Let's think for a second about an amazing party. Think back to a holiday party, a wedding or Bar mitzvah, a great birthday or graduation party, or even a corporate event you attended. Was it fun? *Did it seem magical?* It probably did.

Now, if you've ever had the fortune (or *misfortune*) of planning such an event – what was that like? Was it fun? Was it magical? Perhaps yes, perhaps no, perhaps a little of both. But it was also probably a lot of work, "in the background," to make sure that the party ran smoothly.

Attending a great party if just *fun, fun, fun.*

Throwing a great party is *a lot of work,* and (if it goes right) a feeling of great satisfaction, but still *a lot of work* (behind the scenes).

Great parties have an element of **illusion** in them: they *seem* effortless, while *in reality* (behind the scenes) an incredible amount of strategy, planning, and hard work goes on. Similarly, Internet marketing efforts including strong personal brands online (*think Katy Perry or Lady Gaga, think Bishop Robert Barron or Kevin VanDam, Stephen King or Zak George)*, create an illusion. They (only) "seem" spontaneous, they (only) "seem" effortless. They only "seem" like Greek gods to you and me as mere (online) mortals. However, in the background, a ton of work is going on to promote, manage, and grow these "Internet personal branding parties."

ILLUSION IS COMMON TO PARTIES

With respect to **online personal branding**, this illusion often creates a weird problem for you vis-a-vis your self-esteem and belief that "you can do it." Zak George may be amazing online on his YouTube channel, Steve Blank may be amazing online on Twitter, or Simone Anne may be amazing online on Pinterest. Not to mention Katy Perry or Lady Gaga or other famous personal brands like Ellen DeGeneres.

You, however, know your own faults and limitations, so you get discouraged.

How can you possibly be as cool as one of these amazing personal brands? Or even how can you possibly be as cool as that man or woman who snuck past you to get the interview, get the job, and get the promotion?

Comparing yourself to strong personal brands, in short, may get you discouraged. Please don't get discouraged! Remember these important facts:

- It's only an **illusion**; even famous people like Ellen DeGeneres or Steve Blank must work constantly on their online personal images. They're not better than you, they just "look" better than you.
- **You don't have to run faster than the bear, just faster than your buddy.** Meaning: You're not really competing with the likes of celebrities, but

rather with other real-world job seekers and career-advancers, who have the same level of skill and the same resources as you do.
- With a **systematic plan** and **systematic effort**, you **CAN** do it!

For your second **TODO**, organize a meeting with your team (it may just be "me, myself, and I"). Brainstorm all the things that have to get done to be successful at Internet marketing, ranging from conducting an **inventory** of famous personal brands you like and real-world competitors, to **setting up basic accounts** on Twitter, Facebook, LinkedIn, etc., to **creating content** to share on social media (images, photos, blog posts, infographics, videos), to **monitoring** social media channels on an on-going basis, and finally, to **measuring** your successes in the game of job search and career-building. Educate the team (again, it may be "me, myself and I") that although it might not take a lot of money, Internet marketing does take significant amount of work!

We're planning an awesome party here, people. It's going to take a ton of work, it's going to be a ton of fun, and it's going to be incredibly successful!

Now, don't get discouraged. *Please don't get discouraged.* There's a saying in job search that you should think of "searching for a job" as a "full time job." And I suppose, if you're employed, you should think of building your career as at least a "part-time job."

- Is Internet personal brand-building effortless? No.
- Is it worth it? Yes, yes, yes!

Know the Question and Find the Answer

Once you start to view Internet marketing as a systematic process, a great thing will happen: you'll formulate concrete, specific questions. And, *once you know the question, you can find the answer.* Let me repeat that:

Once you can formulate the question, you can find the answer.

Once you know the "concept" of what you want to do, the step-by-step is easily findable via Google and the help files.

Once you realize, for example, that Facebook allows cover photos, and that great Facebook personal brand-builders swap theirs out from time to time, you can create the "questions" of how do you create a cover photo for Facebook, what are the dimensions, etc. You can simply Google, "What are the dimensions of a cover photo on Facebook?"

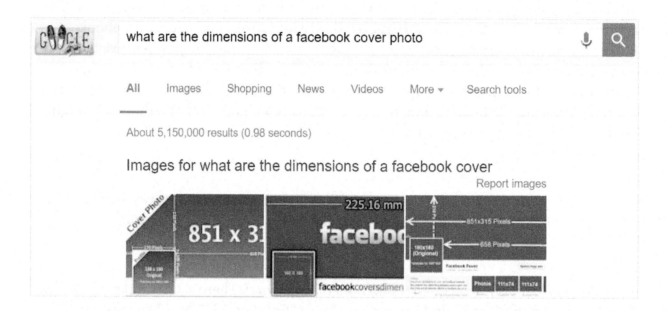

Similarly, once you know that you want a "unsubscribed trailer" to play on your YouTube channel for new visitors, you can go to the YouTube help files, and set it up.

ONCE YOU KNOW THE QUESTION, YOU CAN FIND THE ANSWER.

Once you know you need a personal website or blog, you can Google questions like "What's the best blog-hosting platform," or "How do you feed your WordPress blog to Twitter," and – guess what – you'll find the answers.

≫ REVISIT THE RELEVANT DISCOVERY PATHS

Before we plunge into personal blogging, Facebook, LinkedIn, Twitter, and the gang, it's worthwhile to sit back and ponder the big questions of marketing. Remember to revisit the basics (do this frequently):

- **What is your Personal Branding Statement?** What's attractive about you in the job / career market, in terms of skills and attitude?
- **Who are your target "customers?"** This means: Who are the hiring managers, headhunters, or other critical people who can advance your career?
- **What do you "have" that they "want?"** What are the "connection points" between their needs and your skills? This will usually be some type of informative content like a useful blog post, or great SlideShare presentation.

Next, revisit the **discovery paths**. How might potential employers first find out about you, and second, get so excited about you as to offer you a job interview or even a job or career advancement?

Fortunately, there are only five paths of discovery used by hiring managers. **Only five**. Every way that an employer or hiring manager finds a job candidate to bring in for an interview or identifies a person to promote to a better career position can be categorized by the following five **discovery paths**.

Let's review those, as we begin to think about **content marketing**, and chart out the scenarios of the hiring manager:

Search. The search path occurs when the hiring manager is "searching" for a job candidate. He visits career sites like Monster.com or CareerBuilder.com and searches resumes, or he searches LinkedIn for the profiles of people he wants to headhunt.

> **Scenario**: the hiring manager finds your resume online and thinks, "Wow! This resume exactly matches what I'm looking for, and this candidate looks amazing!"

> **Your job**: know your keywords and embed them into your resume and LinkedIn profile.

Review / Recommend / Trust. The review / recommend /trust path is based on "trust indicators." In it, the hiring manager perhaps already knows about you, or has been given a recommendation about you. In this path, she turns to

Internet searches and other "trust indicators," which indicate you are as wonderful as they say you are. Having an expert-looking profile on LinkedIn can be a "trust indicator" as can a recommendation from a friend or colleague also plays into reviews and trust.

> **Scenario**: the hiring manager checks you out online, finds your amazing personal website, and thinks, "Wow! This candidate is really on top of it — what a fantastic and relevant blog!".

>> **Your job**: create a personal website / blog that validates you as a "helpful expert."

Electronic Word-of-mouth (eWOM)/ Share / Viral. Wow! This candidate is great. Did you read her amazing blog post on the burning issues of our industry? Did you catch her talk at our industry's annual trade show? Or did you see that portfolio of amazing insights on SlideShare? The share path occurs when a person whom a hiring manager trusts loves you so much that they "share" you (or more specifically, your blog post, your YouTube video, your SlideShare deck) on social media — be that via electronic word of mouth, a share on his or her Facebook page or LinkedIn profile, or even a viral video on YouTube.

> **Scenario**: Bob (the technical guy) walks into Susan's office (the hiring manager), and says, "Hey Susan, I know we're freaking out a bit about corporate cyber security. Look at this really cool blog post of ten tips to think about. Perhaps we should reach out to this gal, she looks like she's available in the job market!"

>> **Your job**: create informative online content that the contacts of hiring managers read, and then recommend you to the hiring manager for interviews (or career promotions).

THINK LIKE A HIRING MANAGER

Interrupt. The interrupt path is the bad boy of online marketing. Interrupt marketing occurs in job search most commonly via the unsolicited email. Somehow you acquire the email address of someone who is a hiring manager or one of his colleagues. You reach out, in an unsolicited way. Dangerous? Yes. Successful? At times yes. Likely to provoke a negative reaction? Absolutely.

Scenario: the hiring manager, Susan, gets an unsolicited message from you via LinkedIn, explaining you have just posted a funky YouTube video to your channel explaining why an English Major from the University of Oklahoma knows more about cybersecurity than a computer major from some Carnegie Mellon University. Plus, it has a cat in it. Intrigued, she watches and then contacts you.

> **Your job**: create the "yummy" content that is the "excuse" or "bait" that when she gets your unsolicited contact, she'll take the next steps of "consuming" your content and even reaching out to you with a first step towards a relationship.

Browse. The browse path is a little similar to the interrupt path. In it, the hiring manager is looking for something, reading something, or watching something probably in their industry, and alongside comes something else. For example, they Google search an industry topic such as "the impact of carbon offsets on petroleum refining in California," and they find a few blog articles, one of them, yours. They're not really searching for you – but once they find some of your content, they discover you are awesome enough to reach out to for a potential career advancement.

> **Scenario**: the hiring manager is browsing an industry blog about the travails of background checks on cybersecurity employees, and she finds your blog post about ten questions you might not think to ask. Intrigued, she reaches out to you with an offer of an interview.

> **Your job**: create blog posts, YouTube videos, Instagram photos and other content that might be browsed by hiring managers or their contacts, and then provoke a level of interest that encourages a contact.

For your third **TODO**, download the **Think Like a Hiring Manager worksheet**. For the worksheet, go to https://www.jm-seo.org/workbooks (click on Job Search and Career-building, enter the code 'careers2016' to register if you have not already done so), and click on the link to the "Think Like a Hiring Manager" worksheet."

In this worksheet, you'll brainstorm what hiring managers (or their contacts who can advance your career) are looking for, as well as, the most relevant "discovery paths" by which potential customers find your products. That in turn, will get you to start thinking about which media are the most relevant to your online personal branding efforts.

▶▶ IDENTIFY GOALS AND KPIs (KEY PERFORMANCE INDICATORS)

Marketing is about measurement, and that goes for marketing yourself as a person as well. Are you helping your personal brand image? Are you encouraging solicitations from hiring or promotion managers? How do you know where you are succeeding, and where there is more work to be done? Why are you spending all this blood, sweat, and tears on Internet marketing anyway?

In today's overhyped job search and career-building marketplace, it's easy to be and feel overwhelmed. You may feel like you must have a blog, you must be on Twitter, you must have not only a killer LinkedIn profile but a killer stream of updates to share. *You must, you must, you must.* This feeling is called "Internet Guilt," but the reality is that you should only do those things that actually help your job search or career goals, and throw all the other stuff overboard.

All of the search and social media companies – Google, Facebook, Twitter, Pinterest, Yelp – have a vested interest in overhyping the importance of their platform, and using fear to compel job seekers to "not miss out" by investing in their platform. This goes double for posting your resume to sites like Monster.com, CareerBuilder.com, or sites specific to your industry. Everyone is in the business of overhyping their importance.

Identifying goals and KPIs will help you measure your progress step-by-step, and avoid Internet Guilt as you realize that you want to do ONLY those things that actually help your carrer.

AVOID INTERNET GUILT

Let's identify some common goals for effective online personal marketing. Here are common goals or **Key Performance Indicators** (KPIs):

> **Trust Indicators.** Most hiring managers and those gatekeepers who can advance your career may not know you in person, if at all. Building "trust indicators" is a way to make sure that when they Google you or check you out on LinkedIn, they'll see a positive, reinforcing brand image. **KPIs** here would be things like not only having a LinkedIn profile but growing your connections, endorsements, and recommendations.

eWOM (electronic Word of Mouth). Every ambitious person wants to be talked about in his or her industry. As personal marketers, a common goal for us is to grow and nurture positive eWom. **KPIs** here might be positive conversations on Facebook about you (or your latest bit of content), retweets of your tweets on Twitter or reshares on LinkedIn, Instagram, etc., or even comments on your blog.

Hiring Manager Continuum. First there is interest in you, second there is research, third there is the interview, and fourth there is the rejection or offer. **KPIs** here, for example, would be the number of accesses of your LinkedIn profile or inquiries you receive from headhunters, etc. Keeping track of your phone or in-person interviews is a KPI as well. Also tracking not only rejections but offers is admittedly a key metric for anyone.

One Touch to Many. People may hear about you "one time," for example, if you are lucky enough to speak at a trade show or position a blog post to rank high on a Google search. You want to turn that one touch into many; you want to turn a meeting of you at a trade show into a connection on LinkedIn or a follow on Twitter. Measuring your followers is a **KPI** or goal that measures the growth of your reach to hiring managers and friends of hiring managers.

Promotion, promotion, promotion. No one knows you're in the market for a new job or career advancement, unless you tell them. In some way or another, you have to promote yourself in a professional manner. But it's still promotion. Encouraging social sharing / eWOM / viral marketing is a huge, huge goal for Internet marketing, and this means you have to produce useful content (more on this later) and promote it to widen your shares. **KPIs** here would be the views, comments, and shares of a key post you make to Facebook, LinkedIn, or Twitter.

Note, in particular the desired "virtuous circle" of Internet marketing:

The more connections you have on LinkedIn or Twitter, the more people you can alert about your blog posts or new YouTube videos. The more people you alert, the more people who read these items. The more people who read or view these items, the more they share it with their connections. The more you post the cooler you look, and the cooler you look, the more resources you'll have (in the form of higher paying jobs) to expend on self-promotion. A virtuous personal brand means that your content promotes your shares, your shares promote your content, all of this promotes your online personal brand image, and your personal brand image online advances your career.

NURTURE A VIRTUOUS CIRCLE

Nurturing a virtuous circle is a **major** goal of an effective online personal branding system! And finally, don't forget, that in most cases we want all of these "soft goals" to turn into "hard goals": a positive online personal brand image leads to better interview opportunities, better jobs, and a better career.

For your fourth **TODO**, download the **Job Search and Career-building KPI Worksheet**. For the worksheet, go to https://www.jm-seo.org/workbooks (click on Job Search and Career Building, enter the code 'careers2016' to register if you have not already done so), and click on the link to the "Job Search and Career-building KPI" worksheet.

In this worksheet, you'll identify your "hard" goals and your "soft" goals on search and social media.

» SET UP A CONTENT MARKETING MACHINE

Bring on the chips! Carry out the diet coke! Turn on the band! A great party needs great food and great entertainment, as these are the "fuel" of the successful party. Similarly, great Internet marketing needs the "fuel" of content: interesting (funny, shocking, outrageous, sentimental) blog posts, images, videos, photographs, infographics and instructographics, memes and even videos that will make it worthwhile to "subscribe" to your social channel (like / follow / circle) and keep coming back for more.

To succeed at online personal branding, you must succeed at **content marketing**. You **gotta gotta gotta** create a system for identifying and creating interesting content to share via your social networks.

You need a **content marketing machine**, making *blog posts, images, photographs, videos, shares of interesting content, comments,* and *other items* that constantly keep you "front of mind" in your target audience of employers and hiring managers.

Think for a minute about one of the strong personal brands you've identified. Take someone famous like Lady Gaga. She produces a lot of content! And she has many channels via which to share this content! A song or video might be posted to iTunes or YouTube, shared for free on Twitter or Facebook, and reshared by her adoring fans. She posts quips to her personal website (http://www.ladygaga.com), Tweets them out, shares on Instagram, produces videos, appears on TV... You can see that, she is not only producing her own content, she is commenting on / sharing the content of others, and she is deploying social media channels from YouTube to Facebook to Twitter to get the word out.

CONTENT IS TO INTERNET MARKETING AS FOOD IS TO A PARTY

Leaving aside the channels for sharing content, let's focus on the actual content itself. The "food" and "entertainment" as it were of your own personal branding party. You'll need to create a lot of content. Among the most commonly shared items are:

Blog Posts. An oldie but goodie: an informative, witty, funny, informational, or fact-filled post about a topic that matters to your target hiring managers and/or the contacts of the hiring managers that can recommend you as a candidate for a hire or promotion. You'll need a personal website and/or blog, and you'll need to create content that's witty and useful enough to not only be read but also be shared.

Images. Photographs and images are the bread-and-butter of Facebook, Instagram, and even Twitter. Everyone loves pictures, and one picture is worth a thousand words.

Memes. From grumpy cat to success kid, memes make the funny and memorable, sticky and shareable on social media. This special type of image – used in a tasteful way – can make you memorable as a job candidate.

Infographics and Instructographics. From how to tie a tie to sixteen ways you can help stop global warming, people love to read and share pictures that tell a story, hopefully with facts. Creating something useful in picture format means being "sticky" in the mind of a potential employer.

Slide Shows. From SlideShare to just posting your PowerPoints online, you create a hybrid visual and textual cornucopia of social sharing fun. If you've ever given a presentation – whether to a class in college or to colleagues at an industry trade show – posting this to a service like Slideshare puts it out where all can see it.

Videos. If a picture tells a thousand words, a video can tell ten thousand. YouTube is a social medium in its own right, but the videos themselves are content that can be enjoyed and shared.

In summary, you'll need fuel to power your social media marketing. This fuel comes in two main varieties: **other people's content**, and **your own content**. The advantage of the former is that it is easy to get, while the advantage of the latter is that because it's yours, you control the message. The disadvantage of other people's content is that you do not control the message (and it thereby promotes them to some extent), while the disadvantage of your own content is that its takes time and effort to produce.

> *To be an effective on search engines and as a social sharer, you need both:* ***other people's content*** *and* ***your own content***.

Your goal is to position yourself as a "useful expert," the "goto" person or brand, that people seek out in a very pro-active way to find interesting and useful stuff in your market ecosystem. My own brand, for example, at https://www.jasonmcdonald.org/ is all about sharing interesting, fun, and useful stuff on social media, AdWords, and SEO. That's why I have over 8,000 followers on Google+: *because I'm useful*.

TWO TYPES OF CONTENT

Before you get overwhelmed and think you can never have 8,000 followers on any social network, or you can never be as amazing as Lady Gaga, don't get discouraged. Everyone starts somewhere, and everyone's KPIs are not the same.

Just remember at this point:

- You've realized that **you need content** to "fuel" your personal brand image online.
- You've realized that this **useful content takes many forms**: from blog posts to images to YouTube videos to Slideshares.
- You've realized that smart marketers like Lady Gaga not only produce **their own content**, but they pro-actively **share other people's content**.
- You've realized you need to build a **"content marketing machine"** so that there is enough fuel in your system to power a strong blog, LinkedIn profile, Twitter account, etc.

You've come a long way already. *Don't be discouraged*! Let's turn now to some tools to identify shareable content. Remember you want to be sharing the type of content that your target hiring manager and her friends / contacts want to consume, just as the host of a great party doesn't produce the kind of food *she likes,* but rather the kind of food that *her guests like.* And she produces this systematically, so that the food "keeps on coming" even though the guests think it is magic, or an illusion, or they don't even notice all the hard work and planning that went in to keeping that food coming.

Other People's Content

Your goal here is to identify relevant content produced by other people such as relevant blog posts, images or infographics, videos, etc. By "curating" this content (*identifying the good stuff amidst the whirlwind of bad stuff on the Internet*), you'll provide a useful service to your followers. Like a good editor, you'll identify trends and topics to which they should pay attention vs. nonsense and useless stuff that doesn't merit their attention.

The beauty of the Internet today is that there is a lot of content available from other people. You can identify this content, and share this content, thereby positioning yourself as a helpful expert in tune with the heartbeat of your target industry. Once you set up a system, you'll be surprised at how little time it will take to be a useful sharer of information!

There are wonderful tools to help you systematically identify and share other people's content. (All are listed in the *Job Search and Career-building Resource Book*, content marketing section). Here are some of my favorites:

Feedly (http://feedly.com) - Feedly is a newsreader integrated with Google+ or Facebook. It's useful for social media because you can follow important blogs or other content and share it with your followers. It can also spur great blog ideas of your own.

Buzzsumo (http://buzzsumo.com) - Buzzsumo is a 'buzz' monitoring tool for social media. Input a website (domain) and/or a topic and see what people are sharing across Facebook, Twitter, Google+ and other social media. Great for link-building (because what people link to is what they share), and also for social media.

Easely (http://easel.ly) - Use thousands of templates and design objects to easily create infographics for your blog. A competitor is Piktochart (http://piktochart.com).

Meme Generator (http://memegenerator.net) - Memes are shareable photos, usually with text. But how do you create them? Why, use memegenerator.net.

In terms of other people's content, you want to first identify the "themes" of your personal brand which you want to talk about. A person seeking to advance his career as a tax CPA, for example, might monitor California tax law, small business, and individual tax shelter issues. He can then systematically monitor them via a tool such as Feedly, and use it to easily share other people's content across his social networks such as his Twitter or LinkedIn. A photographer seeking her first job as a wedding photographer at a photography studio might monitor content on trends in weddings today as well as trends in photography, both artistic and technological. By being a "helpful sharer" of this information, she can stay "top of mind" by providing useful content to business owners and hiring managers in the wedding and/or photography industries.

Take a moment and return to a few of the strong personal brands you have identified. Scan their Twitter accounts, for example. How much of that content is their own, and how much is useful content that they have identified or curated from others? Reverse engineer the marketing reason why they are sharing this content to their followers. Who's gaining what?

Simone Anne, for example, a photographer on my list of people with strong online personal brands, shared this tweet for example:

simone anne @_simoneanne · Feb 22

Don't teach girls to be scared (being scared isn't cute!) -

mobile.nytimes.com/2016/02/21/opi...

↩   ⇄ 1   ♥ 3   •••   View summary

Now this tweet is "other people's content" and points to a New York Times article on girls and fear. By sharing this she's building her online brand image, sharing content with her followers that's interesting to them, and staying "top of mind." By identifying other people's content to share, in short, she has "fuel" for her online personal brand image. The content is useful, interesting, and relevant to her brand image as a female photographer.

Now, let's turn to *your own content*, i.e. *content that you produce yours*elf.

Your Own Content

The advantage to your own content is that, because you produce it, it can showcase your personal brand image and tie into your career goals in a very efficient manner. Whether it's a blog post on a timely topic or a photograph of a happy married couple that substantiates you as a budding young photographer, your own content can do amazing things for your job search or career advancement.

Here are the steps.

The first step is to brainstorm a useful content idea (*e.g., an infographic on common ways for small business owners to save on taxes, or sixteen ways weddings can go terribly wrong, or why you as a CPA feel that the Alternative Minimum Tax should be abolished*). The second to create it in whatever format you want (image, infographic, blog post, video), something easier said than done. You'll quickly realize that some types of content such as blog posts or images can be quite easy to create, whereas others such as videos are more complex. You'll also realize that some types of content come naturally to you (e.g. blog posts if you are a good writer, photographs if you are a good photographer) and others do not. Once you have the content itself, your third step is to share it across your relevant social networks.

Let's assume you have an idea about common ways that small business owners could save money. You might have identified things such as using SKYPE for phone calls vs. having a land line, outsourcing some types of jobs to sites such as Fiverr rather than hiring people full-time, and rather than advertising in the print Yellow Pages, using social media sites like Yelp or Google+ to get customer reviews. Next, you need to take this idea and draft it onto one or more of the available content medium:

- **Blog Post**. This isn't that different than a short English assignment in High School. Simply write up a very short essay entitled, "Ten Common Ways Small Business Owners Can Save Money."
- **Image or Infographic**. Take your blog post, and translate it into an infographic image. Use one of the free infographic tools such as Piktochart to create the infographic on top ten ways small businesspeople can save money.
- **YouTube**. Get out your webcam and film yourself counting down the top ten ways small business owners can save money "as if" you were David Letterman or some other TV personality.

You don't have to do all of these, but you do have to do one of them. The concept to grasp, is that the "idea" of the content (e.g., "ways small businesspeople can save money") has to be translated from idea to research to writing and then the "draft content" has to be produced in final form as in a blog post or YouTube video. Just like red wine can fill both a bottle and a glass, the "idea" of content can fill a blog post or a YouTube video.

Next, now that you have your content produced, it's time to share it to your social media networks. (We're assuming you've set up a Twitter account, Facebook Page, LinkedIn Profile, etc.). Turn to my favorite tool for systematic social sharing: Hootsuite (https://www.hootsuite.com/). Hootsuite is a free, cloud-based social media management tool. Hootsuite allows you to summarize and point to content such as a blog post or YouTube video, shorten the URL, simultaneously post it to Twitter, Facebook, Google+, LinkedIn, etc., and to schedule your posts across days, weeks, or months. Best of all it's free for up to three social accounts, and very reasonably priced if you need to share on more than three media.

Here's a screenshot:

The shared content is on the right, and the social networks indicated in blue are on the left. For a great list of the top ten tools for content marketing, please visit http://jmlinks.com/2h. More are included in the *Job Search and Career-building Resource Book*, available of course after you register your workbook.

For your final **TODO**, download and complete the **Content Marketing Worksheet**.

For the worksheet, go to https://www.jm-seo.org/workbooks (click on Job Search and Career-building, enter the code 'careers2016' to register if you have not already done so), and click on the link to the "Content Marketing Workbook."

Once you've started to work on your **content marketing machine**, you'll need a systematic rhythm of content identification, content production, and content sharing:

- **Content Identification (Other People's Content)**. You'll need to spend time at least once a week, if not every day, using tools like Feedly or Google Alerts to browse content that is relevant to your industry, educate yourself about worthwhile content, summarize this content into very short headline / paragraph format, and then share other people's content to your social media network accounts via Hootsuite.
- **Content Production (Your Own Content).** You'll need to spend time brainstorming relevant content of your own that you want to produce, producing it (whether in blog post, image, or video format), and then sharing it via Hootsuite to your Facebook, Instagram, LinkedIn, Twitter, etc.
- **Sharing Content.** You'll need to set aside a time, perhaps weekly, for working with Hootsuite to share relevant content across your networks and respond to any conversations or shares that your content has generated.

If you think of your online marketing like throwing a party, you'll realize that content, like the food or entertainment for a party, is something that you brainstorm, produce in a systematic way, and share with your target audience. When done well, your content will "feed your people" and they will like it (i.e., find it useful), it will position you as a "helpful expert," thereby building your online personal brand, and it will even provoke shares and inquiries, as people find it good enough for them to share with their own friends, family, and business networks.

Content, after all, is king.

» REMEMBER THE BIG PICTURE

At this point, you've begun to transition from thinking about your online job search and career building strategy to actually doing it. You've understood that Internet marketing is about "throwing" the party more than "attending the party." You've realized you need to start "paying attention" with regard to what other strong personal brand-builders are doing on search and social media, with an eye to "reverse engineering" their marketing strategy, so that you have ideas of what you like, and do not like, in terms of search or social media. You've started to brainstorm "discovery paths" and "goals" for your job search and career-building efforts.

And you've realized that once you've identified your goals, identified relevant search or social media, set up your social accounts, the really hard work will be a) promoting your social media channels, and b) creating the kind of content that makes them want to "like you," keep coming back for more, and share your message with their friends, family, and/or business colleagues.

You've understood that **content creation** and **promotion** are the big on-going tasks of successful Internet marketing.

» » DELIVERABLE: A CONTENT MARKETING PLAN

Now that we've come to the end of Chapter 5, your **DELIVERABLE** has arrived. For the worksheet, go to https://www.jm-seo.org/workbooks (click on Job Search and Career-building, enter the code 'careers2016' to register if you have not already done so), and click on the link to the "Content Marketing Plan" worksheet.

Next, we shall drill into individual media, starting with blogging, one of the backbone media of successful Internet personal branding.

>> APPENDIX: TOP CONTENT MARKETING JOB SEARCH AND CAREER-BUILDING TOOLS AND RESOURCES

Here are the top tools and resources to help you with content marketing. For an up-to-date and complete list, go to https://www.jm-seo.org/workbooks (click on Job Search and Career -building, enter the code 'careers2016' to register if you have not already done so). Then click on the *Job Search and Career-building Resource Book* link, and drill down to the content marketing chapter.

BUZZSUMO - http://buzzsumo.com/

Buzzsumo is a 'buzz' monitoring tool for social media. Input a website (domain) and/or a topic and see what people are sharing across Facebook, Twitter, Google+ and other social media. Great for link-building (because what people link to is what they share), and also for social media.

Rating: 5 Stars | **Category:** tool

FEEDLY - http://feedly.com/

Feedly is a newsreader integrated with Google+ or Facebook. It's useful for social media because you can follow important blogs or other content and share it with your followers. It can also spur great blog ideas.

Rating: 5 Stars | **Category:** resource

GOOGLE EMAIL ALERTS - https://www.google.com/alerts

Use Google to alert you by email for search results that matter to you. Input your company name, for example, to see when new web pages, blog posts, or other items surface on the web. Enter your target keywords to keep an eye on yourself and your competitors. Part of the Gmail system.

Rating: 4 Stars | **Category:** service

TAG BOARD - https://tagboard.com/

Hashtags have moved beyond Twitter. This amazing cool tool allows you to take a hashtag and browse Facebook and Twitter and Instagram, etc., so see posts that relate to that hashtag. Then you can find related tags. Oh, and you can use it as a content discovery tool, too.

Rating: 4 Stars | **Category:** tool

Google News - https://news.google.com/

Excellent for reputation management as well as keeping up-to-date on specific keywords that matter to you and your business. First, sign in to your Google account or gmail. Second, customize Google news for your interest. Third, monitor your reputation as well as topics that matter to you. Go Google!

Rating: 4 Stars | **Category:** service

Foter - http://foter.com

Add some color (or monochrome) to your blog posts with Foter. Search over 200 million high-quality, free, downloadable stock photos. Don't forget to copy and paste photo attribution credits included with the images details into your blog post.

Rating: 4 Stars | **Category:** resource

THIS PAGE INTENTIONALLY LEFT BLANK

(PONDER IT)

6
YOUR WEBSITE

Words – in both written and spoken forms – make humans unique. Not surprisingly, a central element in your personal branding strategy for job search and career-building is a **personal website** or **blog**, the foundation of which is the **written word**.

Think for a moment about the things you "do" on the Web – reading newspapers or blogs, sharing posts on Facebook or Twitter, even commenting on images or videos. Fundamentally all of these involve *words*, both words being *written* and words being *read*. Indeed, both a paper resume and an oral job interview rely on words, so it stands to reason that a well-written personal website is an essential component of Internet-based job search and career-building. Moreover, hiring managers search for job candidates by words, and along with key decision-makers they're likely to read your blog on the Web as much as talk with you on the phone.

In this chapter, I will explain and explore why you need a **personal website** or **blog** as the foundation of your personal branding strategy. You'll learn where to set up a website or blog, and how easy this can be. Next, I will connect your website or blog to the "search" function through an explanation of **SEO** "Search Engine Optimization," the art and science of getting your website or blog to rank at the top of Google, Bing, and Yahoo. Finally, I will turn to the **social media purpose** of blogging; blogs give you something to "point to" as well as something for your followers to "share."

Let's get started!

TODO LIST:

>> Get a Blog: Blogging Basics

>> Blogging for Trust

>> Blogging and Personal Websites for SEO

>> Sharing is Caring: Blogging for Social Media

» GET A BLOG: BLOGGING BASICS

To have a serious online brand, one needs a personal website or blog. At the outset, let's get something straight: there isn't really a big difference between a personal website or a blog. What we are talking about, at the most basic level, is:

- **A Personal Website**. A website, preferably at your own unique domain as in http://yourname.com/, is where you can describe your Personal Branding Statement, flesh this out in detail into specific categories and topics, and have a place to "post" content such as in-depth articles, papers, ebooks, and shorter blog posts.
- **A Blog**. A good personal website has a blog, and a good blog consists of short, timely posts where you describe and comment on industry-related topics. In this way, a *personal website* should contain a *blog* (although not all do), and for many people their *personal blog* is their *personal website*.

Since a personal website and blog are so intertwined for anyone seriously working on online personal branding for job search and career-building, I will use them interchangeably from now on. If I say "personal website," or just "website," "personal blog," or just "blog," I am referring to the same thing. It is a place on the Web that you control and also, where you can produce written content as part of your content marketing machine.

YOU NEED A BLOG

To see what I am talking about, take a look at my own personal website at https://www.jasonmcdonald.org/ and my blog at https://www.jasonmcdonald.org/blog/. I practice what I preach. My personal website is the central place where I create content, which I then optimize for search on sites like Google or Bing and share on social media networks like Twitter or LinkedIn. It's the "food" or "entertainment" for my on-going personal brand-building.

Next, revisit some of the personal brands on your list, or visit my list at http://jmlinks.com/9b. Run down the list and click onto an individual. You'll see that in most cases every one of these successful personal branders produces a personal website and/or blog. One of my favorites is marketing guru, Seth Godin, at http://jmlinks.com/9e. Notice how this website not only has a huge photo of him, but also on the right side has links to his blog, books, courses, biography, speaking opportunities, etc. It even says "Click on Seth's head to read his blog!" So click on his head, and you'll end up on his blog at http://jmlinks.com/9c. You can receive his blog via email, as well as follow him on Twitter at http://jmlinks.com/9d. In short, Seth Godin's personal website is his blog, and his blog is his primary strategy for creating interesting and, shareable content that keeps his personal brand "top of mind" among his target audience, in his case buyers of his wonderful books.

> *Best-selling author Seth Godin shows that it's not that difficult: his personal website is very sparse, and his on-going content marketing strategy is to produce daily quips and insights on the world of marketing.*

Return to the list of persons with strong Internet brands, or re-browse your own list. You'll see that almost all the time a personal website and/or blog is at the centerpiece of this online branding strategy.

> You need a website!

Website Basics

If you don't already have a personal website, you need to set one up. Fortunately, it's not hard, and it's not expensive. For most individuals, I'd recommend using Google's free Blogger.com service. Here's how it works:

- Go to **Gmail** at http://jmlinks.com/9f, if you do not already have a Google Gmail account. Follow the instructions to set up a Gmail for yourself. If you already have a Gmail account, log into your Gmail.
- Next, go to **Blogger.com** at http://jmlinks.com/9g. Since you're already signed into Gmail / Google, you'll automatically end up at the blogger creation screen.
- Click on the **New Blog** button in gray at the top left of the screen, and follow the set up instructions by giving the blog a Title, choosing a Web address, and selecting a template. Don't worry you can change the template (which controls the look and feel later).
- Google will then prompt you to "find a domain name for your blog and connect it instantly." For as little as $12 a year, you can have your own custom domain name such as http://www.yourname27.com. An example if my blogger blog at http://jasonplus.org/. You can use GoDaddy's Domain Name checker at http://jmlinks.com/12n to browse available domain names.

It's that easy to set up a personal website or blog, including a personalized domain name. Although I highly recommend you set up a domain for your personal website, you don't absolutely have to have one. You can just use a blogger subdomain. I have set up a sample for you at http://jasonssample.blogspot.com or http://jmlinks.com/9h.

Write Your First Blog Post

To write a blog "post," which is the equivalent of a short article, you simply go to blogger.com, find your blog (if you have more than one), and click on the orange pencil icon. Here's a screenshot:

Jason's Sample Blog

4 pageviews · 1 post, last published on Mar 13, 2016

To see a sample blog post, visit http://jmlinks.com/12p. Within the Blogger platform, to view your blog online, just click on the gray "view blog" link. We'll discuss writing blog posts in more detail as we go further.

Other Blogging / Personal Website Platforms

Blogger isn't the only blogging platform available. It's just easy, cheap, and even free (without a domain name). Also, since it's owned by Google, it's very SEO-friendly and it's well-integrated with Google+. For these reasons, I would recommend that someone who does not have a personal website start up with Blogger.

There are other platforms that compete with blogger, and they include:

- **WordPress.com** at http://jmlinks.com/9j. Not to be confused with the free WordPress.org software, WordPress.com is a "for profit" site that uses WordPress. Like blogger, it has both free and paid versions available. I am not as fond of it as Google's platform because it isn't as good for SEO and has some annoying "lock in" features at a technical level. Check out a sample personal website at http://jmlinks.com/9k.
- **Typepad.com** at http://jmlinks.com/9m. It is no longer free; Typepad has a minimal cost of about $9 / month.
- **Tumblr** at http://jmlinks.com/9n. Like Blogger, it has both free and paid versions and you can either use their domain or register your own. It is also as a social media platform in its own right. It is an excellent choice for more "Artsy" personal brands as it makes it very easy to upload and share image, video, MP4, and other forms of digital content. To see a sample blog, visit http://jmlinks.com/9p.

In addition to these, there are a host of more proprietary solutions that are more like "websites" than blogs. Simply go to Google and type in: Squarespace, Weebly, Websitebuilder, or Jimdo. I dislike, however, how these platforms "lock you in" to their proprietary system. Note: I do **not** recommend WIX, as it is terrible for SEO purposes.

WordPress

If you are serious about your personal website, and you want a platform that can easily be both a strong, structured personal website and a blog, the best platform to use is WordPress. However, the nomenclature is confusing. WordPress.com is their "paid" revenue-generating arm, and engages in quite a few "lock ins," which is why I would prefer Blogger if you are looking for something cheap and easy. WordPress.org is the platform, which can run on many ISPs such as GoDaddy, BlueHost, or WordPressEngine.

THE BEST BLOGGING PLATFORM: WORDPRESS

If you want a robust personal website and blog, here's what you should do. Identify an ISP (Internet Service Provider) that can both host your domain and install the WordPress software. Most provide standard easy-to-use WordPress templates at no additional cost, or you can hire a WordPress developer to really make your website amazing. My favorite hosting service here is GoDaddy's "Managed WordPress" at http://jmlinks.com/9q. They manage set-up, hosting, security, backup and all important technical aspects and even have a few free WordPress themes. (Themes govern the look and feel of a WordPress-based website). You can also go to a site like ThemeForest, ElegantThemes or other sites that sell themes (which control the look and feel of WordPress). Make sure that you choose a so-called "responsive" theme, which is one that looks good on the desktop, mobile phone, and tablet.

In addition to GoDaddy, other popular hosts are HostGator, BlueHost, and InMotion Hosting.

Your first **TODO** is, therefore, to identify which hosting site you want to use, ranging from Blogger to Tumblr to GoDaddy, and follow through on all the set up issues. It is absolutely essential to create a personal website because you need this as a place to "put" the content you need for your online personal brand.

▶▶ BLOGGING FOR TRUST

Now that you've set up your personal website, you need to begin to fill it with content. Here, you're not worried about being found on search engines like Google, nor "going viral" with your posts via Facebook or Twitter. You're simply using your personal website, as a "trust indicator" to verify and validate your credentials as a job candidate or person with a strong Internet brand image.

As you set up your website, I would recommend you conceptualize and lay out the following pages:

- **Your Home Page**. This page should state your Personal Branding Statement so that the user immediately understands who you are and what you can offer them. You should also design your home page as a "jumping off page" to your landing pages and blog posts.
- **Landing Pages**. These pages are "drill downs" into topic areas that anchor your personal brand. If you are going after a job as an accountant, and you have specialties in international tax, tax returns for small businesses, and QuickBooks bookkeeping, you'd create one unique page for each of these topics. Think of these as anchor content that does not change but helps the hiring manager to drill into key skillsets that you offer.
- **Blog Posts**. A good blog post is a short, simple three to four paragraph essay in which you expound on a timely topic. If, for example, you are an accountant and you are looking to build your career in international tax, you might have a blog post on new regulatory requirements of the FBAR (Foreign Bank and Financial Accounts) and what these mean for individuals with foreign assets.

While you will have one, and only one, home page, you may have around three to ten landing pages, and you might end up with hundreds or even thousands of blog posts on timely topics in your industry. Your blog posts will also show that you are educated about issues in your industry and able to make contributions to industry discussions. To see this in action, you can browse my own personal website at https://www.jasonmcdonald.org/. Notice the "one click links" from the home page to my defined landing pages, such as "SEO Consultant" or "Social Media Expert." Also notice the blog, which has many posts on many more esoteric topics.

A BLOG MAKES YOU LOOK LIKE AN EXPERT

In addition to my website, revisit some of the personal websites we have already identified. Take a look, for example, at a strong personal brand like Debbie Grattan (http://jmlinks.com/9r), who is a professional voice-over talent. Her brand is fun yet professional, and her skill is a versatile voice that can be used for TV commercials, corporate videos, and other types of messaging. Notice the structure of her website:

- **Home Page**: explains her Personal Branding Statement, that she is a voice over talent.

- **Landing Pages / Video Examples**. These "anchor pages" give examples of her work in various industry verticals.
- **Blog Posts** (bottom of the home page). These are Grattan's commentary on industry topics and issues of relevance to anyone looking for a voice over talent.

Even if you are looking for a job (as opposed to being self-employed), or you are already employed and seeking to build your brand online, the structure of your website should follow this same basic architecture: a **home page**, explaining your value proposition; **landing pages** drilling down to specific skills; and **blog posts**, commentating on industry topics and showcasing your skills as a "helpful expert."

Using the example of someone who wants to get a job as a photographer, this can be represented as:

Home Page. Explains what your personal website is about, and touches on your keyword themes.

Landing Page #1. This is a "drill down" to a specific keyword area, such as your expertise in wedding photography if you are a photographer.

Landing Page #2. This is a "drill down" to a specific keyword area, such as your expertise in corporate photography if you are a photographer.

Landing Page #3. This is a "drill down" to a specific keyword area, such as your expertise in child photography if you are a photographer.

Blog. This is an on-going place where you put timely content in the form of short blog posts.

Blog Post #1. This might be a short blog post on tips and pointers for how to get kids to smile during a photo shoot.

Blog Post #2. This might be a discussion of whether iPhones or Android phones are better for shooting photos for Instagram.

You the Job Candidate with a Strong Personal Website

Now, returning to the Debbie Grattan website, imagine a scenario. You are being considered for a job or a consulting gig as a voice over artist. Perhaps, it's your first job working at a studio that does voice overs for hire, or perhaps you want to move up the career ladder. The hiring manager reaches out to you for a job interview. The interview goes well. Next, she researches you online. If she finds a website like that of Debbie Grattan, you're hired: she's validated that you know what you're talking about. If she doesn't find anything, or she finds a poorly constructed website, you're invalidated and not hired.

> *The most basic purpose of a personal website, in summary, is as a "trust indicator." It should substantiate you and your personal brand image online. Even if it has only one reader (i.e., the hiring manager who gives you a job or promotion), it will have done its job!*

Remember, you do not actually need to "have a job" to produce a personal website. Even if you are new to the job market, or unemployed, you can (and should) produce a personal website that showcases your professional interest and skills, and commentates on industry issues, etc. Your website validates you as a "helpful expert," whether you have a job or not, or whether you are looking for your first job or a career promotion, etc. Be sure to keep it professional; this is the place for you to look serious and smart, not a place for you to post silly cat videos or controversial opinions about Donald Trump!

Your first chapter **DELIVERABLE** has arrived. Go to https://www.jm-seo.org/workbooks (click on Job Search and Career-building, enter the code 'careers2016' to register if you have not already done so), and click on the link to the "Personal Website and Blog Plan." Complete the first part of the worksheet, focusing on blog goals. Brainstorm whether your blog will be used as a "trust indicator," as an SEO strategy to be found on Google / Bing / Yahoo, for collateral on social media, or all of the above. If there are any other goals for your personal website, write those down as well.

≫ BLOGGING AND PERSONAL WEBSITES FOR SEO: SEO & JOB SEARCH

SEO, or Search Engine Optimization, is a huge topic. (Readers are referred to my companion workbook, the *SEO Fitness Workbook* (http://jmlinks.com/seo), for an in-depth explanation of how to succeed at SEO). You can also take my free short course in SEO at http://jmlinks.com/seomooc. With respect to personal branding, the basics of SEO will go a long way.

Let's first explain what SEO is and how it works, and then touch upon how to use your personal website as an SEO tool, so that you can be more findable on search engines.

SEO, to use a very appropriate analogy, is a lot like the process of getting a job. It has its **resume** (your **website**), its **references** (your inbound **links** and **social mentions**), and its job **interview** (your website **landing pages**).

Understand That SEO Parallels Getting a Job

Let's consider a search for a job. How does the job search market work? People (like you) want to "be found" as the "ideal" candidate for a position. So what do they do? Three important things:

> **Resume - Create a resume.** Job seekers create a **keyword-heavy resume** that explains the job that they want to get, and their qualifications for that job. If, for example, they want a job as a *BMW auto mechanic*, they create a resume that emphasizes keywords like "auto mechanic," "auto repair," and even "BMW repair," by prominently displaying them in the right places, including the subject line of emails they send out to prospective employers. Employers "scan" resumes looking for those resumes that "match" their keywords.

> > **Your resume = your website or blog.** Similarly, in terms of SEO, your website needs to place the keywords hiring managers or employers might type into Google in the proper positions (This is called "On Page" SEO; more on this below). Your **TODOs** here are #1 to identify relevant keywords by which hiring managers or decision makers in your target companies would search on Google, and #2 to embed these keywords strategically into your website pages and blog posts.

> **References - Cultivate References.** Beyond a great resume, the other aspect of job search is cultivating great **references**. Knowing the boss's wife, having the head of the BMW auto mechanic school, or someone else important or influential put in a good word can elevate your resume to the top of the stack. In short, strong references get your resume looked at, substantiate that your resume is factually accurate, and possibly get you the job interview.

> > **Your references = links from other websites to your website.** Similarly, in terms of SEO, Google pays attention to whether other websites link to your website as well as whether your blog or page URLs get mentioned on social sites like Twitter, LinkedIn, or Facebook. Your

TODO, therefore, is to solicit links from other websites to your website, and get other people to mention your URLs on their social media feeds like Twitter (more on this below). (This is called "Off Page" SEO; more on this below).

Job Interview - Work on Interview Skills. Once you get their attention, what's next? The job **interview** is the next step towards landing the job. It's the "free glimpse" of what you have to offer that "sells" the employer on making a financial commitment. A "job interview" is essentially a "free" taste of you as an employee.

The Job Interview = the landing experience. Similarly, in terms of SEO, once you've gotten your website or blog ranked on Google for a target keyword, and gotten the click from Google to your website, you need to persuade the hiring manager to take the next step: reach out to you for a job interview or even offer you the job outright.

The **job search equation** is: **resume > references > job interview > job**.

The **SEO equation** is **on page SEO > off page SEO > website landing > inquiry**.

Now, let's drill down a bit into each of these topics: "On Page" SEO, "Off Page" SEO, and the "Landing Experience." Remember, as you build your personal website and/or an individual blog post you'll want to follow the rules of SEO.

"On Page" SEO

"On page" SEO is the equivalent of a great resume. What are the steps?

First and foremost, **identify your keywords**. As we discussed when writing your *Personal Branding Statement*, you are looking for keywords that connect "what you have to offer" with what hiring managers "are looking for."

Brainstorm the types of keywords a potential hiring manager, employer, or job headhunter might type into Google or LinkedIn. Here are some handy tools to help you brainstorm your most desirable keywords:

Google Autocomplete. Simply go to Google, and start typing in a keyword that a hiring manager might type into the search engine to find a person like you. For example, "accountant" then hit your "A," key, your "F" key, etc., and pay attention to the suggestions Google gives you. Job search sites like CareerBuilder, Monster.com, etc., also often have an autocomplete feature, so pay attention to it.

Google Related Searches. Type in a full search such as "accountant for small business." Scroll to the bottom of the page and look at the "related searches."

AdWords Keyword Planner. Sign up for a Google AdWords account, and use the official Google AdWords keyword planner. Watch a video explaining how to use this tool at http://jmlinks.com/9s. (*Note: you'll need to sign up for an AdWords account in order to use this tool including a credit card, but you do not actually have to spend any money.*)

Your first **TODO**, therefore, is to build a short but focused **keyword worksheet** or list of keywords, by which hiring managers or decision-makers might search Google or job engines like CareerBuilder, Monster or even LinkedIn. A person seeking a job as an entry-level account, for example, would certainly choose the word "accountant," but he might also focus on trending keyword phrases such as "tips to prepare a small business tax return," or "issues surrounding FBAR (Foreign Bank Account Report) for non-citizens." Adjacent areas of expertise such as bookkeeping or the ability to speak a foreign language are also worthwhile. The point of these keywords is to make your personal website more findable via Google searches, and your resume or profile more findable on job engines like CareerBuilder or Monster as well as social media sites like LinkedIn.

In addition, there are more people to influence than just hiring managers or direct employers. Many key employees at a company, for example, will search on Google for industry trends or topics. Something hot and trending like "global warming" or "2017 tax code changes" may spur them to search Google by keywords. Then, if your blog post, video, infographic or other type of content, come ups high in these searches, it's an opportunity for you to showcase your expertise and availability for a new job or promotion. Keywords drive search, in short, and you must know your keywords in a very systematic way!

On Page SEO: Placing Your Keywords into Web Content

Once you've identified your keywords, where do you put them? Well, it stands to reason that you need to write keyword-heavy content on both your website and on your resume or profile. By this, I mean content that is well-written, follows the rules of good grammar, and also contains the keywords by which people are searching Google. In terms of SEO for the Web, you'll need some basic knowledge of HTML Page tags.

The main strategic factors for "On Page" SEO are:

Keyword Density. Write keyword-heavy copy for your web pages, and pay attention to writing quality content. Complying to Google's *Panda* update means placing your keywords into grammatically correct sentences, and making sure that your writing contains similar and associated words vs. your keyword targets.

Page Tags. Place your keywords strategically in the right page tags, beginning with the TITLE tag on each page, followed by the header tag family, image alt attribute, and HTML cross-links from one page to another on your site.

Home Page SEO. Use your home page wisely. Placing keywords in relatively high density on your home page, and, again, in natural syntax, as well as creating "one click" links from your home page to your subordinate pages.

Website structure. Organize your website to be Google friendly, starting with keyword-heavy URLS, cross-linking with keyword text, and using sitemaps and other Google-friendly tactics.

"On page" SEO is all about knowing your keywords and building keyword-heavy content that communicates your priorities to Google, just as a good resume communicates your job search priorities to prospective employers. For a brief tutorial on "On Page" SEO, I highly recommend you download and read Google's official tutorial on SEO entitled, the "SEO Starter Guide," at http://bit.ly/google-seo-starter. This official guide by Google will explain where to place your keywords in your website and blog content.

SEO for LinkedIn

While we haven't yet discussed LinkedIn in detail, I want to point out that there is SEO for Google and there is SEO for LinkedIn. The reality is that many hiring managers and recruiters use LinkedIn to search for job candidates. They search by keywords, in the same way that someone searches Google by keywords.

SEO PRINCIPLES APPLY TO MORE THAN JUST GOOGLE OR BING

For this reason, the basic rules of "On Page" SEO also apply to your LinkedIn Profile, namely:

1. **Identify the keywords** that a hiring manager or recruiter might use to find candidates like you or the job that you want to get.
2. **Place these keywords** in your "professional headline" on your LinkedIn profile.
3. **Populate the content** of your profile, such as your summary, past work experience, skills, etc., with content that reflects and contains these keywords.
4. Solicit **endorsements** and **recommendations** that reflect these keywords.

LinkedIn, like Google, prioritizes the results returned after a search query based on whether these keywords appear in the LinkedIn Profile and whether that person has endorsements and recommendations that support those keywords. The game of SEO, in short, is as applicable to LinkedIn as it is to Google.

A Blog Post Example

Let's leave LinkedIn aside for now, and return to personal websites. For example, let's suppose you are looking to advance your career as a CPA. You have set up your personal blog on blogger with your domain of ray21cpa.com. You know that compliance with the so-called FBAR (Foreign Bank Account Report) is a timely topic in the industry. You are aware that hiring managers and key decision makers at CPA firms are looking for people with knowledge of these sorts of international tax issues.

So you have your keyword: FBAR, as well as some related keywords like "small business." You log into your blogger blog and start a "new post."

- You **embed the keywords into the blog title**, as in "Some Thoughts on FBAR Compliance for Individuals."
- You **write the blog post itself**, making sure to mention both the word FBAR and the spelled-out acronym, "Foreign Bank Account Report," as well as touching on themes like preparing the required tax documents, individuals, etc. Basically, you write **keyword-heavy content** that spits back at Google the keyword phrase you are targeting for SEO.
  - Be sure to use **sub-heads** in your blog post that contain the keywords.
  - Be sure to use **at least one image** and by clicking on the image define the "**alt**" attribute as something that contains the target keyword.

At this point, you've written an SEO-friendly blog post. Similarly, you title the home page of your blog as well as key landing pages using your defined keywords list. Your website home page, landing pages, and key blog posts should regurgitate to Google, the keywords that your target hiring manager or decision-maker might be searching for.

Essentially your personal website should map to your target keywords on a one-to-one basis.

Now, you turn to "off page" SEO.

"Off Page" SEO

"Off Page" SEO is the equivalent of great references. Here, you do not fully control the elements (unlike in "on page" SEO), so the game is played out in how well you can convince others to talk favorably about you and your website. Paralleling job references, the main strategic factors of "off page" SEO are as follows:

Link Building. Links are the votes of the Web. Getting as many qualified websites to link back to your website, especially high PageRank (high authority) websites using keyword-heavy syntax, is what link building is all about. It's that simple, and that complicated.

Your **TODO**: identify the websites of friends, colleagues, family members, professional directories, and even social media site which might describe your personal website and link to it. An example of this is the link from BAVC.org to my personal website at http://jmlinks.com/9t.

Social Mentions. Social media is the new buzz of the Internet, and Google looks for mentions of your website on social sites like Google+, Twitter, and Facebook as well as how active your own profiles are.

> Your **TODO:** identify the friends, colleagues, family members, professional directories, and others who have social media accounts (especially Twitter and Google+), and can share your blog post URLs. In addition, use your own social accounts such as Twitter to share your own URL's. Google sees these "shares" as a sign that you are important, and this helps propel your blog to the top of search.

> **Extra credit**: when a family member, colleague, coworker or friend "shares" your blog content on Twitter, LinkedIn, Facebook, etc., their connections see it and this becomes an opportunity for you to promote yourself as a "helpful expert" who is in the market for a new job or promotion.

Don't overdo this! There are penalties for going extreme in terms of link-building. However, for most of us, just a few links – even as few as ten – can propel our blog to the top of Google.

Landing Page Goals

Now, let's talk about the third element, "Landing Page Goals," the equivalent of great job interview skills. The point of a great website isn't just to get traffic from Google, after all. It's to move that potential hiring manager or employer decision-maker from a blog landing page to an inquiry for a meeting with you.

So in evaluating your website, you want to evaluate each page and each page element for one variable: do they move visitors towards your desired action? It's not enough to write a strong blog post on "FBAR and International Tax Issues." You need to get visitors to see you as an authority on the topic, and to reach out to you for a potential offer of a job or career promotion.

You might as even go so far as to byline your blog posts with a message such as:

Written by Jason McDonald

Currently in the Job Market and reachable at 800-298-4065 or by email to j.mcdonald@jm-seo.net

Don't be shy about the fact that you are "in the market." If you have a job and want to be open to career offers (without notifying your current employer), you might sign each blog post:

Written by Jason McDonald

Got questions? I'm happy to discuss. Call me at 800-298-4065 or email me at j.mcdonald@jm-seo.net

In both situations, you want website or blog visitors to a) Be impressed by how much you know, and b) Realize that they can reach out to you with job offers, offers for career advancement, or just connections.

Your **TODO:** audit every page on your website to verify that it is helping you in your goal of creating a strong online personal brand and encouraging website visitors to reach out to you for a one-on-one contact.

The SEO success equation for your website, in sum, is:

1. **Pre-search**: identify your customer keywords.
2. **On Page SEO**: weave these keywords strategically into your website content.
3. **Off Page SEO**: get links, freshness, and social mentions.
4. **Post-landing**: brainstorm effective landing pages that convert landings into actual sales or sales leads.

» SHARING IS CARING: BLOGGING FOR SOCIAL MEDIA

Now that you have blog use #1 (using your blog as a "trust indicator" to substantiate yourself as a "helpful expert), and blog use #2 (using your blog as a way to get to the top of relevant Google, Yahoo, and Bing searches via basic SEO), you can turn to blog use #3: using your blog as "food" for your personal brand image party. Blog posts, in particular, make great items to share on your Facebook, your LinkedIn, your Twitter, and other social sites.

Blog posts and web pages are, in short, great "food" for your "desired guests," hiring managers and key decision-makers at your target employers.

First, how do you know what people want? Here, again, you need to do keyword research. Revisit the Google tools above to research which keywords have search volume on Google. Are people Googling "international tax," "FBAR," "Foreign Bank Account Report," or even "international tax compliance" or "what to do in case of an IRS audit?" And are hiring managers or employers seeing demand for people who know those issues? If so, the keywords that people search for will also likely be strong magnets for creating social-media-friendly content.

A Blog Post Gives Your Contacts Something To Share

Related to this, you want to keep your eye on trending content. Having set up Buzzsumo (http://buzzsumo.com) and Feedly (http://feedly.com/), for example, keep an eye on industry trends and write quick summaries and responses to them on your blog. Your goals is to become and be seen as an "authoritative commentator" on these trends. Don't get discouraged. If you are looking for an entry level job, just having blog posts on industry trends and having a personal website that focuses on your industry will get you ahead of those candidates who have nothing to substantiate their interests or expertise. If you are looking for a more senior position, then obviously the tone and content of your blog needs to convey more gravitas.

In addition, be sure to follow people who are more authoritative than you are as well as competitors: pay attention to what they write on their blogs, and reverse engineer the content that they are sharing on their Twitter, LinkedIn, Facebook, etc., which is getting a lot of likes, comments, and shares.

Nothing succeeds like success, and nothing tells you what is most likely to be popular and shared on social media, like what is already popular and being shared on social media. In general, things that are shared will hit emotional theme such as usefulness, being counterintuitive or counterfactual, being shocking, provoking fear or outrage, or being funny. It's really all about utility or emotion.

Once you have the keyword target, the next step is to write a catchy headline and write a catchy blog post.

Sticking with our example of international tax issues, we might take the topic of "FBAR compliance," and spin out blog headlines such as:

Why FBAR Matters to Your Clients (Even If They Don't Know It Yet) ("utility").

Why What You as a CPA Don't Know About FBAR Is Going to Cost You ("fear").

The FBAR: An Outrageous Intervention of the Government in our Lives ("shocking")

An FBAR Tragedy: A Small Businessperson Forced into Bankruptcy. ("Outrage or sentimentality")

Fun tools that will help you "spin" blog topics and titles for social media are the Portent Idea Generator (http://jmlinks.com/9u) and Hubspot's topic generator (http://jmlinks.com/9w).

Finally, now that you have a well-written blog post that touches on trending industry themes of interest to key employer decision-makers, it's time to share it. Post it to your blog, and then use a URL shortener like http://bitly.com/ or http://tinyurl.com/ to shorten your long blog URL. Then paste it into Hootsuite, summarize the topic, and post it strategically to your Twitter, Facebook, LinkedIn, and wherever else appropriate. (Hootsuite has its own built-in sharer as well, here's a screenshot:)

The process for **social sharing** of blog posts builds on SEO and is as follows.

1. **Identify the blog concept and relevant keywords**. These define what the blog post is about and which keywords people are likely to search for. Use a tool like Buzzsumo (http://buzzsumo.com) to see what's already being shared on social media sites.

2. **Outline the content and write a rough draft**. Just as in all writing, it's good to write out a rough draft. A good blog post should have about four to five paragraphs of text. "Less is more" when it comes to social media, so make the blog post pithy and informative.

3. **Identify a provocative image**. Whether it's on Instagram, Facebook, or LinkedIn, people respond to images. Use a free image site such as Foter (http://foter.com/) and find an image that conveys the essence of your blog post.

4. **Write a catchy, keyword-heavy headline**. It's no accident that popular sites like Buzzfeed and Huffington Post use shocking or provocative headlines. People react to, and share, content that hits an emotional nerve and the headline is the first step towards a strong emotional reaction.

5. **Finalize the content**. Review your content and make sure it is easy-to-read, preferably with lists and bullets.

6. **Share the content**. Identify the appropriate social media platform such as LinkedIn, Twitter, Facebook, Instagram, etc., and share your post. Use a tool like Hootsuite (https://hootsuite.com/) to organize and schedule your shares.

Your objectives. In terms of job search and career building, your social media objectives are a) to stay "top of mind" among friends, family, colleagues, hiring managers, and others who can help your career, b) to substantiate your brand image as a "helpful expert," and c) to encourage "social sharing" so that friends of friends, and colleagues of colleagues, can become aware of you and possibly offer you a job or promotion. A strong blog post can be great for SEO, great for social media sharing, or great for both.

≫ MEASURING YOUR RESULTS VIA GOOGLE ANALYTICS

Measuring the success or failure of your website or blog is really easy using Google's free "Google Analytics" metrics software. First, you need to establish a Google account and go to https://www.google.com/analytics to sign up for the Analytics software. If you are using WordPress, be sure to use the "Yoast" plugin for Google Analytics, which makes it easy to install the required software on your personal website or blog. (Inside of your WordPress blog, search plugins for 'Yoast for Google Analytics.')

After some time has elapsed and you are either ranking on some target searches or getting traffic from social media to your blog, then you can use Google Analytics to determine:

- **Website Traffic**. You can monitor how many visits per month as well as users per month you are getting plus "slice and dice" them to see their geographic origin, bounce rate, time on site, etc.
- **Traffic Origin**. Using "Advanced Segments" you are monitor where you get traffic from, and in this way determine the relative value of Facebook, LinkedIn, Twitter, and other social media efforts.
- **Goals**. You can define a "goal" such as if someone fills out contact form or sends you an email, and thus monitor how many emails or inquiries your website is getting you.

For information on how to create custom Advanced Segments in Google Analytics, go to http://jmlinks.com/1f. For the Google help files on Advanced Segments go to http://jmlinks.com/1g. The sky's the limit with Google Analytics; check out Google Analytics Academy at http://jmlinks.com/12m for a complete free course on using Google Analytics.

»» DELIVERABLE: A PERSONAL WEBSITE AND BLOG PLAN

To recap, a personal website or blog accomplishes three foundational tasks for your online personal brand:

1. **It substantiates you as a "helpful expert,"** with the knowledge and credentials to be taken seriously for a potential job or offer of career advancement.
2. **It gives you a shot at being found on Google**, Bing, or Yahoo via search, especially for trending industry buzzwords.
3. **It gives you "food" for your "social media party,"** i.e., "content" that you can "share" on social media.

You may achieve only #1, #2, or only #3, or you may hit a *trifecta* and score across all objectives. But regardless, having a personal website is an essential element of your personal branding infrastructure.

Your chapter **DELIVERABLE** has arrived. Go to https://www.jm-seo.org/workbooks (click on Job Search and Career-building, enter the code 'careers2016' to register if you have not already done so), and click on the link to the "Personal Website and Blog Plan." Complete all elements on this worksheet.

≫ APPENDIX #1: TOP SEO JOB SEARCH AND CAREER-BUILDING TOOLS AND RESOURCES

Here are the top tools and resources to help you with SEO. For an up-to-date and complete list, go to https://www.jm-seo.org/workbooks (click on Job Search and Career -building, enter the code 'careers2016' to register if you have not already done so). Then click on the *Job Search and Career-building Resource Book* link, and drill down to the SEO chapter.

GOOGLE SEO STARTER GUIDE - http://bit.ly/google-seo-starter

This is the one, and only, really good resource by Google that is an official guide to what to do when, how, where and why for SEO. It covers mainly 'on page' SEO but definitely identifies basic tasks to accomplish on your website. Highly recommended.

Rating: 5 Stars | **Category:** resource

UBERSUGGEST - http://ubersuggest.org

Do you love Google suggest (the drop-down suggestions displayed when you type into Google)? It's great for keyword discovery. Ubersuggest is even better - it does a variety of things to provide all sorts of keyword suggestions. So it's a wonderful keyword discovery tool!

Rating: 5 Stars | **Category:** tool

SEOCENTRO META TAG ANALYZER - http://seocentro.com/tools/search-engines/metatag-analyzer.html

SEOCentro designed this Meta Tag analysis tool to help webmasters analyze their web pages. This tool analyzes not only Meta Tags but where your keywords are positioned on the page, plus provides information on keyword density. When using Firefox, use CTRL+F to highlight your keywords in the results. In doing so, you can quickly check to see if a target keyword is well positioned vis-a-vis important tags like the TITLE or META DESCRIPTION tag.

Rating: 5 Stars | **Category:** tool

GOOGLE ADWORDS KEYWORD PLANNER - http://adwords.google.com/keywordplanner

Who got the data? Google got the data. Use the Keyword Planner for keyword discovery for both SEO and AdWords, but be sure to know how to use it. Not the easiest user interface, and remember it ONLY gives data for EXACT match types.

Rating: 5 Stars | **Category:** tool

GOOGLE KEYWORD PLANNER - https://adwords.google.com/KeywordPlanner

This is Google's keyword planner. It has now become the primary Google-based tool for keyword research. Be sure to watch Jason's YouTube video on how to use it, as the user interface leaves much to be desired! Still, it is the best tool for researching keyword volume vs. value (CPC) data.

Rating: 5 Stars | **Category:** tool

» APPENDIX #2: TOP BLOGGING JOB SEARCH AND CAREER-BUILDING TOOLS AND RESOURCES

Here are the top tools and resources to help you with blogging. For an up-to-date and complete list, go to https://www.jm-seo.org/workbooks (click on Job Search and Career -building, enter the code 'careers2016' to register if you have not already done so). Then click on the *Job Search and Career-building Resource Book* link, and drill down to the blogging chapter.

TWEAK YOUR BIZ TITLE GENERATOR - http://tweakyourbiz.com/tools/title-generator/index.php

Good blog post TITLES are critical. You should include your keywords for SEO purposes, but add some pizazz, some sex appeal, some please-click-me oomph. This nifty tool gets your ideas flowing for good TITLES.

Rating: 4 Stars | **Category:** tool

PORTENT CONTENT IDEA GENERATOR - http://portent.com/tools/title-maker

Very fun and mind-provocative tool for content ideas and better blog titles. Enter some keywords and the tool will generate some funny titles. So start with keywords and then generate your amazingly, funny and hypnotic blog titles. These then become the HEADLINES on Google by which you can attract more clicks!

Rating: 4 Stars | **Category:** tool

BLOG TOPIC GENERATOR - http://hubspot.com/blog-topic-generator

If you're hurting for blog topic ideas, try this fun tool from HubSpot. Enter three nouns, then watch the tool generate a weeks worth of blog topics. If none of the generated topics pique your interest, hit the back key and try, try again until one does.

Rating: 4 Stars | **Category:** tool

BLOG POST HEADLINE ANALYZER - http://coschedule.com/headline-analyzer

Want to write better blog headlines? Use the Blog Post Headline Analyzer to get a feel for how effective your blog post headlines are. This tool analyzes entered headlines across numerous criteria including keywords, sentiment, structure, grammar, and readability to produce a headline score in an attractive graphical format. Try it and see.

Rating: 4 Stars | **Category:** tool

THIS PAGE INTENTIONALLY LEFT BLANK

(PONDER IT)

7

LinkedIn

If you've ever been to a serious university or college job fair, a big trade show such as the *Consumer Electronics Show* in Las Vegas, or other types of business "meet-and-greets," then you've been to the real-world equivalent of LinkedIn. These events often feature free food and entertainment, a speech or two by a CEO or college administrator, and lots of *schmoozing* between vendors and potential customers, including job-seekers and career-advancers. Dressed in business casual, people listen attentively, are in "learning" mode, and are also ready to introduce themselves and their personal business value proposition or that of their company. Everyone is on their best behavior.

LinkedIn, in short, is the **24/7 online business networking party**. It's not only for job seekers but also for those advancing their careers through groups, online learning, and social networking with potential employers. It's an absolute must for anyone serious about online personal branding and career-building!

To use LinkedIn effectively is to **schmooze.** A quick Google search of *define:schmooze* (at http://jmlinks.com/3f), defines it as to *talk, chat up, converse, mingle, hobnob, network, and work the room.* That's the key purpose of LinkedIn in a nutshell: to *network* with existing contacts and *build relationships* with others (including the contacts of contacts), to learn a little bit, and to self-promote yourself into a better job or better career.

In this Chapter, we'll explore **LinkedIn for Job Search and Career-building**. We'll cover how to optimize your profile on LinkedIn, how to use LinkedIn to network with potential employers and key decision-makers, and how to participate in LinkedIn groups. We'll also cover what to share on LinkedIn as updates and how to post to *Pulse*, LinkedIn's internal blogging platform. We'll conclude with top tools and resources to turbocharge LinkedIn for your job and career goals.

Let's get started!

To Do List:

» Explore How LinkedIn Works

» Create a Strong "Public Resume" on LinkedIn: Opportunity No. 1

» Schmooze on LinkedIn for Job Search and Career-building: Opportunity No. 2

» Share on LinkedIn via Updates and Posts: Opportunity No. 3

» Participate in LinkedIn Groups: Opportunity No. 4

» Follow Companies (and their Employees) on LinkedIn: Opportunity No. 5

» Promote Your LinkedIn Profile, Updates, and Posts

» Measure your Results on LinkedIn

» » Deliverable: A LinkedIn Job Search & Career-building Plan

» » Appendix: Top LinkedIn Job Search & Career-building Tools and Resources

» EXPLORE HOW LINKEDIN WORKS

Let's review the basic structure of LinkedIn:

- **Individuals have LinkedIn profiles**, which function as **online resumes** listing skills, education, and interests. Profiles allow one individual to "connect" with another individual; once connected, any post by individual No. 1 will show in the news feed of individual No. 2. (LinkedIn and Facebook function in a similar way: you send *connection requests* on LinkedIn (*friend requests* on Facebook), and once accepted and connected, you and the other individual can directly check each other out, communicate via direct messaging, and see posts that each other make in your newsfeed).
- **Individuals can join groups.** While groups on Facebook are of limited career interest, groups on LinkedIn are very important. As at a major trade show, LinkedIn has "break out" groups by topic (from petroleum engineering to marketing to advertising to WordPress web design and beyond), that bring like-minded people together in a professional way.
- **Companies can have LinkedIn Pages.** While individuals have *profiles* on LinkedIn (and on Facebook), companies create business *Pages*. Individuals can follow companies, and by doing so, give permission to that company to converse with them. Posts by the company will have a chance to show up in the news feed of individuals who have "followed" a particular company. By following companies of interest, you can learn what's on their agenda and be better prepared for

potential interviews. You can also discover individuals who work at target companies.

- **Posts and the News Feed.** When an individual posts to his or her LinkedIn profile, or a company posts to its LinkedIn Page, those posts show up in the news feed of connected individuals. LinkedIn, like Facebook, therefore has a posting rhythm in which individuals and businesses compete for eyeballs and attention.

Structurally, therefore, LinkedIn and Facebook are very similar:

Profiles: what individuals have on both LinkedIn and Facebook.

Pages: what companies have on both LinkedIn and Facebook

Timelines: what an individual has, and posts to, on both networks.

> However: You post an *update* to your *timeline* on LinkedIn. On Facebook, the structure is the same – but you publish a *post* to your timeline (A *post*, on LinkedIn, refers an article you publish to the *Pulse* blogging platform, internal to LinkedIn, and with no equivalent on Facebook). Despite the different nomenclatures, the effect is the same. You "share" something to your "timeline," and your connection / friend sees it in his "news feed."

News feed. When an individual you are connected with on LinkedIn, publishes an *update* to his timeline, that *update* has a very good chance of showing in your *newsfeed*. The same goes for *posts* by companies to their Pages, and for *posts* to LinkedIn Pulse. Similarly, on Facebook, when a friend *posts* to her timeline, that post has a good chance of showing up in your *news feed*.

Direct Messaging. When you are *connected* to someone on LinkedIn (*friends* with someone on Facebook), you can "direct message" them. In addition, when you "direct message" someone, that person will usually receive an email alert either from LinkedIn or Facebook.

Here's a screenshot of my LinkedIn account, highlighting where I would publish an *update*:

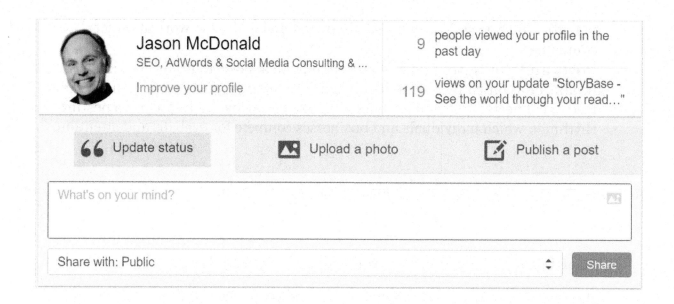

And here's a screenshot of my LinkedIn timeline, showing *updates* from my connections:

And here's a screenshot of a 1st level contact, whom I can message directly on LinkedIn:

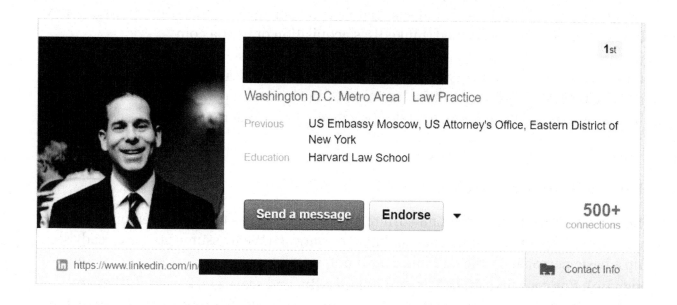

Washington D.C. Metro Area | Law Practice

Previous   US Embassy Moscow, US Attorney's Office, Eastern District of
                 New York

Education   Harvard Law School

Send a message   Endorse   ▼

500+
connections

https://www.linkedin.com/in/   Contact Info

1st

For a more official introduction to LinkedIn visit, http://jmlinks.com/12q.

Similar Structures but Different Cultures

However, the **structural** similarities hide a very different **culture** on LinkedIn. On Facebook, as we shall see, people are engaged in friends, family, and fun. On LinkedIn, in contrast, the center of gravity lies with the personal profiles of employees who are engaged in more serious job and career topics.

Whereas on Facebook, it's impolite to ask what one "does for a living" or to "pitch business ideas," on LinkedIn this not only possible but common. People on LinkedIn, in short, are in **business networking mode** (*whereas on Facebook they are in friends, family, and fun mode*). This makes LinkedIn a fantastic social media platform for job search and career-building!

LINKEDIN IS THE 24/7 BUSINESS NETWORKING EVENT

In addition, **LinkedIn groups** are rather robust, especially in technical areas. For a technical industry such as oil and gas, people increasingly use LinkedIn groups as a way to stay professionally educated. LinkedIn's acquisition of Lynda.com (http://www.lynda.com/) speaks to this growing trend to use LinkedIn as a way to stay up-to-date about an industry. Finally, although **business Pages** do exist on LinkedIn and are increasingly important for business-to-business companies, they have still not broken out to be fully functional and interactive. Their value remains to be seen.

How to Search LinkedIn

First, you'll need to research LinkedIn to identify companies to follow, persons to emulate, and people with whom you'd like to connect. (We'll assume you've already set up a basic personal profile on LinkedIn. If not, visit https://www.linkedin.com/ and sign up). For your first **TODO**, log on to LinkedIn, and search by keywords that are relevant to your job or career interests. Identify a) persons, b) groups, and c) companies that are active on these topics.

Simply type a keyword of interest into the search bar at the top of the LinkedIn page (e.g., "organic food" if you are interested in the food industry, for example, "oil and gas," if you are looking for a job or career promotion in the petroleum industry, or "cybersecurity," if you are looking for a job in computer security). On the left, click on people, jobs, companies, groups, universities, or posts, to narrow down your search and browse what's going on.

Here's a screenshot for the key phrase "organic food:"

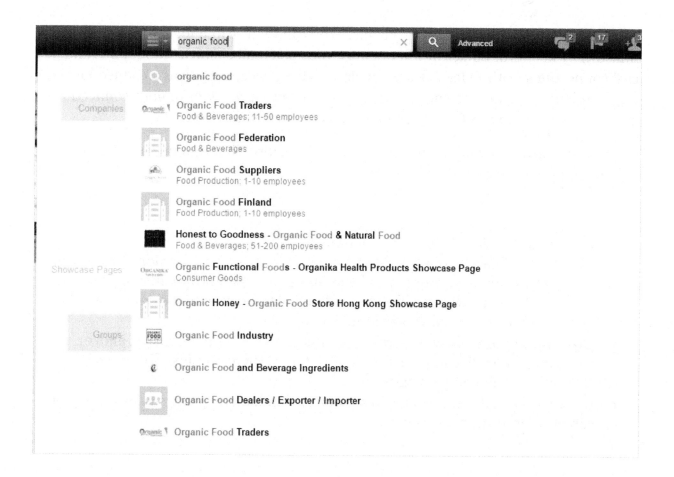

Basically by entering a keyword, you can find companies, groups, and individuals that have that keyword in their summary information.

To drill down to specific people or do other very specific searches, click first on the "Advanced" link to the right of the search bar. Here's a screenshot:

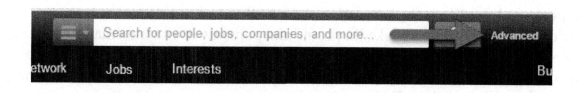

Next, on the left hand side click on "People." You can then search for specific persons on LinkedIn by keyword. LinkedIn will organize your personal contacts into 1st, 2nd, and 3rd level connections, with 1st level being people who have accepted you as a connection (e.g., similar to "friends" on Facebook), 2nd level being *connections of your connections*, and 3rd level being *connections of connections of your connections*.

To get your bearings if you've never used LinkedIn before, first sign up, and then I recommend you search for the following:

- **Individuals**. Identify two types of individuals:
    - Individuals whom you'd like to connect with on a professional basis (e.g., hiring managers, or key individuals at your target companies).
    - Individuals who are like you: individuals who seem to be doing a good job on LinkedIn, and you want to emulate.
- **Companies to follow**. Identify companies in your target industry, and/or companies you'd like to work for. Start to follow them on LinkedIn by clicking "follow" on their company page.
- **Groups**. We'll discuss groups in a moment, but look for groups relevant to your career interests and join them.

As for individuals, if you do not know them, at this point do not connect with them. Just note who they are.

For your first **TODO**, download the **LinkedIn Research Worksheet**. For the worksheet, go to https://www.jm-seo.org/workbooks (click on Job Search and Career-building, enter the code 'careers2016' to register if you have not already done so), and click on the link to the "LinkedIn Research Worksheet."

≫ CREATE A STRONG "PUBLIC RESUME" ON LINKEDIN: OPPORTUNITY NO. 1

The **personal profile** is the foundation of LinkedIn. Just as on Facebook, an individual needs to set up a LinkedIn profile and populate it with information about him or herself. Unlike on Facebook, however, this personal profile is highly visible and acts as a kind of "public resume" for you in your search for a job or a career advancement. A well-optimized personal profile is the foundation of success on LinkedIn.

The **TODOs** here are:

1. **Sign up** for LinkedIn as an individual and set up your personal *profile*.
2. Identify the **keywords** that reflect your Personal Branding Statement, that is keywords that "describe you" as a businessperson and/or your skills and personality traits, such as "WordPress web designer," "CPA," "Petroleum Engineer," "Customer Service Specialist," or "Salesperson."
3. **Optimize** your personal profile so that it –
   a. Clearly and quickly represents your **Personal Branding Statement**.
   b. Is **findable** via LinkedIn search by **keywords** that might be searched on by recruiters, employers, and hiring managers.
   c. Establishes **trust** in you as an authority or "helpful expert" and someone who is worthy of a job or career advancement.

First and foremost, let's focus our attention on **search** and **trust** on LinkedIn. Imagine you are a hiring manager or key employee at one of your target companies.

By **search**, we mean that such people will go directly to LinkedIn (or perhaps to Google) to find potential candidates and/or after they have met you. Recruiters and employers love LinkedIn because it's the world's largest online resume database. It's an excellent way for them to "poach" key employees in their industry from competitors, and "hire them away." So the first aspect of search used by hiring managers or recruiters is **searching by keywords to find employees to hire**.

The second aspect of search is **using LinkedIn to research job candidates once they are already known**. This involves using LinkedIn as a research tool to learn more about you or other potential job or promotion candidates. Once they know about you, employers will "search" you on the LinkedIn with an eye to deciding whether you have any skeletons in your closet, whether you seem knowledgeable about your subject, and whether you seem like a good person to employ. Nowadays, people go to networking events such as trade shows, and return with business cards and email addresses. They then "vet" these people by searching them on Google and on LinkedIn. Indeed, you can optimize your LinkedIn profile to show high on searches for your own name plus keywords.

Think of your LinkedIn profile as your public resume.

To see my LinkedIn profile (*which I humbly submit to you as a model*), visit http://jmlinks.com/3g. Note that my LinkedIn profile appears in about position four on a Google search for *Jason McDonald SEO*. Here's a screenshot:

Jason McDonald | LinkedIn
https://www.linkedin.com/in/**jason**eg3 ▾
San Francisco Bay Area - SEO, AdWords & Social Media Consulting & Expert Witness
- San Francisco Bay Area
View Jason McDonald's professional profile on LinkedIn. LinkedIn is the ... SEO,
AdWords & Social Media Consulting & Expert Witness - San Francisco Bay Area.

The concept here is when someone meets me (or meets you, or meets a key employee), you want to use LinkedIn to show prominently in a search for your name plus keywords, plus you want your LinkedIn profile to show off your expertise and talents. Just like a "real" resume, your LinkedIn "resume" should be optimized to be found and to put your best foot forward. It should also be publically viewable without the necessity of being logged into LinkedIn.

Optimize Your LinkedIn Profile

Now, let's turn to the steps to **optimize** a LinkedIn profile for **search** and **trust**.

> **Define your target keywords.** What value do you provide for others in a business relationship? Using your **Personal Branding Statement** and **keywords** identified earlier, you'll want to embed these in strategic locations in your LinkedIn profile. For example, I want to rank, and be trusted as the *Jason McDonald* that can help you with **SEO**, **Social Media**, and **AdWords**. Thus, I embed those keywords in my profile, and write it well enough to convey my value as a helpful expert in those areas.

> > **Once you have identified your keywords, weave them strategically into your LinkedIn profile.**

To access these features, click on *profile > edit profile* while logged in to LinkedIn. Hover over an area, and click on the pencil to edit.

Professional Headline. This is the most important text on your LinkedIn profile for search discoverability. It should answer the question, "What can you do for me" and **must** contain a few of your most important **keywords**.

Here's a screenshot of mine:

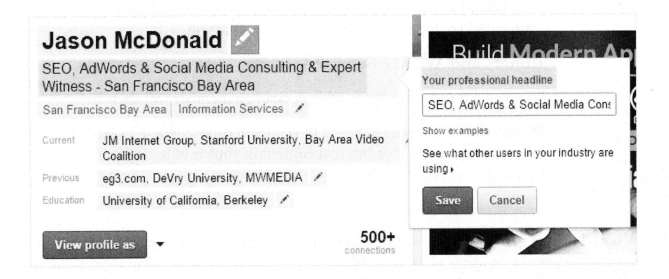

Current (Position). This is your current job, if you have one, or your last job or education if you do not, so state it well. Always "think like an employer" and write in the style of what you can do for them.

Summary. Like a real resume, this describes your skills and experience. Use ALL CAPS and other ways to break up the content. Populate it with relevant keywords that hiring managers or recruiters might search on LinkedIn, and make it easy to read. It should state your personal branding statement succinctly. Write this "as if" you were explaining to someone at a job or career event what you do, and how this is relevant for what they might need in an employee.

Experience. Here's where you input your current and past employment. If your current employer is on LinkedIn with a company page, a logo will be available. Again, write succinct summaries of current and past employment that contain logical keywords (do not overdo this), and explain how you can help a hiring manager to accomplish something of business value for his company.

Languages. Input any languages you speak.

Education. Don't be shy. Populate your education section with your educational achievements, not only degrees but any awards or extra-curricular activities.

Additional Info. Fill out as indicated, especially the "advice for contacting" so that it's easy for prospects to find you.

Honors and Awards. Got any? Add them.

Groups. LinkedIn groups to which you are a member will show here.

Other Media. You can also add links to YouTube videos, SlideShare presentations, and other Internet content in your profile. To learn how, visit http://jmlinks.com/11a.

A word about groups: at this point, we are optimizing your LinkedIn profile for **search** and **trust**. In terms of groups, therefore, you might consider joining groups not because you plan to actively participate in them but because they convey your interests and skills. For example, I am a member of both the Harvard and UC Berkeley alumni associations really just to convey that I am smart, and attended these prestigious institutions (not because I actively participate in those groups). Similarly, I am a member of Ad Age and WordPress experts groups to convey my interest and expertise in those topics (*I don't actually participate in these groups in any serious way – I'm too busy!*). Think of groups as you would think of college extracurricular activities on your resume: to convey interests and skill.

Profile Visibility

At this point, scroll back up, just under the blue "View profile as" button and click on gear icon, next to the LinkedIn logo on the left with the https:// web link. Here's a screenshot:

By clicking on the gear icon, you open up the privacy settings of LinkedIn. These appear on the right hand side.

Your public profile URL. Set this to be something short and easy to remember; this becomes what is visible on a Google search.

Customize your Public Profile. Here, you can control what is viewable to anyone either on LinkedIn or via a Google search. (For anyone actively searching for a job, my recommendation is to make EVERYTHING public on LinkedIn).

Your public profile badge. Click here, and LinkedIn will give you the code to place on your blog or website, so people can easily view your profile. To see it in action, visit https://www.jasonmcdonald.org/ and click on the LinkedIn icon on the right.

A word about privacy. For most of us, we want to be highly **visible** *(non-private)* on LinkedIn. We want potential employers, friends or colleagues, business associates, hiring managers, or even recruiters or headhunters to easily find us. Therefore, set your public profile as "visible to everyone," and check all of the boxes below. *If, for some reason, you do NOT want to be publically visible on LinkedIn, then set the visibility and check boxes accordingly.*

One of the more common mistakes people make is to think of the LinkedIn profile like the Facebook profile: whereas on Facebook, you may want to be *invisible / private* to hiring managers or employers, on LinkedIn you often want to be *visible / public* to hiring managers or employers. Therefore, setting your LinkedIn to **private** defeats the purposes of **search** and **trust** as part of your LinkedIn marketing strategy.

For most people, therefore, I recommend to set LinkedIn to fully *visible / public*.

GENERALLY, LINKEDIN IS A *PUBLIC* PROFILE, WHILE FACEBOOK IS A *PRIVATE* PROFILE

Now close your settings window, go back to the basic profile page, and click on "Contact info" on the far right. Here, you'll see your email, phone, IM, and address as well as social media links. Here's a screenshot:

Generally, I would not put your physical address here (*too many crazy stalkers on the Internet*), but I would put your email and phone. As for the social icons, LinkedIn has a direct link to your Twitter account. As for websites, you can either use their standard descriptions, or if you click "other" you can set these to what you like. I have set mine, for example, to "Contact Jason," "Read Jason's Blog," and "Follow Jason on G+." Here's a screenshot:

You'll need to know the http:// link for each.

IMPORTANT: When enabled, this makes it easy for anyone to contact you on LinkedIn. Importantly, this means that anyone will be able to contact you: 1st level, 2nd level, and even 3rd level connections. If you leave these items blank, then only 1st-level connections will be able to easily contact you via LinkedIn.

Therefore:

> *If you want to be highly findable and easy-to-reach via LinkedIn, be sure to enable the Websites section under your contact information.*

At that point, you're done with populating and optimizing your LinkedIn profile for **search** and **trust**. Congratulate yourself, as you've successfully optimized your LinkedIn public resume!

For your second **TODO**, download the **LinkedIn Profile Worksheet**. For the worksheet, go to https://www.jm-seo.org/workbooks (click on Job Search and Career-building, enter the code 'careers2016' to register if you have not already done so), and click on the link to the "LinkedIn Profile Worksheet."

Recommendations and Endorsements

While building out your profile, you'll notice that some people have many **recommendations** or **endorsements**. **Recommendations**, like references for a resume, are generally all positive. *After all, you ask for them and you control them.*

Why ask for a reference from a boss or coworker who won't give you a glowing endorsement? Similarly, LinkedIn will prompt you (and your connections) to complete **endorsements** for each other concerning relevant skills. These build out like "merit badges" on your profile, making you look trustworthy.

Note: you control whether recommendations show on your public profile; you can suppress any you do not like.

Solicit Recommendations and Endorsements

Your **TODO** here is to ask for recommendations and endorsements from friends, coworkers, college professors, and business colleagues. One of the best ways to get them is to preemptively do them for other people. After completing a project with an outside connection such as a customer of your current employer or even a professor at your college, for example, connect to that person on LinkedIn and write him or her a glowing recommendation and endorsement. Often, they will reciprocate. *(This is called "pre-emptive" recommendations in LinkedIn lingo.)* Or after a successful project, just email or ask, "Hey, it was great working with you. I'm currently looking for a career change; so could you write me a recommendation on LinkedIn?"

Here's a screenshot of two of my recommendations:

▾ 13 recommendations, including:

Rob Seide
National Director, Communications - Finance & Shared Services at Kaiser Permanente

Jason knows how to get results! He helped CPMC's SEO/SEM efforts and our ranking and page views shot through the roof! Jason... View

Frank Motola
SEO & Web Design Expert | Delivering Trackable Results by Combining Expert Web Design, SEO, Branding, PR & Web Marketing

Jason McDonald is a respected authority on SEO and someone you can trust with this important work. View⤓

And here's a screenshot of some of my endorsements (which are very short, sort of like "merit badges" in the Boy Scouts or Girl Scouts):

Regardless of how you get them, getting many positive *recommendations* and *endorsements* will make your LinkedIn profile position you as a "helpful expert."

» SCHMOOZE ON LINKEDIN FOR JOB SEARCH AND CAREER-BUILDING: OPPORTUNITY NO. 2

Now that you've optimized your LinkedIn profile for search and trust, you're ready for the next level: **schmoozing** via LinkedIn. "Schmooze" is a Yiddish word for meeting and greeting, helloing and goodbying, shaking hands, and basically connecting or networking with anyone and everyone who might help you advance your career. *Networking* is the most important activity on LinkedIn for job searchers and career-builders, whatever you call it.

> *Schmoozing is another word for business networking: expanding your circle of job / career contacts, nurturing their respect for you, and keeping top of mind so that when they have a career opportunity, they think of you.*

By nurturing your 1st level contacts and being active on LinkedIn, you can use LinkedIn as your online social rolodex, extending beyond just people you actually know to people you'd like to know for your career advancement goals.

Let's investigate schmoozing on LinkedIn, namely:

1st level contacts: these are people who have accepted your connection requests on LinkedIn.

2nd level contacts: these are 1st level contacts of your 1st level contacts (friends of friends, so to speak).

LinkedIn Connections: What's Your Bacon Number?

Your "bacon number" is a term coined to humorously point out that nearly everyone on the planet is connected to actor Kevin Bacon. Google, for example, has a funny hidden Easter egg: go to Google and type in a famous person's name followed by "bacon number," for example: "Cher Bacon Number" or visit http://jmlinks.com/3h. Cher has a Bacon number of two because she and Jack Nicholson appeared in *The Witches of Eastwick*, and Jack Nicholson and Kevin Bacon appeared in *A Few Good Men*.

So Cher is a 1st level connection with Jack Nicholson, and a 2nd level connection with Kevin Bacon. That means I have a Bacon number of 5, because I know my Mom, my Mom knows Cher, and Cher knows Jack Nicholson, and Jack Nicholson knows Kevin Bacon.

How does the Bacon number concept relate to LinkedIn? LinkedIn uses the same system universally: you can *direct message* or *see the email* of your 1st level connections, and you can use your 1st level connections to get introduced to your 2nd level, for example:

Cher can message via LinkedIn or email Jack Nicholson, directly.

Cher can "see" that Jack Nicholson is connected to Kevin Bacon, and ask Jack to "introduce" her to Kevin.

I can message via LinkedIn or email my Mom, directly.

I can "see" that my Mom is connected to Cher, and ask my Mom to introduce me to Cher (but she won't because my Mom is way too cool for that).

Similarly, on LinkedIn, you can directly message / find the email of anyone who is your 1st level connection. Or, you can ask a 1st level connection to introduce you to a 2nd level connection. For example, simply search on LinkedIn for the name of someone with whom you are already connected. Then:

Click on the **blue** "Send a message" box. This sends them a message via LinkedIn, and in most cases, will also send them an email alert that they have a message waiting on LinkedIn.

or –

Click on the "**Contact info**" tab and you can view their email address, phone number, and address.

Or, let's assume you're trying to find a connection that has a particular interest that matches your skillset. Rather than typing a person's name into the search box, click on the "Advanced" text to the right of the search, then click on "people" to get to a "people search" on LinkedIn. Type your keyword / key phrase into the keywords box as in "hiring manager" or "professional recruiter" or perhaps "accounting hiring manager" and hit search. Here's a screenshot:

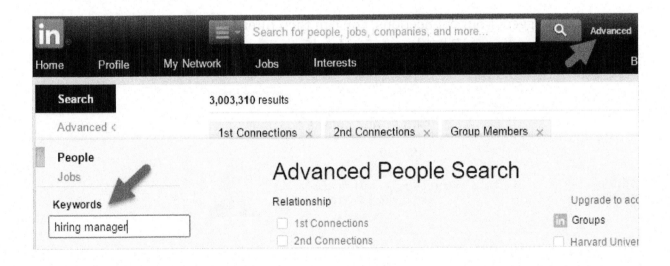

You can also filter for 1st, 2nd, and 3rd level connections. (Remember: you can directly email 1st level connections, and ask 1st level connections to introduce you to 2nd level connections).

Tagging Connections on LinkedIn

Furthermore, you can "tag" 1st level connections by affixing keywords to individual connections. For example, you can create a "tag" that indicates a "real-world friend" or a "tag" that indicates an industry trade show connection or a "tag" that designates a "hiring manager." Once tagged, you can then sort or filter your connections by tag. To "tag" a connection, simply click on a connection (which must be a 1st level), click on the "relationship" tab, and next click on "Tag." Here's a screenshot:

Once you've "tagged" your connections, you can then filter them. To do so, click on My Network > Connections > Filter by > tags. Here's a screenshot:

Next, if you like you can message these contacts "as a group." Simply filter for the "tag," and then you can go one-by-one to each contact and copy / paste a message. You can also send to groups of fifty, but (unfortunately) LinkedIn no longer allows this feature to be managed via tags.

Here's a screenshot of a group message:

Essentially, you are able to use LinkedIn as a searchable rolodex of 1st and 2nd level business contacts: define what type of person you want to contact (or prospect), search for them, and reach out directly. And for 1st level contacts, you can email / message them via LinkedIn as well as sort them via tags.

Many people are not aware that when you message a person via LinkedIn that message also generally generates a real email to that person. So you can use LinkedIn to "email" contacts. Here's a screenshot of how that looks in Gmail:

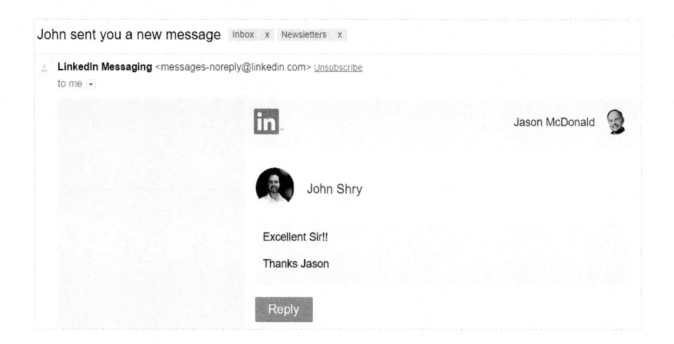

LinkedIn is a very powerful online rolodex and schmoozing tool!

Working with 2nd Level Connections

While you can direct message (send emails or see the email addresses of) 1st level connections, this is not true of 2nd level connections (who are the 1st level connections of your 1st level connections). However, LinkedIn allows you to ask for an "introduction" from a 1st level connection to a 2nd level connection.

Here's a typical scenario.

Let's suppose you have just graduated from Carnegie Mellon University with a degree in biology and you are interested in the field of proteomics. (*Proteomics is the large scale study of proteins and is used heavily in industry to analyze organic materials*). You have a very exciting term paper from your Senior Year entitled, "Using Proteomics on Organic Food for Residue Detection," which is a way to validate just how organic a food item truly is.

You'd like to use LinkedIn to discover 1st and 2nd level connections that share your interest in proteomics and might give you your first job. So you have:

- An interest in proteomics and so do they;
- A "yummy yummy" content item in the form of your term paper, a.k.a. an *excuse to connect.*

1st Level Connections: Use Your "Carrot" to Reach Out to Them

Next, you need to find 1st and 2nd level people who are hiring managers, key personnel at target companies or otherwise potential employers.

- Your 1st level connections, you can simply message or email via LinkedIn something to the effect of "Hi, I have this interesting paper on proteomics that I completed Senior Year, and I was wondering if you'd be interested in reading it and possibly giving me some feedback." Just search for contacts who have "proteomics" in their profile, and you can even "tag" them for future reference.

The idea here is that you have the "content" that provides the "excuse" for you to contact / email them with the hope that they will so like your paper that they may begin a conversation that ultimately leads to a job offer.

2nd Level Connections: Ask for an Introduction from your 1st's

But what about your 2nd levels? You cannot directly message them. So you turn to your 1st level connections to get to your 2nd levels by way of **introduction**.

Here's how.

Although you cannot see the contact information on the 2nd level connections, you can ask for an introduction from a 1st level connection. This is akin to being at a job fair or career event, going up to a 1st level connection who knows someone whom you want to get to know, and asking for an introduction. Then your 1st level walks over to your 2nd level (his 1st level), and introduces you. Susan (your 1st level) introduces you to Bob (her 1st level, and your 2nd level connection):

"Hey Bob, I'd like you to meet Jason. He's a recent CMU graduate in biology with a really interesting paper on proteomics and the validation of organic food. I thought you two might get to know each other."

Or structurally:

First level > reason to ask for an introduction > introduction to 2ⁿᵈ level > and (hopefully) the 2ⁿᵈ level becomes a 1ˢᵗ level (accepts your request).

Essentially, do your search, click on the person's name, and use the chevron (pull down menu) next to the blue **connect**, and select "Get introduced." Here's a screenshot:

After you click on "Get Introduced," you'll be able to select which 1st level connection you're going to ask for the introduction to the 2ⁿᵈ level connection, and what message you are going to send to them. Here's a screenshot:

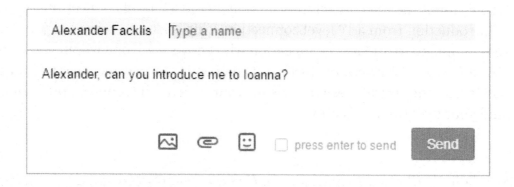

Sometimes this doesn't pop up correctly – in that case first click on the target person's name, and then on the far right, you'll see your 1st level connection, and then click on "get introduced." Here's a screenshot:

Alternatively, you can send an InMail (see http://jmlinks.com/3m) with a paid LinkedIn account, but it's probably more effective to "get introduced" as it would be in a real-world business encounter. After all, people trust people they know more than a "cold" call or a "cold" InMail / email.

It's not what you know (in business). It's who you know.

In this way, you use your 1st levels to get to your 2nd levels, and you have some "yummy yummy content" that gives you the reason to connect in the first place. It's not that different than asking a person whom you do know to invite a person whom you do not know to your personal business networking event. "Who knows who?," and "Why should they come?" are the relevant questions.

The bottom line, therefore, is to use your 1st level connections to get to your 2nd levels by way of a "content excuse," and the **TODO** for LinkedIn is to constantly be expanding your 1st level network, but how?

How to Expand Your LinkedIn Connections

If having many connections is the name of the career game on LinkedIn, how do you grow your connections? Here are some strategies:

Ask. Continually ask every business person you meet for their email, and then look them up on LinkedIn. Next click the Connect button and then fill out the information as indicated (you'll need their email and then write a note as to how you met them). Here's a screenshot:

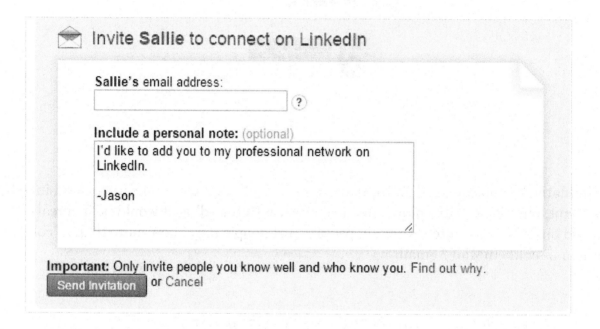

I recommend customizing your personal notes, such as *"Hi Sallie! You and I met at Proteomics world last week, and I'd like to connect with you on LinkedIn."* If she accepts, she becomes a 1st level connection.

No Spamming. Do not contact people you do not know because spamming on LinkedIn can lead to your account being deactivated.

Lifetime Limit. Indeed, there is a lifetime limit of 5000 invitation requests, designed to prevent connection spamming.

Get People to Ask You. Even better than asking people to connect to you, is to get them to ask you. Ideas for this would be:

- **Real World to LinkedIn**. If you give a presentation at a trade show, write an excellent blog post, or post an amazing professional video to YouTube, ask attendees to connect with you on LinkedIn. Include LinkedIn on your business cards, and literally mention LinkedIn when you meet business associates in real life.
- **Your Website or Blog**. Place the LinkedIn icon on your website or blog, and encourage visitors to connect.
- **Other Social Media**. Connect your LinkedIn to your Twitter, Facebook, Google+, etc., and encourage people who already follow you on Twitter, for example, to connect with you on LinkedIn.

The point is to do everything you can to encourage possible career contacts to connect with you on LinkedIn, because the more you grow your 1st level contacts, the more you can directly connect to them, and the more you can use them as introductions to their 1st level contacts, i.e., your 2nd level contacts.

The more 1st and 2nd level connections you have on LinkedIn, the wider your job search and career network. The wider your network, the more likely you are to be considered for jobs or promotions.

Who Should You Connect With?

There are different strategies in terms of reaching out, or accepting, the connection requests of others on LinkedIn. If you are desperate for a job, you should not be very choosey. If you are a senior level computer programmer, you might connect only with those persons whom you know in real life and/or seem very likely to advance your career.

Are Paid LinkedIn Accounts Worth It?

If you are actively looking for a job or career promotion, I recommend setting up a paid LinkedIn account. The main advantages of a paid LinkedIn account (of which there are several types) are:

- Enhanced cosmetics for your profile, such as a larger photo
- Better positioning when applying for a job
- Access to everyone who's viewed your profile in the last 90 days
- Ability to see 3rd degree profiles
- Additional search filters, and the ability to filter and save search results (great for sales prospectors)
- Up to 10 - 15 InMails per month to directly contact anyone on LinkedIn, even if you are not connected; (depending on the package you get)
- More detailed analytics

To learn more about LinkedIn Premium, visit https://premium.linkedin.com/. For a very helpful comparison of accounts, visit http://jmlinks.com/3n.

Your **TODO** here is to **brainstorm a logical connection philosophy**. If your purpose on LinkedIn is to use it for heavy schmoozing, then connecting with anyone or everyone makes sense. If your purpose is more passive or more secretive, perhaps just using LinkedIn as a public resume, and/or to keep up-to-date on industry trends, then connecting only with real-world connections makes sense. There might be different levels of openness when you are "in the job market" vs. when you "have a job."

Remember, once you accept a connection request, you become a 1st level connection, meaning that person can directly contact you via LinkedIn and email, as well as see your contact information. Similarly, he or she can see your 2nd level connections (unless you block that in settings). So, if you need to be more secretive, then be more judicious about whom you connect with. If not, don't worry about it. There is no right or wrong connection strategy: just pre-think a strategy that makes sense for your marketing objectives.

Also, remember that in the long run, you want to build your connections on LinkedIn *all the time, 24 hours a day, 7 days a week even when you have a job* because connections cannot be forged in a day. **Career-building doesn't stop just because you have a job!**

Brainstorming a Schmoozing Strategy

For your third **TODO**, download the **LinkedIn Personal Branding Worksheet**. For the worksheet, go to https://www.jm-seo.org/workbooks (click on Job Search and Career-building, enter the code 'careers2016' to register if you have not already done so), and click on the link to the "LinkedIn Personal Branding Worksheet." Complete the sections on goals, themes, 1st and 2nd level connections, and LinkedIn as rolodex.

❯❯ SHARE ON LINKEDIN VIA UPDATES & POSTS: OPPORTUNITY NO. 3

In the real world of career-building, it's a truism that you need to "look active." People respect people who are involved and engaged, and look down on people who seem to be doing nothing. Similarly, on LinkedIn, it is important to present at least the appearance of activity. By being active, you "look active" (a **trust** indicator), plus you have new ways to reach out to folks who can give you a job and/or advance your career thereby staying top of mind and generating career-building connections and inquiries.

Posting frequently (as well as being active in LinkedIn groups (see below)), in short: a) makes you seem active (and therefore trustworthy), and b) gives you more opportunities to be top of mind among hiring managers or key employees, thereby increasing opportunities for connections and job offers. I'm not saying you should be fraudulent. Nevertheless, just as at a business networking event, be active and engaged in a serious way. Participation is important!

Updates and Posts

The first way to do this is to post informative content to LinkedIn on a regular basis via *updates* and *posts*, and the second, is to participate in LinkedIn Groups. Let's look at each in turn.

Just as on Facebook, if you share an update to your profile (what most of us would call a "post," although in LinkedIn lingo this is called an "update,") and I am a 1st level connection, then that post has a good chance of showing up in my news feed. The news feed on LinkedIn is the first content that greets me when I login.

Here's a screenshot of my news feed highlighted in yellow:

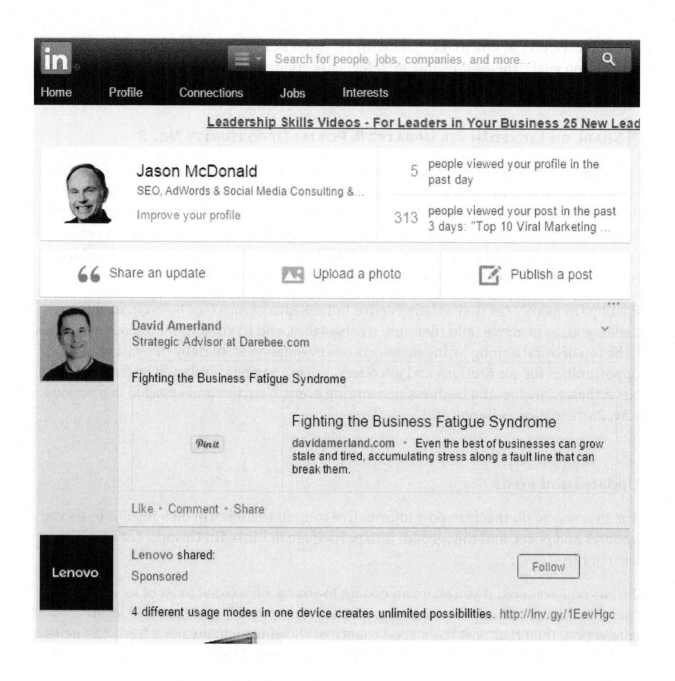

David Amerland, with whom I am a 1st level contact, posted an update, namely a link on LinkedIn to his blog post on "Business Fatigue." He posted his update, and it showed in my news feed. So the process is:

Identify items of interest to your business contacts (your own blog content or that of others) > Post updates on them to LinkedIn > Your connections see them in their news feeds (and hopefully get excited about doing business with you and/or your company).

Content is king, queen, and jack on LinkedIn as it is on all social media. Turn back to your Content Marketing plan, and remember you'll need both other people's content and your own content to post as updates or as posts to *Pulse* (more below):

- **Blog Post Summaries**. To the extent that you have an active blog and are posting items that fit with LinkedIn's professional focus, post headlines, short summaries and links to your blog.
    o Note that the first or "featured" image will become the shareable image, and that the META DESCRIPTION will become the default description when sharing. Choose striking, fun images for your blog posts!
- **Quotes**. People love quotes, and taking memorable quotes (on business themes) and pasting them on graphics is a win/win.
- **Infographics and Instructographics**. Factoids, how to articles, top ten lists, 7 things you didn't know lists, especially ones that are fun yet useful, are excellent for LinkedIn.
- **Quizzes, Surveys, and Response-provoking posts**. Ask a question, and get an answer or more. Great for encouraging interactivity, especially when the interaction is business-oriented. A great idea is to mention a project you are working on, and ask for feedback before, during, or after.

Turn to the content marketing section of the *Job Search and Career-building Resource Book* for a list of tools that will help you find other people's content and create your own. Remember that I recommend Hootsuite (https://www.hootsuite.com/) to manage all your social postings across platforms, including LinkedIn. I recommend Feedly (http://www.feedly.com/) as a way to organize industry blogs and the content of other people, so that you can be a useful sharer of third-party information on LinkedIn. And I also recommend Buzzsumo and Google Alerts as still other ways to find interesting content from other people to share via LinkedIn.

LinkedIn *Pulse*

One opportunity not to be missed on LinkedIn in terms of posting is *LinkedIn Pulse* (https://www.linkedin.com/pulse). LinkedIn is aggressively trying to grow its role not only for job seekers but for the fully employed. *Pulse* is LinkedIn's internal blog, and anyone (including you) can easily post to *Pulse*. Think of posting to *Pulse* as you would post to your own blog:

1. **Identify a topic** that will interest your target hiring managers and/or key employees at your target companies or industry, such as an industry trend or a common "pain point" in your industry or more generally in business.
2. **Brainstorm and identify keywords** using tools like Google suggest, Ubersuggest, or the Google AdWords Keyword Planner. (Don't forget trending topics culled from Google Alerts, Feedly, and Buzzsumo).
3. **Write a strong post with a great headline**, catchy first paragraph, and some substantial content that will be useful to readers / followers / potential employers / business contacts and position you as a "helpful expert."
4. **Tag your *Pulse* post with relevant tags** – these influence whether your *Pulse* post will show in their news feed and/or relevant searches.
5. **Google the LinkedIn Editorial Calendar**. LinkedIn produces one each year (e.g., for 2016), and if your post is timed with their interests, this has a better chance of being picked up "officially" by LinkedIn Pulse.
6. **Tweet Your Post to LinkedIn Marketing**. Use Twitter to alert the LinkedIn Marketing Team (https://twitter.com/linkedinmktg) that you've published something that fits into their calendar.

Inside of LinkedIn, *Pulse* lives under the beige button "+*Write a new post*". Here's a screenshot:

Pulse Reaches Beyond Your Connections

LinkedIn *Pulse* also allows individuals with whom you are NOT 1st level connections on LinkedIn to "follow you." It is also visible on the Internet even to people who are NOT on LinkedIn. Even better, when you share your *Pulse* Post on other social networks (e.g., Twitter, Facebook, Google+) and encourage people to cross over to LinkedIn, LinkedIn monitors this activity. If you get enough momentum, a *Pulse* Post can "go viral," and really supercharge your LinkedIn connections!

Therefore, a strong *Pulse* posting strategy can position you as a "helpful expert" to new people, and is not an opportunity to be missed!

For your fourth **TODO**, download the **LinkedIn Posting Worksheet**. For the worksheet, go to https://www.jm-seo.org/workbooks (click on Job Search and Career-building, enter the code 'careers2016' to register if you have not already done so), and click on the link to the "LinkedIn Posting Worksheet."

As much as it is fun and easy to post, the reality of LinkedIn today is that outside of job seekers (meaning you), not everybody checks LinkedIn on a daily or even weekly basis. Recruiters and headhunters probably do, but busy employers and busy hiring managers might not. So while posting frequently to LinkedIn is a good idea, it is not nearly as dynamic as Facebook in terms of active engagement. Keep that in mind when you measure the ROI of posting frequently on LinkedIn.

How frequently should you post?

Now that the LinkedIn news feed is very crowded (and the reality is that only few people outside of job seekers and outbound marketers check their feed daily), you can safely post quite frequently: even several times a day. But this differs with your audience, so pay attention to your updates, by monitoring thumbs up and comments (*for LinkedIn updates*) and stats (*for Pulse posts*). Your goal is to be interesting, informative, useful, and friendly as trust indicators and hopefully get social spread amongst new contacts, especially via *Pulse*. Note that you can see who responded to your *Pulse* posts, and this gives you an opportunity to connect with them with an eye to your career.

>> PARTICIPATE IN LINKEDIN GROUPS: OPPORTUNITY No. 4

With LinkedIn's growing emphasis on "professional learning," it should come as no surprise that LinkedIn has a growing ecosystem of groups on every topic imaginable. Compare LinkedIn groups to the "break out" sessions at your industry trade show: interested parties show up, listen to each other, participate in discussions, and showcase their questions (and answers) on professional topics. Oh, and occasionally, they use groups as yet another opportunity to **schmooze** *(surprise!)*. By participating tactfully in LinkedIn groups you can grow your prestige (and put the word out that you're pro-actively looking for a job or open to offers of career advancement). It's a soft sell environment; however, anyone who is a member of a group that you are a member of is a good prospect to become a LinkedIn 1st level connection.

To find relevant groups, simply search LinkedIn by keyword and then click on "Groups" on the left hand column in the resulting pop up. Or, first click on "Advanced" to the right of the search box, and then on "Groups" in the left-hand column. Then enter keywords that are relevant to your skillset and career-building needs.

Here's a screenshot:

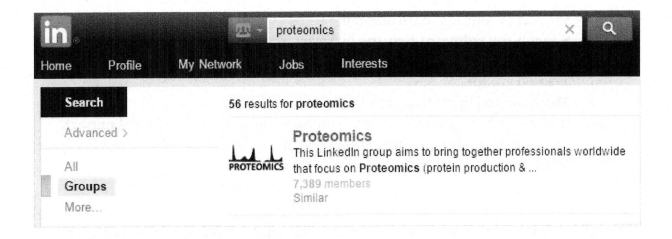

Note that there are two types of groups: **closed** and **open**. When you try to join a "closed" group, LinkedIn will ask you for some additional information. This goes to the group moderator, and if you are accepted, you've successfully joined the group. Open groups are easier (but probably of less technical or lower quality); just join them.

Group Self-promotion Strategy

LinkedIn is a serious social media platform; so please don't "spam" groups with self-promotional "hire me" messages! Instead, join relevant groups, pay attention to the on-going discussions, and post informative and useful content. It's a **soft sell environment**; let group members realize how smart and useful you are, and then reach out to you directly with job offers.

Don't hide the fact that you're looking for a job, or open to offers for career advancement, but don't be overly aggressive either.

Another strategy is to participate in groups to make connections, and then (over time) inform the connections that you are in the job market. First build the relationship and then mention that you're in the market for a job.

As you research (or join) groups, pay attention to the quality of the discussions. Some groups are fantastic: full of motivated, informed, honest people. Other groups are quite spammy with everyone talking, and few people listening. Just as at a professional trade show, be choosy with your time and efforts. Not all groups are created equally.

Your **TODOs** for groups are simple:

- **Log on** to your LinkedIn account.
- **Search for relevant groups** by keyword.
- **Identify** interesting and useful **groups**, and join them (or apply to join if it's a closed group).
- **Monitor** and begin to **participate**.
- Diplomatically position yourself (and your company) as a **helpful expert**.
- Carefully **broach the subject** that you are looking for a job or open to career offers.

❱❱ Follow Companies (and their Employees) on LinkedIn: Opportunity No. 5

Like Twitter, Google+, and Facebook, LinkedIn offers company Pages. And like Facebook or Google+, you must first have an individual profile to follow a company page.

Here are some examples of effective LinkedIn company pages:

- Thermo Fischer Scientific at https://www.linkedin.com/company/thermo-fisher-scientific.
- Intel Corporation at https://www.linkedin.com/company/intel-corporation
- Hewlett-Packard at https://www.linkedin.com/company/hewlett-packard
- Monsanto at https://www.linkedin.com/company/monsanto
- Social Media Examiner https://www.linkedin.com/company/social-media-examiner

To find companies to emulate, either search LinkedIn directly by keywords, or use this Google trick. Go to https://www.google.com/ and enter:

site:linkedin.com/company {keyword}

site:linkedin.com/company {company name}

as for example:

site:linkedin.com/company "organic food" at http://bit.ly/1NxviIZ

You'll find that LinkedIn is fast becoming a better home for more "serious" or even "boring" companies than Facebook; companies whose business value proposition is more *business-to-business* rather than *business-to-consumer*, and whose customers engage when they are in their work / professional / business mode. If the career you seek is in B2B, then LinkedIn companies are especially relevant!

Identify Employees Who Work at Your Target Companies

For any company on LinkedIn, you can see the employees that work there, and you can see your connection level (1st, 2nd, 3rd). First, find the target company's LinkedIn Page by searching for it in the LinkedIn search box. Then on the right hand side, you'll see a box showing the employees at the company and how you are connected to them.

Here's a screenshot:

If you click on the "See all" link, you can literally browse employees of those companies. Then, assuming you have an excuse or reason to reach out to your 1st or 2nd level connections, you can effectively schmooze the employees inside a company and look for job opportunities. Many companies also post jobs on LinkedIn, and other career opportunities. Look to the tab marked "Careers."

So your **TODOs** here are:

- **Identify target companies** for your job or career search objectives.

- **Follow them** on LinkedIn.
- **Browse to find employees** at these companies, and look for "reasons" to reach out to them such as new content of your own that is relevant to their company, your reactions to posts by the company, trade show events, or industry trends.
- Or, **follow the company's career tab** for events and offers that are posted officially.

Just as in real-world career-building, it is far better to have an "insider" recommend you for a position than to apply cold. Following relevant companies on LinkedIn is a fantastic way to keep your eye on target companies and key employees.

▶ PROMOTING YOUR LINKEDIN PROFILE, UPDATES, AND POSTS

Once you have established your individual profile, you should begin to share updates or posts to LinkedIn *Pulse*, send connection requests to all relevant friends, family, and colleagues, identify companies and key employees to follow, and begin to populate your account with updates and posts on a regular basis. It seems like a lot, but you are systematically growing your connections and establishing a "posting rhythm" for sharing content on the network.

Remember: social media is a **party**, so don't stop the party!

You must have yummy yummy food and entertainment for people to show up, and stick around. So as you promote your LinkedIn **content**, always keep front and center "what's in it for them" – what will they get by connecting with you LinkedIn or following your posts or updates?

Generally speaking, people on LinkedIn are looking for informative, educational, useful, and professional content relevant to their industry and job, so that they can stay informed and educated. If on Facebook the name of the game is *fun*, on LinkedIn the name of the game is *useful*.

FACEBOOK IS ABOUT FUN; LINKEDIN IS ABOUT USEFUL

Assuming your profile, updates, and posts have lots of useful content, here are some common ways to promote your LinkedIn accounts:

- **Real World to Social.** Don't forget the real world! Connect with everyone you meet in a professional or semi-professional capacity. Remember they need a reason to connect with you on LinkedIn *Why connect with you? Because they'll get insider tips, industry news, free eBooks and webinars – stuff that will keep them abreast of the industry, and better informed at their jobs.*
  - o Collect business cards and email addresses and use those to connect via LinkedIn after a real-world business networking event.
- **Cross-Promotion**. Link your personal website or blog to your LinkedIn profile, your blog posts to your profile, your Twitter to your profile, etc. Notice how strong personal brands on the Internet do this: one digital property promotes another digital property.
- **Email**. Email your contacts and ask them to "connect" with you on LinkedIn. Again, you must have a reason why they'll should do so: what's in it for them? Give away something for free like an eBook, write an in-depth industry article, share your white paper on a key industry topic, produce an informative YouTube video or SlideShare, or otherwise motivate them to click from the email to your profiles, and then connect.
- **LinkedIn Internal**. Using your profile on LinkedIn, you can promote yourself in an authentic way to grow your follower base. LinkedIn *Pulse* is especially useful for this, as are LinkedIn groups.
- **Use LinkedIn Plugins**. LinkedIn has numerous plugins that allow you to "embed" your LinkedIn content on your website, thereby nurturing cross promotion between your blog (for example) and LinkedIn. To learn more about plugins, visit https://developer.linkedin.com/plugins. In this way, your blog can promote your LinkedIn content, and your LinkedIn content can promote your blog. Similarly, your YouTube videos can promote your LinkedIn Profile, and your LinkedIn updates and *Pulse* posts can promote your YouTube Videos and vice-versa.
- **Leverage Every Connection**. People who already have connected with you are your best promoters. Remember, it's *social* (!) media, and encouraging your connections to share your content is the name of the game. You want to leverage your connections as much as possible to share your content. On LinkedIn, it's all about being useful! Indeed, a timely post to LinkedIn *Pulse* can be picked up by key influencers, go viral, and exponentially increase your attractiveness as a job candidate.

GET YOUR CONTACTS TO HELP PROMOTE YOUR LINKEDIN CONTENT

Advertise. Advertising is increasingly important to success on LinkedIn. While you can't advertise your LinkedIn profile directly, there is a workaround. Create your own "company" on LinkedIn (e.g., the *Jason McDonald Consulting Agency*), and then use the company Page to promote your personal updates or posts. How do you do this?

First, create a company website and a company domain such as *thejasonmcdonaldconsultingcompany.com* including an email address at that domain. Second, set up the company Page on LinkedIn. And, third, have the company share your personal update via its Page on LinkedIn. Finally, promote your personal blog post, YouTube videos, or other content on LinkedIn. Your company page can also promote your Pulse Posts (but you can't do this directly). To see the requirements and how to do this, visit http://jmlinks.com/9z.

The steps are:

- Set up a **Company Website** (e.g., on Blogger) with a unique domain.
- **Use your domain email address** (i.e., the domain you used to set up your personal website or blog) to verify that company.
- **Create a company page**, such as your own consulting business. Requirements are not very intense.
- Have the company Page "**share**" your LinkedIn update (e.g., your blog post or new YouTube video).
- **Advertise** your personal posts or updates to demographically specific targets by using your company page.

LinkedIn is hungry for advertising, and so it doesn't really matter how active or serious your consulting company is. For all they know, it could be a really serious business or just a startup. Who knows: if it succeeds well enough, perhaps you'll be an independent consultant. But regardless, you can use a company Page to promote your personal Profile's posts on LinkedIn.

Visit LinkedIn's advertising center at https://www.linkedin.com/advertising to view their official information on how to advertise. Here are some ideas:

Promote your Updates. Create your own "consulting company" page, find an update from your profile. At the bottom of the update, click on the gray "Sponsor Update" button and follow the instructions. You can demographically target advertising on LinkedIn in a very focused way: people who are members of a group, people who follow specific companies, etc.

Advertise Directly. You can create direct ads on LinkedIn to promote either offsite web content, or connect back to your Page or Posts. In terms of LinkedIn promotion, therefore, you can use LinkedIn advertising to grow your LinkedIn company followers by advertising your Page and/or posts.

» MEASURE YOUR RESULTS ON LINKEDIN

Measuring the success or failure of your LinkedIn personal branding efforts can be a challenge. Let's look at it from the "bottom up" in terms of items a job searcher or career builder might want to know or measure vis-a-vis LinkedIn:

- **Job Interview Leads**. Have your LinkedIn profiles, updates, or posts resulted in actual conversations or even job interviews?
- **Branding / Awareness**. Has LinkedIn increased your personal brand awareness and/or improved your personal brand image?
- **Top of Mind / One Touch to Many**. Has LinkedIn helped you to stay "top of mind," by reminding potential hiring managers of your value as a potential employee?
- **LinkedIn Update / Post Interactivity**. Have people read your updates or posts? Interacted with your posts or updates by liking, commenting, or sharing them?
- **LinkedIn Profile**. Is your connection count increasing, and if so, by how much and how fast? Where are your followers physically located, and what are their demographic characteristics?
- **Recommendations / Endorsements**. Are you gaining recommendations or endorsements from connections? From whom, and how fast?

The last of these is the easiest to measure: simply record your LinkedIn connection count each month, and keep a record of it month-to-month. I generally do this on my *Keyword Worksheet*, where I also track inbound links to my website, and my review count on review media such as Google+ and Yelp. (Watch a video on a Keyword Worksheet at http://jmlinks.com/1l).

Analytics Inside of LinkedIn

Inside of LinkedIn, click on the "who's viewed your profile" on the far right column. Here's a screenshot:

The click on the "Who's Viewed Your Profile" link and you'll get to analytics about your LinkedIn profile. At the top of that screen, you'll see three tabs: "Who's viewed your profile," "Who's viewed your posts," and "How do you rank for Profile views."

Google Analytics

If not a direct job interview lead, most of us want to drive traffic from LinkedIn to our personal blog or website. Google Analytics will measure how traffic flows from LinkedIn to your website, and then what happens upon arrival.

Sign up for Google Analytics (https://www.google.com/analytics) and install the required tracking code on your personal blog or website. Inside of your Google Analytics account on the left column, drill down by clicking on Acquisition > Social > Overview. Then on the right hand side of the screen you'll see a list of Social Networks. Find LinkedIn on that list, and click on that. Google Analytics will tell you what URLs people clicked to from LinkedIn to your Website, giving you insights into what types of web content people find attractive.

You can also create a custom Advanced Segment to look at only LinkedIn traffic and its behavior. For information on how to create custom Advanced Segments in Google Analytics, go to http://jmlinks.com/1f. For the Google help files on Advanced Segments go to http://jmlinks.com/1g.

In summary, inside of LinkedIn you can see how people interact with your LinkedIn profile, updates, and posts. Inside of Google Analytics, you can see where they land on your website and what they do after they arrive.

▶▶▶ DELIVERABLE: A LINKEDIN JOB SEARCH AND CAREER BUILDING PLAN

Now that we've come to the end our chapter on LinkedIn, your **DELIVERABLE** has arrived. Go to https://www.jm-seo.org/workbooks (click on Job Search and Career Building, enter the code 'careers2016' to register if you have not already done so), and click on the link to the "LinkedIn Personal Branding Plan." Complete the sections on promotion and content strategy.

▶▶ APPENDIX: TOP LINKEDIN JOB SEARCH AND CAREER-BUILDING TOOLS AND RESOURCES

Here are the top tools and resources to help you with LinkedIn marketing. For an up-to-date and complete list, go to https://www.jm-seo.org/workbooks (click on Job Search and Career Building, enter the code 'careers2016' to register if you have not already done so). Then click on the *Job Search and Career-building Resource Book* link, and drill down to the LinkedIn chapter.

LINKEDIN HELP CENTER - https://www.linkedin.com/help/linkedin

> Learn about all the different features on LinkedIn. From a brief overview to detailed tips, you'll find them here. Learn about profiles. Find out how to get a new job. Use LinkedIn on your mobile phone. Learn how to build your network. Get answers to your questions with Answers.
>
> **Rating:** 5 Stars | **Category:** overview

LINKEDIN LEARNING WEBINARS -
http://help.linkedin.com/app/answers/detail/a_id/530

>LinkedIn hosts live learning webinars on a variety of timely LinkedIn topics.
>Alternatively, users can view pre-recorded sessions. Topics are designed for a
>variety of audiences including, job seekers, corporate communications
>professionals, and journalists.
>
>**Rating:** 4 Stars | **Category:** resource

LINKEDIN COMPANY PAGES FAQ - http://linkd.in/1BbOokZ

>Interested in setting up a business page on LinkedIn? Here's the official FAQ on
>LinkedIn company pages.
>
>**Rating:** 4 Stars | **Category:** resource

RAPPORTIVE - http://rapportive.com

>Rapportive is a Gmail plugin that works with LinkedIn (and other social media
>sites). So when you're exchanging email with someone, you can see their
>LinkedIn profile details. It's sort of a bye-bye privacy app that helps you know
>how 'important' someone is with whom you are interacting.
>
>**Rating:** 4 Stars | **Category:** tool

OFFICIAL LINKEDIN BLOG - http://blog.linkedin.com

>The official LinkedIn Blog...lots of detailed information on what's happening
>when, where, and how on LinkedIn by LinkedIn staff.
>
>**Rating:** 4 Stars | **Category:** blog

LINKEDIN PULSE - https://www.linkedin.com/pulse/

>Need ideas for your next blog post? Look no further than LinkedIn Pulse where
>top business influencers post their thoughts daily. Even better, you can post to
>LinkedIin Pulse and become a LinkedIn superstar as well. Even even better: post
>to both LinkedIn Pulse and your own blog.

Rating: 4 Stars | **Category:** resource

8
FACEBOOK

Facebook is the largest social media platform, with over 1 billion active users. Nearly everyone is on Facebook: moms, dads, you, your friends, your high school teachers, employers, hiring managers, recruiters, the police, stalkers, and everyone in between. That's the *good news*. (Well, *except for the stalkers*). The *bad news* (from a job search or career-building perspective) is that they're not generally on Facebook for serious business or career goals. Rather, they're on Facebook for the F's: *friends, family, fun, photos*, and *fake*. (I'll explain *fake* in a moment).

Facebook, in a nutshell, is all about friends and fun. Friends connect with friends via *friend requests*, and friends share *status updates* or *posts* (especially photos and videos) on their timeline, which show in their friends' *news feeds*. Friends then *like, comment,* and/or *share* these posts, and the circle continues with the intervention of *Edgerank*, Facebook's secret algorithm that determines who sees what in their timeline.

People spend a lot of time on Facebook, and so do companies! It's clearly where the consumer audience is, so many consumer-facing companies such as Whole Foods, REI, Disney, and others maximize their involvement with Facebook. Unfortunately for a job-seeker, companies are on Facebook primarily to connect with customers, not to recruit new employees.

Nonetheless, Facebook is a tantalizing opportunity. In this Chapter, we'll explore Facebook from the perspective of how it can be used to look for a job and/or advance one's career. We'll cover how to set up your profile on Facebook, how to use Facebook to network or *schmooze* with friends, family, friends of friends, and even potential employers. We'll also cover what to share on Facebook as posts, with an eye to keeping the *Internet You* looking fantastic and out of trouble. We'll conclude with top tools and resources to leverage Facebook for your job and career goals.

Let's get started!

TO DO LIST:

» Explore How Facebook Works

» Be on Your Best Facebook Behavior

» Audit Your Facebook Privacy Settings

» Use Your Facebook Profile for Job Search and Career-building: Opportunity No. 1

» Set up a Facebook Page: Opportunity No. 2

» Follow Companies on Facebook: Opportunity No. 3

» Promote Your Facebook Profile, Page, and/or Posts

» Measure your Results on Facebook

»» Deliverable: A Facebook Job Search & Career-building Plan

»» Appendix: Top Facebook Job Search & Career-building Tools and Resources

» EXPLORE HOW FACEBOOK WORKS

To understand Facebook as a social media platform is to understand the "F's": *friends, family, fun, photos, and "fake."* You're probably already a Facebook user; technically what you have as an individual is called a "Profile," while companies have what is called a "Page." But if you're not on Facebook, it's easy to sign up: simply visit the Facebook help section at http://jmlinks.com/11b, and click on "Getting started on Facebook" on the left hand side. Facebook is easy to join and to use.

Before we start exploring how to use Facebook for career building, let's step back and look at the big picture:

> *What are people doing on Facebook? Why do they use it? What are they sharing and interacting with? Are your target hiring managers, recruiters, or employers on it, and if so, what are they doing? How will you interact with them in a compelling, fun and non-obtrusive way to support your career?*

Basic Set up

Once you sign up as an individual, you'll have a Facebook **profile**. Choose a nice-looking, job-appropriate picture of yourself as your "profile picture," and choose a larger job-appropriate photo that you can set as your "cover photo." Also fill out the information about yourself as required. If you're already on Facebook, audit your profile picture, cover photo, and descriptive text with an eye to how it might look to a potential employer. Don't use anything over-the-top, inappropriate, or controversial. All of this can (and should) be in the theme of "fun," but the reality is that *controversy* isn't what you want to advance your career. So be *fun* but *safe* with how your Facebook profile, cover photo, and description describes the *Internet You*.

Next, you're ready to investigate Facebook from the perspective of job search and career-building. I assume you have a few friends and family that you've already connected with on Facebook. If not, or to expand your circle of friends, search for real-world friends or family, send them "friend requests," and let them do the same to you. Next, login to Facebook on your desktop or your phone, look at your "news feed." Your news feed will show you the posts of the friends and family with whom you are connected: when they post a picture or text paragraph to their "timeline," it will show in your "news feed" (with some caveats about *Edgerank*, more about this later). Similarly, when you post to your timeline, those posts will show on the news feed of your friends when / if they log into Facebook whether on their computers or their phones. For example, post some photos of your family, your dog, your trip to Las Vegas or whatever you're up to in such a way that they are about friends, family, or fun (and are job-appropriate!). *In summary, your posts will show up in the timelines of your friends; and vice-versa, all day long.*

As you are posting things to Facebook, and paying attention to what others post that shows up your own timeline, pay attention to the "culture" of Facebook, and you'll soon realize that all those photos, videos, and text updates generally fall into the themes of *friends, family,* and *fun.*

Structurally, here's an example of how Facebook works:

Johnnie and I are **friends** on Facebook.

Johnnie **posts** a picture of his Labrador retriever puppy on his Facebook **timeline**.

When I login to Facebook and check my Facebook **news feed**, I see Johnnie's post of his puppy.

I **like** the post and/or **comment** on the picture: "Oh that is such a cute puppy!"

My friend, Robert, *sees my comment on his timeline*, and **comments**, "Pugs are cuter than labs!"

Johnnie gets "**tagged**" in his photo by his friend, Michael, and Michelle (one of Johnnie's other friends) sees a notification in her news feed that Johnnie was "tagged" (with the photo showing).

My other friend, John, sees the picture, comments on it, and **shares** it with his friends, and then his *friends* (such as Susan and Rachel) can chime in with likes of the post, comments, or shares of their own. Everyone can like, comment, and share this Facebook-thread about Lab puppies vs. Pug puppies.

This can go on a long time as *friends, family* and importantly *friends of friends* upload, comment, and share their pictures and posts...

The reason that it's called a *social network* is that one simple post can essentially ripple outwards through circles of friends and friends of friends.

Another good way to think of Facebook is that it is really a **huge interactive scrapbook**. When you post photos and writings to your timeline, your friends, family, and even friends of friends see them in their news feed, where they can like, comment, or share them. And vice-versa: when your friends post to their timeline, you see it in your news feed.

Facebook Saves Everything

Everyone can see and participate in this scrapbook, and Facebook stores this scrapbook so that you (or other people) can go back in time and see your past posts. (*This historical storage is often what causes trouble for people in job-search mode*).

FACEBOOK IS A SOCIAL SCRAPBOOK

THAT ALMOST NEVER FORGETS

Another way to think about Facebook is that it is like a big, never-ending, non-stop, 24/7 family and friends *party* **that is being recorded**. People post messages about their lives, families, social events, causes they like/dislike, etc., 24 hours a day, 7 days a week. As you pay attention to what people are sharing on Facebook, you'll see it falls into the themes of *friends, family, fun*, and *photos*:

- **Photos.** Photos dominate Facebook! Photos of friends at the beach, at Universal Studios Hollywood, graduating from High School, new babies, silly and strange selfies. People are constantly posting photos with short commentaries, generally about friends, family, and fun.
- **Videos.** Whether shared in photo format, as a video, or as plain text, Facebook is a place where people share image and text content generally about their friends, family and activities. The video shares are similar to the image shares.
- **Text.** People can share updates about where they are, what they're doing, or their state of mind. In most cases, these text updates will be accompanied by a photo or a video.
- **Memes.** These are funny photos, images, or videos often with quotes that focus on universal hopes, desires, humor, social causes, etc. Some of these "go viral," meaning they get extensively shared among individuals across Facebook.
- **Games, Social Contests, Groups.** For some people, Facebook is a place for social games. There are also groups on Facebook which allow people to collaborate and communicate; for example, a "group" of people taking a High School class in US History or a "group" of people who are passionate about cat rescue in Milwaukee.
- **Social Causes and Endorsements.** People often "endorse" causes they care about (e.g., Breast Cancer awareness, Gay & Lesbian issues, Save the Whales) and share "outrage" about issues that they disagree with. They can simply post and share messages on these themes, or join Facebook groups devoted to their particular cause.

As a quick assignment, log in to Facebook using your own personal Facebook profile, and spend some quality time, just bopping around Facebook and observing what people are "doing" online. Imagine Facebook is a party, and you have attended not to "have fun" but to "observe," and report back to a group of strange aliens to explain "what is going on" at this party. Then, you'll brainstorm (by yourself or with these imaginary aliens), how you might use the goings-on at the Facebook party to advance your job search and career goals. The career-building goal is to understand the vibe and culture, of Facebook so that your personal branding message will blend in, be seen and interacted with by others, and ultimately leverage the opportunities on Facebook to promote your job search or career goals.

Employers are on Facebook (as People)

The **good news** is that hiring managers and bosses are on Facebook. Bosses, hiring managers, recruiters, senior executives, and other key persons at nearly every company have a personal life (*yes, they really do; I know, it's hard to believe*) and in most cases, they are using Facebook just like you are. Your boss or potential boss might be a grandfather or grandmother, friend of friends of yours, a participant in a Church group or social cause, be a lover of beagle puppies (*especially her own*), have a spouse with whom she just went to Rocky Mountain National Park, and so on and so forth. These boss figures and others who can advance your career are just as likely as you or I are to be on Facebook and to be using Facebook for friends, family, and fun.

The good news is that your target employers are on Facebook.

Here's the **bad news**, however. They're not really in "let's-find-people-to-hire" mode when they are on Facebook. So you have to be careful, and you have to be clever. You can't be too forward on Facebook, and just start spamming everyone you know or might know that you're looking for a job or to advance your career. You can't shamelessly talk about your (boring) career or job issues, and you certainly shouldn't trash your employer, act trashy in other ways, or use inappropriate language. You have to see Facebook as having three purposes: 1) to be used for friends, family, and fun, 2) to be used to nurture the *Internet You* in such a way that it advances your personal brand and personal job / career goals, and 3) to be used to "spread the word" among friends and friends of friends that you are "in the market" for a new job or career promotion. With some skill, finesse, and subtlety, you can leverage Facebook for your personal brand and job search.

GOOD & BAD NEWS ABOUT FACEBOOK

But for now, let's sum up the Facebook reality:

The good news: nearly everyone is on Facebook, including hiring managers and employers. Even better, many people check Facebook once a day or more, and most check it at least a week. (For a research study on how heavily Facebook is used by various demographic groups, see http://jmlinks.com/11c).

The bad news: they're not doing much in the way of job / career recruiting, but are rather in "fun" mode, browsing pictures of their grandkids and discussing their family trips to Walt Disney World or Boston. They're not directly interested in any shameless self-promotional career / job messages you may want to share.

Facebook and Fake

Let's talk for a moment about Facebook and "fake." By "fake," I mean that people (especially older people!) generally do not share *embarrassing* news or *controversial* or *depressing topics* on Facebook. People are very likely to share photos of their family trip to Yosemite or New York's Empire State Building, their new Siamese cat with kittens, or their endorsement of the San Francisco Red Cross or GreenPeace. If they climb Mount Everest, or canoe the Grand Canyon, you can be sure they'll take a selfie at the summit or the bottom, and post it to Facebook. They are not likely, however, to share news about their family struggles, their pending divorce, or their shameful addiction to candy corn and weight problems. Neither will smart people be sharing truly controversial topics such as which religion is better than the others, or which politician or political cause is obvious to anyone but idiots. Very few people share this kind of information, and few go on to Facebook with the goal of listening to negative information.

In general, people put their best foot forward on Facebook; it's a social scrapbook in many ways about how life "should be," rather than how life "is." If you imagine your behavior on Facebook as how you might behave at a first meeting of your boyfriend's or girlfriend's family at a formal Thanksgiving dinner, you'll be in the right mode to be fun and family-oriented without creating problems for your personal brand image.

Businesses on Facebook

Turning to businesses, because Facebook's culture is about fun, it's a natural place for fun consumer brands like Whole Foods, REI, and Disney Cruises. It's a great place to share recipe ideas by Martha Stewart and Rachel Ray. It's a great place for both companies and consumers to share "how to" videos on how to pitch a tent, or enjoy a cruise with your kids. It's not such a great place for posts on taxes, divorce issues, how to buy an industrial fan for your pig farm and the like. Some companies will blend easily into the vibe of Facebook, while others will blend only with some brainstorming about how to be "fun" even if the product or service isn't that fun (dentistry? plastic surgery? insurance?). And 99% of the time these companies are not looking for new employees on Facebook, but rather looking for new customers.

Stay Positive on Facebook

This "fun" vibe makes posting on Facebook about your job search or career-building goals, a bit of a challenge. A bit of advice: stay positive! No one wants to read "Debbie Downer" posts of how depressed you are about getting a job, about how much you hate the job you have, or how much you detest your boss.

In fact, I **strongly advise against any sort of negative post** (especially against your boss and/or current employer / company). That includes posting or talking about controversial issues: you may "hate" your boss, you may be "for" Donald Trump or "for" Hillary Clinton, but you don't know the politics of a possible supervisor who might impact your promotion. You might be "for" or "against" Gay Marriage, but the same situation exists. Do you really want to be passed over on a promotion because you are "for" Catholicism's view of Christianity, "for" LGTBQ rights, or "for" government restrictions on carbon pollution? Or maybe "against" any or all of the above?

> *Yes, I know that it's not politically correct to advise that you keep your politics and religion to yourself, but the reality is that (unfortunately) a future employer may take you off her list if she doesn't agree with your politics, religion, or current cause about which you are "outraged." Ditto if she sees some trashy or inappropriate pictures or behaviors. The safe strategy is to stay positive, polite, and politically neutral on Facebook.*

Edgerank on Facebook

In terms of who sees which posts, it's time to discuss the Facebook algorithm. (Think of an algorithm as the "computer brain" that governs how Facebook works). Historically, the Facebook algorithm (or at least the component that controls who sees what) has been called *Edgerank*. Essentially, the *more* a person interacts with the posts of another person's Profile or a company Page on Facebook by liking, commenting on, and sharing its posts, the *higher* the *Edgerank* of that person or company. The *higher* the Edgerank, the *more* likely it is that others will see and continue to see posts by that person.

With an eye to the future, you want to start thinking about posting items that encourage interactivity, so that your own *Edgerank* improves and therefore more of your friends and family start to see your posts.

> *Essentially, the more you and your posts receive likes, comments, and/or shares on Facebook, the higher your Edgerank, and the higher your Edgerank, the more people will actually see your posts.*

(Technically, Facebook no longer officially uses the term "Edgerank," but in practical terms it is very clear that the Facebook algorithm rewards interactivity. To read a more technical discussion of Edgerank, visit http://jmlinks.com/11f.)

Here's the beginning of a Facebook job search strategy: you post frequently to Facebook, and you post items that are fun and interactive, so that your friends and family click like, comment, or share your posts. That increases your *Edgerank*. Next, you "use" the *Edgerank* accumulated via this fun posts by posting an announcement with a fun picture of you, announcing that you're in the market for a new job or career advancement. Your strategy in a nutshell is:

Expand your circle of friends, family, and friends of friends by connecting with everyone you know on Facebook.

Post many (80%) posts that are fun and interactive so that your Facebook connections like, comment, and share your posts (expanding your reach).

Post a few (20%) career-oriented posts that are both "fun" and yet explain that you are "in the market" for a job or career advancement.

By posting many "fun" posts and just a few "I'm in the market for a job" posts, you maximize the probability that your family, friends, and friends of friends will see that you are available for a new or better job.

» BE ON YOUR BEST FACEBOOK BEHAVIOR

They say that an elephant never forgets, and the same is certainly true for the Internet and for Facebook as well. Remember that post you made in 2014 about the Frat party in which you got so drunk, and danced nearly naked on the front lawn? *Oops.* Remember that politically incorrect post you made about so-and-so after such-and-such? *Oops.* Remember how you chastised Grandpa because he was so out of touch with the important needs of twenty-somethings to not have to repay college loans? *Oops.* Remember how you vented and trashed your ex-employer after you got fired? *Oops, oops.*

Here's the rub: many of us, especially but not only young people, don't think very hard about the ramifications of what we post on Facebook (or what we like or share). We might not have much of a "Facebook filter," and in our college days, or in our unemployed days, we might have shared some posts, some photos, or even some videos that we'd really rather not be seen by our potential employers. We may have left some damaging items that have a negative impact on our *Internet You.*

Oops.

What is to be done?

Think Before You Post. From now on, when you post ANYTHING on ANY social network, especially Facebook, ask yourself how this might look to a future employer? If you'd be ashamed that they'd see it, I strongly recommend AGAINST posting it. If you think it might be offensive to ANYONE, do NOT post it. I don't want to be a *prima donna*, but the reality is that some posts that to you seem like "no big deal" on Facebook, might appear to a potential employer as so heinous as to cost you your job before or even during employment.

Conduct a Facebook Audit. Log onto Facebook (preferably on your computer or tablet), and click on your name on the top left. This gets you out of your news feed and into your profile / timeline. Scroll down through your posts year by year with an eye to anything embarrassing. If you find a post you'd rather get rid of, click on the down chevron on the right side of the post, and select "Delete." Here's a screenshot:

Jason McDonald

March 14 at 9:04am · Fremont, CA, United State

I believe the Chinese have a saying to the effect
interesting times." We are approaching the End

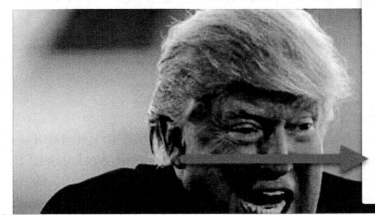

Save link
Edit Post
Change Location
Change Date
Turn off notifications for this post
Refresh share attachment
Hide from Timeline
Delete
Turn off translations

Your mission is to go back in time, and delete any and all posts that you'd rather not
have an employer see. When you're done with this exercise, you will have deleted all
potentially embarrassing posts. And, for the future, you should make the following
solemn promise that whenever you post to Facebook (as well as ANY social media),
you'll ask the question:

> *If a potential employer sees this post (or a potential key employee who might
> recommend me for a job or career advancement sees this post), will I be
> embarrassed? Will it hurt my career prospects? If so, I will NOT post it.*

OK, right now, I'd like you to stand up from your chair, hold out your right hand with
three fingers up, and repeat after me:

> *If a potential employer sees this post (or a potential key employee who might
> recommend me for a job or career advancement sees this post), will I be
> embarrassed? Will it hurt my career prospects? If so, I will NOT post it.*

See how easy that was? You've now sworn to be a "Goody Two-shoes" on Facebook.

BE ON YOUR "BEST BEHAVIOR" ON FACEBOOK

Your first chapter **DELIVERABLE** has arrived. Go to https://www.jm-seo.org/workbooks (click on Job Search and Career-building, enter the code 'careers2016' to register if you have not already done so), and click on the link to the "Facebook Audit Worksheet." By completing this worksheet, you'll audit your Facebook account to ensure that you have a good handle on your preferred privacy settings. Print out this audit, and work through it as your read the steps below.

Timeline Audit

There's an easier way to do your Facebook audit, including not just your own posts but also posts in which you've been tagged, photos of you by others, etc. To do this, you'll conduct a "Timeline Audit." Here's how:

- Log into Facebook.
- Click on your name on the top left to get to your timeline.
- Click on "View Activity Log," which is the gray button at the top right.
- On the left hand column, scroll through each item, including "Posts You're Tagged In," "Posts by others, etc."

Here's a screenshot:

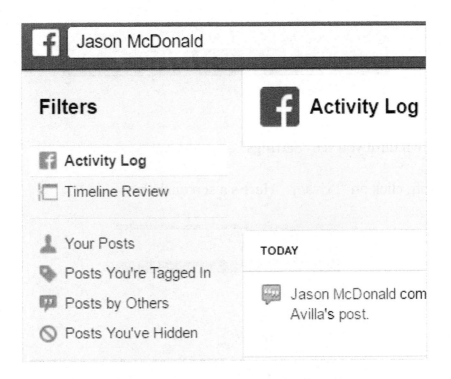

You can also enable "Timeline Review," which gives you more control of whether you can be tagged by others in photos and comments, and have those elements shared on your Timeline. ("Tagging" means that a friend of yours identifies you in a picture or post, essentially helping Facebook know who is who on posts to the network). This function is on the left hand column as shown above.

» AUDIT YOUR FACEBOOK PRIVACY SETTINGS

For most of us, we'd like to use Facebook only for friends and family. We don't want the "prying eyes" of employers to be analyzing our Facebook posts, even though we've just solemnly promised not to post anything that might potentially hurt our careers.

The next step, therefore, is to do a **privacy audit** on Facebook and make sure that the privacy settings are set so that only our friends and family can see us on Facebook. Here's how:

Log in to Facebook, and click on the top right downward chevron. Here's a screenshot:

Scroll down until you see "Settings"

On the left, click on "Privacy." Here's a screenshot:

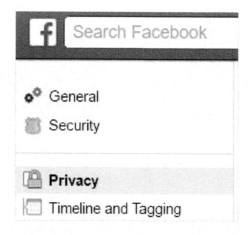

Go through each item, and set to the maximum level of primacy, namely:

Who can see my stuff? Click on "edit," and set this to "friends."

Review all your posts and things you're tagged in. Review posts that friends tagged you in. If your friends are a bit crazy, I recommend clicking "Use Activity Log," finding a post you've been tagged in, click on the "gear" icon in the top right, and change "Timeline Review" to "enabled." This will then require that you "approve" any posts in which you are tagged.

Limit the audience for posts you've shared with friends of friends or Public? Click "Limit old posts," and this will reset all old posts to be visible only to friends.

Who can send you friend requests? If you are still expanding your Facebook friends, you can leave this at everyone. Just be careful as you review "friend requests" that you truly know each person, so that a potential snoopy employer can't request to be a friend, you approve him or her, and bingo – they can see everything on your account.

Who can look me up? Again, you can leave this open to everyone, or change to just friends if you want to be very restrictive. The same goes for anyone who has your phone number.

Do you want search engines outside of Facebook to link to your profile? Be sure to set this to "no."

Next, scroll down on the far left to "Followers." Then find "Who can follow me?," and change this from "Everybody" to "Friends." This prevents employers from being able to follow you without being your friend. For extra privacy, you can also change "Who can comment on your public posts?" to just "friends." You should also NOT have your Facebook connected to your Twitter account, as Twitter is 100% public and ANYTHING posted to Twitter is visible by ANYONE.

Very important: do not connect Facebook to Twitter.

At this point, you have done a complete "Privacy Audit" on Facebook and ensured that your privacy settings are set to their maximum. You can review the Facebook help information on "privacy checkup," at http://jmlinks.com/11d.

Conduct a Facebook Friend Audit

Be careful who you're friends with! Over time, you may have become Facebook friends with employers, former employers, coworkers, business colleagues, or other persons that you aren't really friends with and there is little value in having them exposed to your posts. Or, they may be doing stupid and embarrassing things and you do not want "guilt by association" in the eyes of an employer.

A good example might be if you are Facebook friends with a coworker at work, and you post something "politically incorrect" to your Facebook timeline. That coworker might see it, and start office gossip that ultimately hurts your chances of career advancement. Or that coworker may be out doing stupid things, and you like, comment, or share one of his posts and you have just become "guilty by association." Or, you're Facebook friends with a former employer, and they might not like what they see on Facebook, thereby nullifying their interest in giving you a good job reference.

> *Your first line of defense is being "on your best behavior" on Facebook in terms of what you post, like, comment, and/or share.*
>
> *Your second line of defense is restricting your privacy settings.*
>
> *Your third line of defense is auditing your Facebook friends, and restricting your friends to people you can trust.*

Friends as Security Risks

So it's time to audit your friends on Facebook and unfriend those who are "security risks" (in a very mild sense of the word.).

AUDIT YOUR FRIENDS

What's a "security risk?" A good example would be a supervisor, ex-employer, or coworker at your current place of employment. Suppose you (stupidly) post a picture of yourself getting arrested at a professional baseball game, acting a bit too crazy. This Facebook post might become office gossip, and thereby hurt your chances at a career advancement. Or suppose (really stupidly) that you trash your employer / ex-employer in a Facebook rant, and that employer is your friend (you had forgotten about that). *Oops.* You might lose your job, or be passed over for a career advancement. I am recommending two levels of security here:

- **Don't post stupid things to Facebook** such as pictures that you're not comfortable having an employer see, remarks such as criticisms of employers or supervisors, controversial political or religious beliefs, etc. Be on your "best behavior" from now on on Facebook.
- **Unfriend all risky people** who might share / spread / comment on your posts in such a way that these unflattering posts might be seen by employers / potential employers.

To see your current friend list, simply type "My Friends" into the Facebook search box and click on the magnifying glass to search. Here's a screenshot:

Once it loads, be sure to click the "more" button at the bottom. Here's a direct link to this function: http://jmlinks.com/11e.

Scroll down the list and review each friend. For those who are "security risks" (again in the mildest sense of that word, I am indicating those who might share / expose unflattering items about you to potential employers), simply "unfriend" them. Here is a screenshot:

At this point, you've removed any "security risks" from your friend list on Facebook. This, in combination with your new "best behavior" strategy of posting and your tightened privacy settings, should help prevent negative information about you from being discovered by potential employers.

And, again – to remind you – I am not advocating lying or being deceitful on Facebook. I am just advising you that in constructing an advantageous *Internet You*, you want Facebook to reflect you on your best behavior.

Revisit your first chapter **DELIVERABLE** has arrived. Go to https://www.jm-seo.org/workbooks (click on Job Search and Career-building, enter the code 'careers2016' to register if you have not already done so), and click on the link to the "Facebook Audit Worksheet." By completing this worksheet, you'll audit your Facebook account to ensure that you have a good handle on your preferred privacy settings.

» USE YOUR FACEBOOK PROFILE FOR JOB SEARCH AND CAREER-BUILDING: OPPORTUNITY NO. 1

Now that you've done a Facebook audit and upgraded your Facebook behavior to put your best Facebook face forward, it's time to shift from being passive on Facebook to being pro-active. You can use Facebook as part of your job search and career-building efforts.

Follow along by opening the next **DELIVERABLE** for this chapter. Go to https://www.jm-seo.org/workbooks (click on Job Search and Career Building, enter the code 'careers2016' to register if you have not already done so), and click on the link to the "Facebook Job Search and Career Building Marketing Plan." By filling out this plan, you will establish a vision of what you want to achieve via Facebook.

Let's get started

Notify Your Friends and Family That You're Looking for a Job

Facebook is really all about friends and family, and these are the people most likely to help you out in finding a new job. *Hopefully they like you! And hopefully they'll help you out!*

NOTIFY FACEBOOK FRIENDS YOU'RE LOOKING FOR JOB

The trick is to realize that when they are on Facebook, they're not in "help you out" mode but rather in "check out the pictures of my grandkids" mode. This is especially true when you realize that the people who are ablest to help you with a job search are generally older than you, and that older people on Facebook really use it as a social scrapbook. Appeal to their sense of family duty, and appeal to them to help you out in your job search. The first way to do this is to use Facebook to directly message each and every person on your contact list who might be able to help you find a job:

- **Reach out directly to people you know on Facebook**. You can chat or message people directly on Facebook, and after identifying those who might be able to assist you, message them just to say, "Hey, I'm in the job market, and if you know of any openings – let me know."

To do so, first type the person's name into the Facebook search box, next click over to their Facebook Profile, and then click on the "Message" box in gray in the top right of their cover photo. *Be polite, and not pushy but ask for help.*

Post Smart and Advance Your Career

In addition, you can use your posts in a clever fashion to constantly remind your contacts that you are "in the market." Here are some ideas on how to do this:

- **Post short summaries and even pictures ("selfies") of you on your job search**. For example, let's say you score a job interview. You've put on your best clothes, and you're waiting in the reception area. Pull out your iPhone and snap a "selfie" of you, waiting for your job interview. Post a message that says something like, "Here I am – nervous and crazy, waiting for my next job interview. Wish me luck!" In that way, you've notified friends and family that you're in the market for a job, and those that might be able to help you, might reach out.

- **Post short summaries and even pictures ("selfies") of you when you get rejected.** Let's say you just got rejected from the job. Post a selfie of yourself, looking a bit down-in-the-mouth with a message like, "Oops, didn't get that job. Never give up, never surrender – that's my job search motto"). You're positive in a tough situation, and you've implicitly notified friends and family that you're looking for a job.
- **Post updates about your job search.** You can use your blog to chronicle your search for a job, and then post updates to Facebook as you chronicle this process. Today's society is more open than ever, and many people might actually enjoy reading about your journey. So be open; share your job search journey to your blog and to Facebook.
- **Post updates on your industry of interest to a general audience.** Let's suppose you're not actively looking for a job, but you're open to career offers. Use your blog to comment on industry trends, and cross-post those articles that have a more general interest, have a fun spin, or share insights of interest to the general public to Facebook. Don't bore everyone with every single blog post, but do share those insights that you have as an expert that less skilled people might find interesting.
- **Write or Research a Long Article or Book.** Once you have a blog, you now have an "excuse" to do "research" for articles. For example, if you're looking for a job in accounting, research and article on "10 Things I Wish I knew at My First Accounting Job." Reach out to friends and family on Facebook and ask for tips and insights from their work experience. This is a polite way to inform them you are looking for a job, get information for a truly good article for your blog, and make yourself look active and insightful as a job candidate: win, win, win, win.
- **Post useful items about careers and jobs.** As you are searching for a job and you find (or produce) articles, photos, infographics and other fun-oriented items that nevertheless related to career-building, post these to Facebook. Ask friends and family for comments, and you'll be sharing in a subtler way that you are "in the market" for a new job or promotion opportunity.

BE CREATIVE IN WHAT YOU POST

- **Ask to be shared.** Post to your friends and family, that you are looking for a job, describe yourself and your career goals (perhaps link over to a more detailed small essay on your blog about your Personal Branding Statement and career goals), and pro-actively ask friends and family to share this message with their contacts. The friends of your friends may know about job opportunities that your friends do not. *Alternatively, ask your Mom or Dad to share this message for you, and then complain in the comments that they've shared it!*

- **Post items that get shared**. The items that get shared on Facebook are generally *emotion, emotion, emotion*. Post funny photos, sentimental items, shocking statistics, and indicate that the reason you are doing so is that you are "in the market" for a job or a career promotion. Your goal is to get friends to share with friends, and thereby broaden the circle of people who know you are in the market.
- **Post questions and surveys**. Rather than simply posting that you need a job, post questions. Such as, "I'm off to a job interview. What do you recommend I wear? Post suggestions in the comments." Or, "I'm 22, and just graduated from Carnegie Mellon. I'm beginning my job search for a career in engineering – any suggestions from my elders?"

These are just a few ideas. Take a moment and brainstorm posts that you might make to Facebook that can assist in your search for a better job or a better career.

Your second chapter **DELIVERABLE** has arrived. Go to https://www.jm-seo.org/workbooks (click on Job Search and Career Building, enter the code 'careers2016' to register if you have not already done so), and click on the link to the "Facebook Job Search and Career Building Marketing Plan." It starts with your personal posting rhythm; so fill out that first section, now.

Posting Rhythm and Edgerank

Remember that Facebook rewards posts with *Edgerank*, its algorithm that chooses which posts to display in the news feed of Facebook members. Thus if you only post self-serving messages about your job search and your friends or family members don't "like," "comment," or "share" these messages, your *Edgerank* declines and they are less likely to see your messages. Therefore, post items that are fun and interactive frequently and items that are a bit more self-serving less frequently.

Post 80% fun stuff, and 20% stuff that says you are "looking for a job."

A posting rhythm might follow the 80/20 rule: 80% fun stuff and 20% stuff about your job search. For example, you might post about your Labrador retriever puppy, photos of you and your friends hanging out at college, photos of sunsets, old photos of you as a kid, humorous photos about current events and happenings, etc. Your posting rhythm would be posts that are:

Fun, fun, fun, useful, fun, humorous, fun, useful, fun, I-am-looking-for-a-job, fun, fun, useful, fun, humorous, fun, useful, fun, I-am-looking-for-a-job, fun, etc.

In this way, your posts are likely to be seen by more friends and family, including those that help you in your job search.

EDGERANK REWARDS INTERACTIVE POSTS

Employed but Looking for a Better Job

If you already have a job and are looking to advance your career, the situation can be trickier. If you don't want your employer to know you're looking, then it is a bit dangerous to announce your search for a better job on Facebook. So you'd have to be subtler, posting items about your career and perhaps queries about how others have thought about advancing their careers over time. You can also direct message / private message via Facebook your friends and family in a more private way.

If it's OK with your current employer that you're planning to leave, then it's OK to post your positive, upbeat, but *can-you-help-me-out-I-am-looking-for-a-new-job* messages to Facebook.

In all cases, the trick is to post fun items more frequently than self-serving ones, and when you do post something that should assist you in your job search, "spin" it in a way to make it fun. People are on Facebook for friends, family, fun, and photos, so leverage that reality, as you use it to announce that you are looking for help in advancing your career.

» SET UP A FACEBOOK PAGE: OPPORTUNITY NO. 2

In addition to using your Facebook profile as part of your job-search and career-building journey, you can go to the next step: setting up an official Facebook Page. Here's the scoop on Profiles vs. Pages:

Real persons have profiles. A real person has a "profile" on Facebook, and Facebook's official policy is to verify (to the extent possible) that you are a real person. Profiles can interact with each other on Facebook (e.g., when you share a selfie of yourself at a job interview, your Mom sees it on her Facebook news feed), but a "profile" must first send / or / accept a "friend request" from another profile for this interactivity to occur.

A Facebook Page is an entity such as a business or public figure. A Facebook "Page" is not a real person but rather a brand such as Whole Foods or a public figure such as Bishop Robert Barron. A "Page" is open for the whole world to see, and any individual can simply "like" a "Page." Once that is done, posts by the Page will show in the news feed of persons who have "liked" that Page.

Note: All of this is mediated by *Edgerank*, and the higher your *Edgerank*, the more likely friends and family are to see your posts in their very busy and very crowded news feeds on Facebook. In addition, the *Edgerank* of Profiles is significantly higher than the *Edgerank* of Pages.

That said, Pages have one huge **advantage** over Profiles: they can **advertise** and therefore reach people who are NOT connected to them. Here's an idea for you:

- **Create a Page** Entitled "My Job Search" or "Tips on Accounting by a Person Seeking a Job" or "A Humorous Take on Being 22 and Searching for a Job," etc. Essentially devise a "concept" for something that fits with Facebook's focus on friends, family, and photos and yet markets your personal brand or personal job search. Cross-linking this to a blog is a great way to leverage both your blog and Facebook without having to generate additional content.
- **Post interesting / funny / shocking / emotional items to this Page**, and promote this Page not only to friends and family but to any demographic group on Facebook that might assist you in your career.

Remember that in doing this, what you are doing is 100% public (Pages are NOT private by design), and that it must fit with Facebook's personality of friends, family, and fun.

Something boring like "My Accounting Journey" won't do as well as "Selfies from My Accounting Job Search." To learn more about setting up a Page on Facebook, visit http://jmlinks.com/11g. Of the Page types available, here are the most relevant:

Artist, Band, or Public Figure. An example here would be to have a "public" Page of you-as-job-seeker or you-as-creative-web-designer-type or you-as-engineer. Click on this Page type, and then select a category from the pull-down menu. Categories include entertainer, entrepreneur, author, blogger, public figure, etc.

Cause or Community. Choose this category if you want to have a Page only during your job search. To be a bit tongue-in-cheek, you could call yourself "Jason's Job Search," or "Help Antonia Get Her First Job." In that way, you can enlist the emotional and other support of people around the Internet to help you find a job.

Once you've set up your Page, populate it with a fun "cover photo" and a fun "profile picture." Your Page will appear on the left-hand menu when you login to Facebook. Click on your Page, and then on the top right, click on "Settings." You can change the privacy and other settings here, but remember, unlike your personal Profile, you probably want your Page to be very public. Finally, you can then invite friends and family to "like" your Page.

Page Posting

At this point, you're ready to start posting. You'd probably post many of the same items I listed above if you are using the Page to directly support your job search. Or, if you're going a bit off the map, you might have a "fun" page of you as a young accountant (for example), sort of a Dilbert-esque view of the world. You need to brainstorm the tone you want for your page, and then brainstorm posts such as links to blog posts, infographics or instructographics, photos or images, Memes, etc. Remember, Facebook is all about friends, family, and fun, so even though you have a Page, the posting strategy is the same.

Another important point to understand is that the Edgerank of your Profile is generally much higher than that of your Page, so be sure to continue to post to your Profile. In fact, I would say that the main advantage of a Page, is that it can advertise to anyone on

Facebook. In this way, you can reach many people that you cannot reach with a Profile. So don't think of it as Profile OR Page but rather Profile AND Page.

> ***Important***: *generally speaking, your Facebook Profile as an individual has much more reach to friends, family, and friends of friends than a Facebook Page.*

Use my list of persons with powerful personal brands online at http://jmlinks.com/persbrands and browse those persons who have strong Facebook Pages. A good example is Dr. Will Courtenay at http://jmlinks.com/11h. Dr. Courtenay's focus is on being a "therapist for men." Notice what he posts and brainstorm why. He shares both other people's content, and his own content all on the theme of masculinity in today's society. Or take a look at Max Michael, a professional shooter at http://jmlinks.com/11j. His goal is to build a personal brand around being a professional athlete in the shooting sports. You can also take a look at your own list of brands-to-emulate and start to brainstorm how you, too, could have an effective personal brand page on Facebook.

(*We're going to look at advertising and promoting your Facebook Profile and/or Pages, but let's turn to following other companies, first*).

» FOLLOW COMPANIES ON FACEBOOK: OPPORTUNITY NO. 3

Many companies have their own Pages on Facebook. While most of them will be in friends, family, and fun mode (not career mode), you can still identify, "like" them to follow them, and then interact with their posts, as a way to both learn about their company culture and also ingratiate yourself with the company. This is especially relevant if you want a job at a consumer-facing company.

Let's say, for example, that you wanted a job at a company selling organic food. You'd first identify local companies that are your target employers. Then, you'd "like" their Pages on Facebook. Finally, you'd interact with their posts and subtly hint that you're in the market for a job at their company.

Here are the steps:

1. **Keywords.** Using your keyword list, search Facebook to find relevant companies. To do this, login to Facebook and type one of your keywords into the search box such as "organic food." Scroll to the very bottom, and click on "See all results for 'Organic Food.' Find the 'Page' section and click on 'See More.'
2. **Identify and Follow.** Identify interesting companies from this search and "like" their pages.
3. **Monitor**. Monitor your news feed for posts by these Pages, and interact with them.
4. **Use the Pages Feed**. Alternatively, sometimes you won't see posts by your target company Pages, so login to Facebook and on the left menu find "Pages Feed." Clicking on this link will show you a specific news feed of ONLY Pages that you have liked. (If you have trouble finding it, click on http://jmlinks.com/11k while logged into Facebook).

Another way to find Facebook pages is to use Google and type *site:facebook.com {your keywords}* as in site:facebook.com "organic food" Cleveland Ohio. To see an example, visit http://jmlinks.com/11m. Remember there is NO SPACE between site: and facebook.com! What's nice about using Google is you can specifically type in a city or region to find local companies.

Once you've built a list of relevant companies to follow, monitor them and interact with their posts by liking, commenting, and sharing them. Look for opportunities to find and Facebook-friend employees at the company by interacting with the Facebook Page. Over time, politely indicate you'd love to learn more about the company as you are in "job search mode." Some local companies will have enabled "Facebook Reviews," and you might write a review since companies pay a lot of attention to reviews. Depending on your own personal brand and comfort level, you might indicate that you really love the company and its products or services, and while looking for a job, would love the opportunity to work there.

You don't have to be that shameless, but hey, why not? It depends on how aggressive you want to be in your job search. Remember as well that by following a company on Facebook, you'll learn about its corporate culture and gain some insight into whether that culture is a good fit for you.

≫ PROMOTE YOUR FACEBOOK PROFILE, PAGE AND/OR POSTS

Once you have optimized your individual profile, begun to share posts, and possibly created a public Page that corresponds to your online Personal Brand, it's time to brainstorm ways to promote yourself on Facebook. In and of itself, nothing on Facebook is truly self-promotional.

Remember, social media is a **party**. You must have yummy yummy food and entertainment for people to show up, and stick around. So as you promote your Facebook **content**, always keep front and center "what's in it for them" – what will they get by interacting with your Profile and/or Page? Keep in mind:

FACEBOOK IS ABOUT FUN; LINKEDIN IS ABOUT USEFUL

Assuming your profile and posts have lots of fun, useful content, here are some common ways to promote your Facebook Profile and/or Page:

- **Real World to Social.** Don't forget the real world! Ask Mom, Dad, whomever for the email addresses and names of all those long-forgotten Aunts, Uncles, and old family friends. Grow your Facebook friend list by reaching out to these people. Since 80% of your posts will remain friends, family, and fun, most of them will be happy to "friend" you on Facebook.
- **Cross-Promotion**. Link your personal website or blog to your Facebook Profile (or explain how a true friend can connect with you on Facebook) and/or Facebook Page, your blog posts to your profile / Page, your Twitter to your profile / Page, etc. Notice how strong personal brands on the Internet do this; one digital property promotes another digital property. Use **Hootsuite** (https://hootsuite.com/) to make this cross promotion easy.
- **Email**. Email your friends and family and ask them to "connect with you" on Facebook. Again, you must have a reason why they should do so; what's in it for them? What are you posting that's in the vein of fun?
- **Use Facebook Plugins**. Especially for Pages, Facebook has many Plugins that connect your website to your Page. To view a list of official Facebook plugins, visit http://jmlinks.com/11n.
- **Leverage Every Connection**. People who already have connected with you on Facebook are your best promoters. Remember, it's *social* (!) media, and encouraging your friends and family to share your content is the name of the game. By creating fun content that still increases awareness that you are in "job

search mode," you can enlist their support and networking capabilities in your quest.

GET FRIENDS & FAMILY TO SHARE YOUR FACEBOOK CONTENT

Advertise. Advertising is increasingly important to success on Facebook for Pages (not Profiles). Just a few years back, Pages could really grow organically and be seen organically in the news feed. With the news feed increasingly crowded, Facebook has clearly prioritized content from real people over content from brands, and all but hidden the brand Pages. In many ways, Facebook has become *pay to play* for Pages.

However, a *Page* can advertise on Facebook while a *Profile* cannot. Here are ways you can promote your Page and posts through advertising.

> **Promote Your Page**. When you log in as a Page administrator, you'll see a blue button called "promote your Page." Click on that, and then follow the instructions to demographically target potential customers. Facebook will then suggest your Page to people, as a Page to "like." You can even specifically target certain demographic groups (such as your followers of one of your target companies).

> **Boost your Posts**. When you make a post to Facebook, a blue boost button will appear on the bottom. If you click boost, you can demographically target an audience, as well as "boost" your Post to people who already like your Page.

The great thing about Facebook advertising is that it is demographically targeted. However, be careful as you can quickly exhaust your budget. Advertising is expensive! Therefore, I'd probably not advocate advertising your Page unless your job / career targets can be identified in a very focused manner.

Employer Targeting via Facebook Ads

For some of the larger companies, you can literally target people who "work" at a specific company. To do that, you have to set up a Facebook Ad, and then under "Detailed Targeting," first enter the name of one of your target companies, and find "employers" on the right hand side. Once you've found at least one company that has the "employer" feature available, you can get to Demographics > Work > Employers and search employers available on Facebook.

Here's a screenshot:

Click on the "employers" link, and then you'll see:

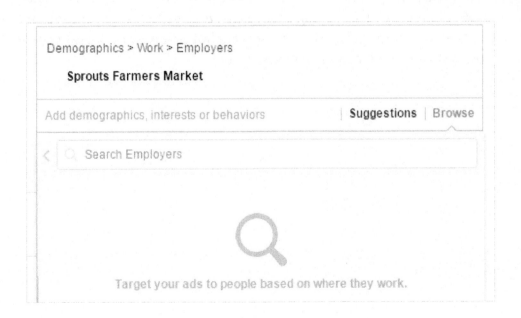

This allows you to search for employers (i.e., companies you'd like to work at) and build a list of them. You can then advertise a blog post, link to your website, infographic, YouTube video, etc., in the hopes that key employees who work at these specific companies will see them and learn about you (and your career availability).

To learn more about Facebook ad targeting options, go to http://jmlinks.com/11p. To learn more about Facebook advertising, visit https://www.facebook.com/advertising.

>> MEASURE YOUR RESULTS ON FACEBOOK

At the **Profile** level, Facebook does not provide much information on how successful you are as a personal brand marketer. The most you can do is monitor the likes, comments, and shares of your posts.

If you've set up a **Page**, however, Facebook does provide a lot of information not just on advertised items, but on everything. Here's the scoop:

Inside of Facebook, click on the **Insights** tab at the top of your Facebook Page (when you're logged in, of course). Here, you'll find an overview to your Facebook activity, and a post-by-post breakdown of the reach of a post and the engagement. A graph will tell you when your fans are most engaged. You can select "Pages to watch," – even down to which posts of theirs were the most interactive.

For any of your posts, click on the post, and a popup window will give you drill-down information. Remember, you are trying to improve *Edgerank*, so pay attention to the positive and negative interactivity. Here's a screenshot of a post of "other people's content" to the JM Internet Group Facebook Page:

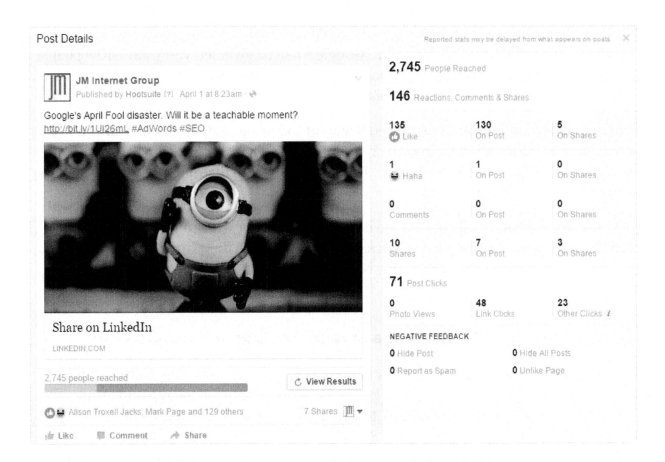

Pay attention to the reach, the likes, the comments, the shares, and clicks; all of this is influencing *Edgerank* and you are trying to propel that as high as possible.

Back to the top tabs, you can also drill down into people, to see the demographics of who is interacting with your Page. All in all, Facebook provides excellent insights into who is interacting with your Page. Use this information to make your Page better and better!

Google Analytics

If not a direct job interview lead, most of us want to drive traffic from Facebook to our personal blog or website. Google Analytics will measure how traffic flows from Facebook to your website, and then what happens upon arrival. (This includes both Profiles and Pages on Facebook).

Sign up for Google Analytics (https://www.google.com/analytics) and install the required tracking code on your personal blog or website. Inside of your Google Analytics account on the left column, drill down by clicking on Acquisition > Social > Overview.

Then on the right hand side of the screen, you'll see a list of Social Networks. Find Facebook on that list, and click on that. Google Analytics will tell you what URLs people clicked to from Facebook to your personal blog or website, giving you insights into what types of web content people find attractive.

You can also create a custom Advanced Segment to look at only Facebook traffic and its behavior. For information on how to create custom Advanced Segments in Google Analytics, go to http://jmlinks.com/1f. For the Google help files on Advanced Segments go to http://jmlinks.com/1g.

In summary, on Facebook you can see how people interact with your Facebook Page, updates, and posts. In Google Analytics, you can see where they land on your website and what they do after they arrive (for both your Profile and your Page(s)).

>> >> DELIVERABLE: A FACEBOOK JOB SEARCH AND CAREER BUILDING PLAN

Now that we've come to the end of our chapter on Facebook, your **DELIVERABLE** has arrived. Go to https://www.jm-seo.org/workbooks (click on Job Search and Career Building, enter the code 'careers2016' to register if you have not already done so), and click on the link to the "Facebook Job Search and Career Building Marketing Plan." By filling out this plan, you will establish a vision of what you want to achieve via Facebook.

>> APPENDIX: TOP FACEBOOK JOB SEARCH AND CAREER-BUILDING TOOLS AND RESOURCES

Here are the top tools and resources to help you with Facebook marketing. For an up-to-date and complete list, go to https://www.jm-seo.org/workbooks (click on Job Search and Career Building, enter the code 'careers2016' to register if you have not already done so). Then click on the *Job Search and Career-building Resource Book* link, and drill down to the Facebook chapter.

FACEBOOK HELP CENTER - http://facebook.com/help

> The 'missing' help pages on Facebook. Useful for learning everything on the king of social media. Links on advertising, business accounts, connect, Facebook places and more.
>
> **Rating:** 5 Stars | **Category:** overview

FACEBOOK LIKE BUTTON FOR WEB -
https://developers.facebook.com/docs/plugins/like-button

> The Facebook Like button lets a user share your content with friends on Facebook. When the user clicks the Like button on your site, a story appears in the user's friends' News Feeds with a link back to your website.
>
> **Rating:** 5 Stars | **Category:** tool

FACEBOOK SOCIAL PLUGINS (LIKE BOXES AND BUTTONS) -
http://developers.facebook.com/docs/plugins

> Make it easy for your Facebook fans and fans-to-be to 'like' your company and Facebook pages you create. The best Facebook resource for all plugins to integrate Facebook with your website, including the Like, Share & Send Button, Comments, Follow Button and others.
>
> **Rating:** 5 Stars | **Category:** tool

FACEBOOK ADVERTISING - http://facebook.com/advertising

> Facebook advertising opportunities. Run text ads on Facebook by selecting the demographics of who you want to reach. Pay-per-click model.
>
> **Rating:** 4 Stars | **Category:** overview

TAG BOARD - https://tagboard.com/

> Hashtags have moved beyond Twitter. This amazing cool tool allows you to take a hashtag and browse Facebook and Twitter and Instagram, etc., so see posts that relate to that hashtag. Then you can find related tags. Oh, and you can use it as a content discovery tool, too.
>
> **Rating:** 4 Stars | **Category:** tool

9

TWITTER

Do you Tweet? Should you? How can you use Twitter for job search and career building? Twitter can be quite confusing not only to job seekers and career builders, but to just about anyone trying to understand this chirpy little medium. On the one hand, Twitter dominates news and pop culture, giving it a brand presence second only to Facebook. *Ellen DeGeneres tweets. Barack Obama tweets. CBS News tweets.* And so, the logic goes: *you better tweet, too.* However, on the other hand, Twitter is so full of noise, news and craziness, that it might not be a good marketing venue for job searchers or career builders. In fact, there are so many fake and/or dormant accounts on Twitter and the Twitter feed moves so fast, that you might be tweeting, and no one will actually be listening!

Here's the **big picture** on Twitter.

The first really relevant use of Twitter for career building is simply as a **trust indicator**; it doesn't really matter whether anyone is actually reading your tweets. To hiring managers and employers (especially in the professional services, technology, and non-profit sectors), a robust Twitter account (*one with many followers and frequent tweets on topics related to your target industry*) signals that you are a serious person with some street credibility. You tweet, in short, to sound and seem important (*and you don't care if anyone is really listening*). The second relevant use of Twitter is more significant. **If you know what you're doing, Twitter can be used to network with real people, spur conversations, and thereby grow your job and career network**. For example, few people realize that you can use Twitter to talk with literally *anyone*: a recruiter, a hiring manager, employees at a company you want to work for, or even the CEO or CFO at a Bay Area start up. Indeed, you can tweet to journalists, effectively pitching them with story ideas that showcase your personal brand image.

In this chapter, you'll learn how Twitter works, how to figure out if Twitter is a good opportunity for advancing your career goals, how to set up your Twitter account, and – most importantly – how to use Twitter effectively at a technical level. Throughout this chapter, I will point you to free tools and resources on Twitter as well as worksheets to guide you step-by-step.

Let's get started!

TODO LIST:

>> Explore How Twitter Works

>> Ponder Twitter's Curious Culture

>> Twitter Basics

>> The *Private You*, The *Internet You*, and Twitter

>> Identify Twitter Accounts to Emulate

>> Twitter Goals: Trust, Networking, or Both?

>> How to Use Twitter for Job Search and Career Building

>> Brainstorm & Execute a Tweeting Strategy

>> Grow Your Twitter Reach

>> Measure your Results

>> >> Deliverable: A Twitter Job Search & Career Building Plan

>> >> Appendix: Top Twitter Job Search & Career-building Tools and Resources

>> EXPLORE HOW TWITTER WORKS

One way to understand **Twitter** is to think of Twitter as a **micro blogging** platform. Just as your personal blog should have posts about your professional interests, including commentary on and analysis of current events in your target industry, so should your Twitter account. It should also provide commentary on industry trends, just in a shorter, quicker, more headline-style fashion.

Twitter is just a lot shorter than blogging - 140 characters, to be exact.

Let's compare writing a blog post and composing a tweet.

When you write a blog post, you –

a. Conceptualize a **topic** (*hopefully of interest to your target career audience*).
b. Write a **headline** and the **blog post** itself.

c. **Promote** your blog post.

Similarly, within the constraints of a 140-character tweet, you –

a. Conceptualize a **topic** of interest to your (potential) audience.
b. Write a **headline / tweet** (they're basically one-and-the-same on Twitter).
c. **Promote** your tweet.

A, b, and c are essentially the same steps, just in a shorter format on Twitter.

TWITTER IS MICROBLOGGING

One difference apparent right from the start, is that on Twitter, a tweet often points outward to an in-depth blog post, a video, an infographic, or an image. A tweet can often be just a "headline" pointing out to the "rest of the story," but many tweets are self-standing as well. Twitter's most common usage is as a "headline service," often pointing to blog posts, YouTube videos, infographics or images, and other more robust content on another website.

Twitter is Like Facebook (and LinkedIn and Pinterest...)

Structurally speaking, Twitter also shares many similarities with other social media. Like Facebook, LinkedIn, Pinterest and other social media, your Twitter account (a.k.a., "Page") can be "followed" ("liked") by others, who are alerted in their news feeds when you tweet new items. In addition, tweets can be searched for via Twitter search or discovered through *#hashtags*. And, people can *retweet* (share) your tweets, respond to them, or even favorite them, thereby drawing the attention of their followers to you.

The **names** may have changed, but the basic **structure** of Twitter is not unlike that of Facebook:

- Individuals have *accounts* on Twitter ("profiles" on Facebook).
- Companies have *accounts* on Twitter ("Pages" on Facebook).
- If an individual *follows* your account on Twitter ("likes" your Page on Facebook), then when you tweet it will show up in the *news feed* of that individual.
- Individuals can
  - *favorite* a tweet – "like" a post on Facebook;
  - *respond* to a tweet – "comment" on Facebook; and/or
  - *re-tweet* a tweet to their followers (reshare posts on Facebook).

Tweets are short (less than 140 characters), and consist usually of text but can include links, graphics and videos. As of 2016, there is talk of expanding Twitter's character limit. In addition, Twitter increasingly allows not only text but also images and videos to be hosted natively on Twitter, thereby making it converge with and compete with services like Instagram or Facebook. In addition, as on Facebook, you can share just a few sentences, share a link to a blog post or textual item, or share a link to an image or video. When you share an image or video, Twitter will create a thumbnail image in your tweet, automatically.

» PONDER TWITTER'S CURIOUS CULTURE

Twitter has a curious culture. First and foremost, Twitter is the most **open** of all the social media. Anyone can set up a Twitter account in literally minutes, and start tweeting – there's no real authentication, policing, or censorship (compare that with the controlled culture of Facebook or the uptight culture of LinkedIn). Indeed, *anyone* can listen in. There's no required *friending* or *connecting* as on Facebook or LinkedIn. Even people who do not follow you can easily find and read your tweets. *Even complete strangers can contact you via Twitter, without your pre-approval.* In addition, Twitter's tone is all over the map: it can be serious (talking about industry issues), funny (talking about silly jokes, memes, or pop culture), political (arguing about the politics of the day), or friend-to-friend (sharing the details of one's daily life). Twitter is a chameleon, able to be anything to anyone.

TWITTER IS 100% OPEN

Twitter's openness is really important to job search and career-building, so let me emphasize:

> **Anyone** can instantly set up a Twitter account and start tweeting; no authentication required.
>
> **Anyone** can listen in to anyone on Twitter; no friending required.
>
> **Anyone** can talk to **anyone** via Twitter; it's completely open!
>
> **Anyone** can talk about **anything** on Twitter; there is no censorship.

Twitter is Open, Really Open

Twitter is like a massive 24/7 talk radio station, or a water cooler conversation; anyone can talk, and anyone can listen. No authentication is required, and there is no requirement that the person talking has any expertise or intelligence on the matter.

> *Twitter is as open as talk radio. In fact, it's even more open: not only can anyone "listen in," anyone can also "broadcast."*

Twitter's Curious Culture

What stands out about Twitter's culture? First, Twitter is fast-paced and used primarily to share news (about everything) and/or to share gossip (about pop culture, politics, and social controversy). Twitter moves at the speed of news, with little concern about social status, fact-checking, or the credentials of the speaker. This makes it a great place for sensationalism, tabloid journalism, and rumors without foundation. Second, Twitter users as a whole, are known to "gang up" and "bandwagon" for or against certain topics, making Twitter the origin of many of the Internet's great social protests as well as many crazy and zany viral trends. Third, and most significant for job search, Twitter is a place where the movers and shakers of many industries go to publish and be heard on timely industry trends. The three aspects (speed, viral waves, and the goings-on in specific industries) compete and contrast with each other at any given moment. Like talk radio or cable TV, everything is on Twitter – the silly, the outrageous, the dangerous, the political, and the important – making Twitter the noisiest and craziest of all the social media.

The Dangers of Twitter

With its fast-paced, somewhat anonymous culture, Twitter is a lightning rod for social criticism and controversy. Whether a controversy is police brutality, a criminal event, or a faux pox by a celebrity that strikes against "political correctness," Twitter can be a rough-and-tumble world of impolite conversation. The strangest things have gone viral and spurred controversy on Twitter!

Seen through the lenses of a job seeker or career builder, you are well advised to steer clear of public controversy on Twitter, or at least dive in eyes wide open. Approach all of social media, but Twitter especially, with the attitude of ***anything you tweet, can and might be used against you*** in a job interview or opportunity for advancement in your career! Not only is everything you say on Twitter essentially on the public record but also you never know whether something you say could become the whirlwind center of a strange and embarrassing political moment. Be on your best behavior.

THINK BEFORE YOU TWEET

To this end, I recommend that you read the February 12, 2015, article by Jon Ronson in the *New York Times* entitled, "How One Stupid Tweet Blew Up Justine Sacco's Life" (http://jmlinks.com/8j). Without passing judgement on the events that transpired, the concepts for job seekers and career builders here are: a) Anything posted to Twitter should be considered 100% public, b) You never know what might "go viral," and c) The reaction of the Twitter masses might be quite crushing to your personal brand and future career prospects.

The lesson of Justine Sacco isn't just that obnoxious racial prejudices have no place in a civilized society. It's also to "think before you tweet." If Ms. Sacco had thought, for just a moment, that she was *publically broadcasting* her politically incorrect opinions (even as jokes), she would have saved her public image and her career. As your Mom hopefully told you, if you don't have something nice to say about someone (or a group of people, a social or political phenomenon, or anything else), or if there is significant controversy about a person or a social / political trend, don't say anything.

Silence can be golden, especially on Twitter, and especially for those building their careers in the 21st century.

» THE *PRIVATE YOU*, THE *INTERNET YOU*, AND TWITTER

All of this brings us to the possible tension between the *Private You* and the *Internet You* as experienced on Twitter. Whereas on Facebook, you have a reasonable expectation that your personal profile isn't easily visible to employers (although you should, of course, be on your best behavior on Facebook, too), you have no such expectation on Twitter. Twitter is 100% public.

What, then, should you do if the *Private You* already has a pretty public (and embarrassing) Twitter account, or if you want to be able to enjoy Twitter as a private individual and yet use Twitter for career purposes?

Let's face it: some of us like to party, share inappropriate pictures or jokes, and have a significantly non-serious side to our personality. Our private hopes, dreams, aspirations, and foot-in-the-mouth moments might not decline to the level of Justine Sacco's *faux pas*, but our private self on Twitter might still be something we'd like to keep private.

> The answer here is to have **two** Twitter accounts: one for the **Internet You** and one for the **Private You**.

You might have (and want) a personal (private) Twitter account to follow sports teams, celebrity figures, fashion trends, or even inappropriate humor (of which Twitter is full). You might want and have a personal Twitter account to interact with friends and family in pretty crazy ways. You might even use this personal Twitter account to tweet about all sorts of silly and crazy things, from your sister's latest embarrassing selfie to your own mashed makeup and unforgiving hair, after last weekend's camping trip without a shower.

> *But, do you want a hiring manager to discover this over-the-top, Katy Perry "Last Friday Night" (*http://jmlinks.com/8h*) personal video you shared on*

Twitter? Or your feelings about politics, pop culture, or whether diet Coke is better than diet Pepsi? Perhaps not, in fact probably not.

So how can you have your Twitter bird seed and eat it too? Here's how.

Strategy #1: Modify Your Twitter Privacy Settings

So, if you have that type of Twitter account and/or want to separate the *Private You* from the *Internet You*, then your first **TODO** is to mask this account by making it private, changing your profile to remove connections to the *Internet You*, or un-SEO it, so it's difficult to find via Twitter and/or Google search.

To make your Twitter account private, log on to Twitter (http://twitter.com). Next, click on *settings*, then click on "Security and privacy" and change your privacy settings. For example, you can click "Protect my tweets," and therefore only people you approve will see your Tweets. Here's a screenshot:

Tweet privacy   ☐ Protect my Tweets

> If selected, only those you approve will receive your Tweets. Your future Tweets will not be available publicly. Tweets posted previously may still be publicly visible in some places. Learn more.

In addition, you can turn off "Discoverability" by unchecking the boxes that allow people to find you via your email address or phone number. Here's a screenshot of that:

Discoverability   ☐ Let others find me by my email address
                       ☐ Let others find me by my phone number

Delete Tweets

Now that you've realized hiring managers might browse you on Twitter, you can also go back through past tweets and delete ones that are embarrassing. Just scroll through, find tweets you'd wish you had not tweeted, scroll to the bottom of the tweet, and click on the three gray dots. Then hit delete, and "poof," that tweet is now gone.

Here's a screenshot:

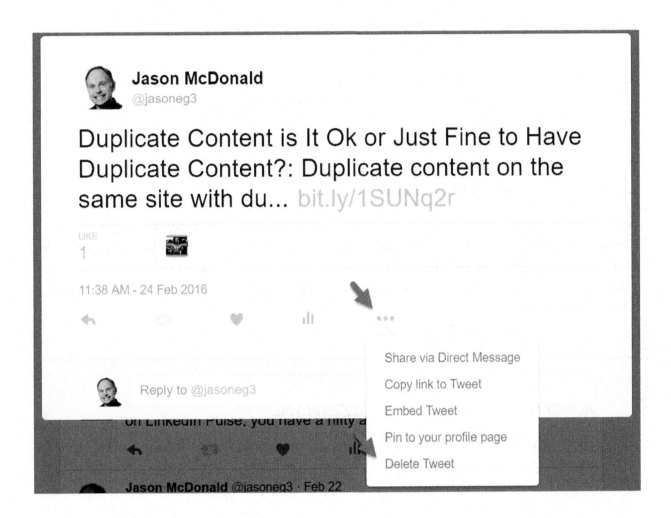

Go Incognito

Another option is to modify your existing *Private You* Twitter account by changing your name, picture, summary and even outward Web link to something non-recognizable so as to still be *public* and yet be *incognito* to anyone but friends and family.

You might use a nickname known only to close family and friends for your *Private You* Twitter account, and then your real name for your *Internet You* Twitter account. In that way, you can be *easy to discover* for friends and family, and *hard to discover* for hiring managers or employers doing research.

And, of course, if you want a *Private You* Twitter account, then de-link it from your *Internet You* blog, LinkedIn account, Facebook, etc. Essentially de-couple the elements of the *Internet You,* from the *Private You* when it comes to Twitter.

So in this way, you have made your potentially embarrassing *Private You* Twitter account *private* and/or *incognito*, and you can then set up an *Internet You* Twitter account for your professional life and employers.

(It may be true that the *Private You* is so non-controversial that this is a non-issue, in which case you have nothing to worry about, other than to refrain from saying embarrassing things on Twitter!)

Be Private Not Falsified or Illegal

Note: I am not saying to falsify your identity, but I am saying that for many people, a strong separation between their *Private You* and *Internet You* on Twitter is a **good** idea for effective career building. It's OK to have a crazy let-your-hair down Katy Perry "Last Friday Night" self on Twitter, and keep that private. There's nothing wrong or immoral, after all, about privacy.

> *Remember: It's OK to keep the Private You private.*
>
> *Remember: The Private You isn't a Secret You.*
>
> *Remember: The best practice is to consider anything you tweet as 100% public, including visible to employers.*

Now let's turn to Twitter for the *Internet You.*

» TWITTER BASICS

If you haven't already signed up for Twitter, or are in the process of splitting the *Private You* from the *Internet You,* simply go to http://jmlinks.com/1h and follow the steps to set up a Twitter account for the *Internet You.*

The basics of a Twitter account are as follows:

- **Your Account / Your Username / Twitter Handle**. A username such as **@jasoneg3** becomes your Twitter handle or URL (http://twitter.com/jasoneg3) and shows up in your tweets. Choose a short user name that reflects your personal brand identity. **Shorter names are better** because tweets are limited to 140 characters and your username or "handle" counts as characters. As with most social media, you need an email address to sign up, or you can use a mobile phone number; unlike Facebook pages, you can only have one email address / password / user – or you can use third party apps like Hootsuite (http://www.hootsuite.com/) or Tweetdeck (http://www.tweetdeck.com/) to let multiple people access your account. Note: if you are going to have two Twitter accounts, you'll need two email addresses and possibly two mobile phone numbers.
- **Profile Photo**. This is essentially the same as a profile photo on Facebook. The recommend images size is 400x400 pixels. It shows on your Tweets when viewed in a follower's news feed.
- **Bio**. You have 160 characters to explain your personal brand. Be sure to include a http:// URL link to your public blog or website, and summarize your Personal Branding Statement.
- **Header Image**. Similar to the Facebook cover photo, you get 1500x500 pixels to run as a banner across your account page.
- **Pinned Tweet**. You can "pin" a tweet to the top of your Twitter account, so that it shows first when users click up to your Twitter page. For example, compose a tweet that puts your best foot forward in a career sense.

Here's a screenshot of how to "pin" a Tweet:

Jason McDonald @jasoneg3 · 1h
Free tools for social media marketing.
Social Media Toolbook. Coupon code:
social3762 jm-seo.org/?p=1103

 Jason McDonald @jasoneg3 · 1
"Is Donald Trump   ian 4
Scam?" #marketi

jamesaltucher.co   n...   View

Share via Direct Message

Copy link to Tweet

Embed Tweet

Pin to your profile page

Delete Tweet

Essentially, find the tweet you want to pin, click on the *dot dot dot* icon, and then click on "pin to your profile page."

Extra Credit: create a tweet that explains you are looking for a job, and have it linked to your personal website and your online resume. Then pin this tweet to the top of your Twitter account.

To access any of the other settings and features, go to your page on Twitter (as for example, http://twitter.com/jasoneg3), be sure you are logged in, and click on the "edit profile" button in the far right of the screen. Also note that by clicking on your (small) Twitter profile picture at the top right of the screen, you can access your account settings (or go here: https://twitter.com/settings/security when logged in).

Here's a screenshot:

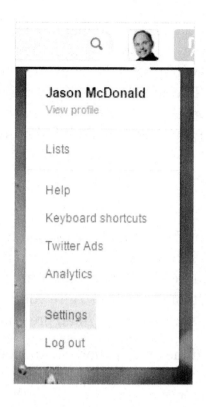

Not much can be customized, but in this day of Internet hacking and cybercrime, I recommend that you turn on **login verification** (http://jmlinks.com/8k), which will require a mobile phone verification code for any new login.

Following and Followers

Now that you've set up your account, you can "follow" people or brands on Twitter by finding their Twitter accounts and clicking on the "follow" link. Similarly, people can follow you on Twitter by doing the same.

> ***Word to the wise***: *choose to follow brands and people who substantiate your personal brand image. If you want to follow silly or inappropriate Twitter accounts, confine those to your (hidden) private Twitter account, not your Internet You account! The reason for this is that anyone can see who you are following on Twitter; that, too, is 100% public.*

The structure of Twitter's news feed is very similar to Facebook's news feed; when people follow you on Twitter, they see your tweets in their news feed subject to the clutter of the rapidly-moving Twitter news feed and a secret algorithm in Twitter that attempts to prioritize the best Tweets to the top (e.g., similar to Facebook *Edgerank*). Similarly, you can share the tweets of others (called *retweeting* or *RT*) to your own followers and others can share your tweets to their followers. It's *social* media after all.

Understand a Tweet

Tweets are the heart and soul of Twitter, and correspond to posts on Facebook, or posts on a blog. A tweet is limited to 140 characters, and as you type your tweet into your Twitter account, it will give you a convenient countdown of the remaining characters. If you use an app like Hootsuite, that app will also give you a character count. Or you can use a service like http://www.lettercount.com/ and pre-count your characters.

Think of a tweet as a news headline or very short micro blog post with just a little supporting information. If you tweet a link to a blog post or other Web page, use a URL shortener like http://bitly.com, http://tinyurl.com/, or the "shortlink" feature in WordPress, so as not to waste characters. To read Twitter's own description of how to tweet, visit http://jmlinks.com/1j. You can create a self-standing tweet, or you can tweet "outlinks" to blog posts, videos, or images.

Here's a screenshot of a tweet:

Twitter is becoming more image-friendly, so you can now tweet an image and/or if you tweet an outbound link to many websites, their thumbnail images will display on Twitter.

Understand Hashtags

A hashtag (#) in a tweet indicates a keyword or theme and is clickable in a tweet. Think of a hashtag as a keyword / subject / theme about which people are talking: *sports, the Oakland A's, global warming, the 2016 presidential campaign, the Academy awards* etc. Hashtags should be short, and CANNOT include spaces. Anyone can create one, and the success, or failure, of a hashtag is a function of whether many, or just a few, people use them. And, yes because Twitter is totally open there is no control: anyone can use them for any purpose, and a hashtag can overlap two discussions.

> *Anyone can create a hashtag! Anyone can chime in on a hashtag! No one controls a hashtag!*

How it's used, however, is a function of the crowd. The crowd decides what the hashtag really means.

Identify Relevant Hashtags

To find existing hashtags, use http://hashtagify.me or simply search Twitter using the # hashtag in front of a topic such as *#organicfood* or *#free*. Note that hashtags CANNOT include spaces. So it's *#organicfood* not *#organic food*. You can also search Twitter by keyword and look for the # hashtag symbol. For example, here's a screenshot of a tweet with the hashtag for *personal branding* highlighted in yellow:

Hashtags (which do not allow spaces and are always preceded by the "#" sign) are clickable in a tweet, and are a way to "listen in" to the worldwide, 24/7 conversation on a topic occurring on twitter. For example, to "listen in" to the conversation about #personalbranding, visit http://jmlinks.com/8m.

I recommend that you research, identify, and maintain a running list of *hashtags* that are important to your personal brand, especially ones to which potential employers might be listening into, or ones to which the employees of your target industry or companies might find important. If, for example, you are looking to advance your career in biofuels, you should monitor hashtags such as #biofuels, or #cleanenergy.

#Hashtags Designate Conversations on Twitter

Chime In on Relevant Hashtags

You can not only listen in to hashtags, you (or anyone else) can broadcast via hashtags. By including hashtags in your Tweets, you can be found by non-followers who are interested in, and following, that topic on Twitter. For example, if you are a looking for a job or seeking to advance your career in the area of *computer security and networking*, you might tweet with hashtags as follows:

> *Just completed my infographic on quick steps for consumers for #cybersecurity and #computersecurity. Check it out at http://bit.ly/1234*

By including hashtags, you have contributed to the content and conversation on Twitter on that topic. In summary, finding popular, relevant hashtags and tweeting on them is a good promotion strategy on Twitter.

> *Remember, however, that you have to stand out and get attention amidst all the noise! Just because you're talking, doesn't mean anyone is listening!*

Understand the @ Sign or Handle

The @ sign designates a Twitter account, often called a "handle" on Twitter. When included in a tweet, it does two things:

- It becomes **clickable**. Anyone who sees this tweet can click on the @*handle* and go up to that account, to view the account and possibly follow that person on Twitter; and
- It **shows up in the news feed of that person** and **sends an email alert** to him or her, that they have been mentioned. This is called a *mention*. A *mention* means essentially that: someone has spoken about you (or your Twitter account) in a Tweet.

Here's a screenshot:

 Rachel Miller @rachelloumiller · Jan 15
#CMAD --> Let's talk #personalbranding! w/ @LorrieGuerrieri @suzimcc @CarlosGil83 @wutangbunny Jan 25th 8am PT
ow.ly/X7glG

 **Pros and Cons of Personal Branding for Communi...**
Join us January 25, 2016, at 11:00 EST (16:00 GMT) to discuss the pros and cons of personal branding for Community Managers.
communitymanagerappreciationday.com

↩   ⇄ 9   ♥ 4   •••

Rachel Miller (@rachelloumiller) has tweeted to her followers an alert about a Google hangout to discuss personal branding for community managers. She's working with @LorrieGuerreri, @suzimcc, @CarlosGil83, and @wutangbunny on the event. Anyone seeing this tweet can click "up" to any of the Twitter accounts she mentions with the @ sign. In addition, each of those persons mentioned with the @ sign would have received a notification in his or her account that they had been "mentioned," and also possibly an email alert. In all probability, they are also tweeting out the event, so this "team" of people is seeking to create publicity for a common event.

USING THE @ SIGN, YOU
CAN TWEET TO ANYONE

Importantly, Twitter's openness combined with the @ sign functionality means that you can tweet "to" anyone on Twitter. It's completely open, and unlike Facebook or LinkedIn – you do not need "pre-approval" to converse with someone via Twitter (more about this later, when we discuss promoting your Twitter account).

Again, when your Tweet contains the @handle of someone else, that generates an alert in their news feed and often via email. ***Via Twitter, you can tweet to anyone!***

Within reason, therefore, you can tweet "to" job targets by merely mentioning them in your Tweet. For example, if you'd like to get a job at IBM, you can tweet "to" IBM US Recruitment by including @IBMUSjobs (http://twitter.com/IBMUSjobs) in your tweet. It's as easy as clicking on the purple Tweet to IBM US recruitment button on their Twitter account (while you are signed in to your own account) or just including their handle (@IBMUSjobs) in your tweet. Here are screenshots:

First, Twitter has made it super simple to tweet "to" someone. Simply find their account, and then click on the "Tweet to" button on the left side.

Second, here's an example of tweeting "to" @IBMUSjobs

Now, just because you can tweet "to" IBMUSjobs, doesn't mean that they're actually listening or will reach out to you. Like the telephone before it, Twitter gives you the capability to communicate with nearly anyone on the planet; it's your job to make that initial query interesting enough, to spark a two-way conversation.

Understand Mentions and Retweets

We've already explained a **mention**. When someone includes your @handle in their Tweet, that's called a *mention*: clickable by anyone following them, to go "up" to your account and learn about you or your business.

A **retweet** is a special type of mention. In it, person *A* retweets the tweet of person *B*. Meaning, he takes your tweet and tweets it out to his followers. Imagine if Ellen DeGeneres recapped your joke on her TV show, or announced that you were seeking a career as a standup comedian. That "retweet" of your joke would spur her followers to learn about you, and might result in a massive increase in your follower count.

Here's a screenshot of Ellen retweeting Justin Bieber:

Ellen DeGeneres ✓
@TheEllenShow

Yeah I did. RT @justinbieber: I think today was our best hang out yet. @TheEllenShow u got me. Lol

Ellen is "retweeting" Justin Bieber's tweet about how great their interaction was on her TV show. In this way, her fans see Justin Bieber's Twitter account *@justinbieber* and can learn about him, and possibly follow him, thereby increasing his follower count. Ellen and Justin are essentially having a public conversation via Twitter.

You don't have to be a Hollywood star to do this. Identify important people in your industry and converse with them via the @sign (handles). If they respond, your followers can see this conversation, and their followers can see it too (if the person responds to you) – thereby cross-pollinating your accounts. (See technical details below).

Who Sees Your Tweets?

Here's some esoterica about mentions or retweets. When you tweet directly at someone (by including their account (@sign) <u>at the beginning of your tweet</u>), that tweet is visible to only those folks who <u>follow both accounts</u>.

Alternatively, if you put a dot "." before the @ sign, your tweet shows up in the news feed (officially called your "timeline" on Twitter, but not to be confused with the "timeline" of Facebook) of all of your followers, even if they do not follow the mentioned account. For example, if I tweet:

@katyperry love your music, give me free concert tickets!

(This tweet shows to ONLY those people who follow @jasoneg3 AND @katyperry) and it shows in Katy Perry's own timeline (if she actually checks it)).

vs.

.@katyperry loved your concert, give me free concert tickets!

(This tweet shows to ALL people who follow @jasoneg3 AND it shows in Katy Perry's own timeline (if she actually checks it)).

Extra Credit. What's nifty here is if you want to keep tweeting to various hiring managers, key persons, etc., and *you do not want those tweets to go to all your actual followers*, simply start your tweet with the "@" sign (no "." dot), or use Twitter's built in "Tweet to" button that appears on the left hand side of any account.

To read more about the "dot" in front of the "@" sign in more detail, visit http://jmlinks.com/2k. For the official Twitter help files, visit https://support.twitter.com/.

▶▶ IDENTIFY TWITTER ACCOUNTS TO EMULATE

Now that you understand the basics of how Twitter works, it's time to identify persons on Twitter to emulate. You're looking for people "like you" or people who you want to "be like" (in a job or career sense), so you can reverse engineer their Twitter strategy. You're also looking for media sites and companies in your target industry to follow (to stay informed, and/or to at least look like you want to stay informed). And you're looking for the accounts of key employees at your target companies (again, to not only follow them, but to have the capacity to tweet "to" them).

Find Accounts on Twitter

Log in and stay signed into your Twitter account.

Next, there are several ways to find accounts of persons to follow on Twitter (and "reverse engineer"):

- **Visit their Blogs or Websites**. If you have already identified persons to emulate, simply visit their blogs and often they will have a direct link to their Twitter account. For example, if you are looking for a career in cybersecurity, you might follow Bruce Schneier (https://www.schneier.com/) – simply visit his website, click on the Twitter icon and you'll be redirected to him on Twitter at https://twitter.com/schneierblog/. Also, visit the websites of companies you want to target, and look for a page that has the Twitter account of key persons.
- **Search Google**. Google is the world's best search engine, and so you can use a specific site: command to search Twitter for the accounts of key persons. Here's an example to identify Twitter accounts of Wells Fargo employees (http://jmlinks.com/8q).
- **Search on Twitter**. While logged in to your account, go to the top right of the screen and in the "Search Twitter" box, enter your keywords. To find stuff on Twitter about cyber security, just type in "cyber security" into the search box. Then, when you find an account you like, just click "follow" and you are now following him or her. Similarly, you can do a search for a company name. Here's an example for Wells Fargo on Twitter (http://jmlinks.com/8r).
- **Advanced Search on Twitter**. You can find Twitter Advanced Search by first doing a search, then in the results

Here's a screenshot:

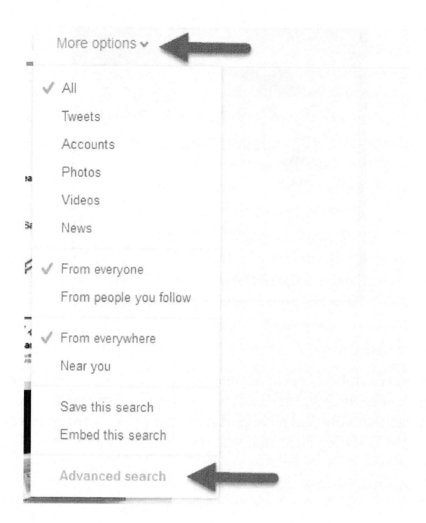

You can also just visit this link: https://twitter.com/search-advanced.

Once you follow individuals, you can browse their Twitter pages easily by clicking on the "following" link at the top left of the page while you are logged into your Twitter account. Here's a screenshot –

Note that Twitter is completely open: anyone can see who you follow via your public Twitter account (unlike on, say, Facebook, where only you know whom you are following). You can therefore find an important person at a company you are targeting and then see who is following them, and who they follow. Twitter, after all, is a *social* network.

Inventory Likes and Dislikes

Your **TODO** here is to identify persons or companies on Twitter, both in and outside of your industry, so that you can not only follow them (and research their followers as well as who they follow), but also inventory what you like and dislike about their Twitter strategy.

Here are some inventory questions:

- **Username**. Usernames should be short yet convey the personal brand. Do you like / dislike the usernames of the persons or brands that you see?
- **Profile Picture**. As is true in all social media, the profile picture shows when viewed on someone else's timeline. Do you like / dislike the profile pictures of various persons-to-emulate on Twitter? Why or why not?
- **Header Photo**. Similar to the Facebook cover photo, this wide banner dominates that account visuals. How are persons-to-emulate using the header photo on Twitter?

- **Pinned Tweets**. Are any persons-to-emulate using the pinned tweet feature? If so, how?
- **Account Bio**. How are persons-to-emulate using their bio to market via Twitter? Do you see any opportunities or pitfalls here?

Posting or Tweeting Strategy

You'll quickly realize that Twitter offers little customization, and that most of the action on Twitter has to do with *posting strategy* or what would precisely be called *tweeting strategy*. What are persons-to-emulate tweeting, and why? What is their *posting rhythm*? Similar to all social media, the idea is to spur interactivity, get shares (retweets), and drive traffic to desired actions such as job interview or consulting requests.

Pay attention to companies in your industry, as well as hashtags (see below) in your industry, all the while asking the questions. "Are your potential employer targets on Twitter? Are key employees active on Twitter? Is your target industry on Twitter, and if, so, what are they tweeting about?"

Let's review some accounts on Twitter and reverse-engineer their posting strategies. Do the same for businesses that you like and/or competitors in your industry.

Twitter Marketing: Common Uses

Here are people using Twitter for personal branding, and thus worthy of emulation:

- Katy Perry (https://twitter.com/katyperry)
- Justin Bieber (https://twitter.com/justinbieber)
- Hillary Clinton (https://twitter.com/hillaryclinton)
- Barack Obama (https://twitter.com/potus)
- Bill de Blasio (https://twitter.com/billdeblasio)
- Steve Blank (https://twitter.com/sgblank)
- Max Michel (https://twitter.com/Max_Michel)
- Bishop Robert Barron (https://twitter.com/BishopBarron)
- Michelle Zaffino (https://twitter.com/michellezaffino)
- Will Courtenay (https://twitter.com/themensdoc)
- Tom Silver (https://twitter.com/tomsilver)

IDENTIFY PERSONS WHO DO TWITTER WELL, AND REVERSE ENGINEER THEM

For your second **TODO**, download the **Twitter Job Search and Career-building Marketing Worksheet**. Go to https://www.jm-seo.org/workbooks (click on Job Search and Career-building, enter the code 'careers2016' to register if you have not already done so), and click on the link to the "Twitter Job Search and Career-building Marketing" worksheet.

In the first section, you'll answer questions as to whether your potential employers are on Twitter, identify persons and brands to follow, and inventory what you like and dislike about their Twitter set up and marketing strategy as well as look for connection points between their interests and your own.

» TWITTER GOALS: TRUST, NETWORKING, OR BOTH?

Twitter can be a strange beast. On the one hand, it is used by millions of people each day, in anything ranging from broad pop culture topics, serious social controversies to micro discussions on the future of carbon offsets or other industry topics. On the other hand, it is chock-full of noise and nonsense. It is both important and unimportant, believable and not-to-be-believed.

This brings us to your job-search and career building goals on Twitter (for your *Internet You* account), namely:

1. Do you want to use Twitter solely to substantiate your seriousness as a job candidate (i.e., "**trust indicator**"); and/or
2. Do you want to use Twitter to **communicate** and **network with** potential peers and employers in your target industry?

You can do just one of the above, or you can do both. The reality in many industries is that potential employers may check you out on Twitter to confirm you have a sufficient number of followers, an active stream of industry-relevant tweets, and that you are following "relevant" trade shows, media sites, and companies in the industry. In this way, they are using Twitter as a "trust indicator" that substantiates you as a serious career contender.

In **Scenario One**, it may not be very relevant if people are actually engaging with your tweets. In fact, there are even cases wherein people simply Google "Buy Twitter Followers" and beef up their account with fake followers to look "more important" than they really are. (For example, during the 2012 Presidential Campaign, candidate Mitt Romney was accused of buying fake Twitter followers so that he would look more competitive against Barack Obama (http://jmlinks.com/8n)).

I am not recommending that you buy fake Twitter followers, but I am pointing out that using Twitter as merely as part of a "trust indicator" – growing your follower count, following relevant industry websites and companies, and tweeting your blog posts out – can be an appropriate Internet personal branding and career building strategy.

Scenario Two is not incompatible with this approach. In it, you use Twitter in an additional way as a platform to have Twitter conversations with "movers and shakers" in your industry and even to pro-actively reach out to hiring managers and individuals at target companies. You can post interesting and provocative content to relevant Twitter #hashtags. You can also use Twitter to directly start conversations with key people that might ultimately lead to relevant job interviews. This is less likely than Scenario One, but especially in professional service industries, can be a way to get one's foot in the proverbial door. Remember that by using #hashtags and @handles on Twitter, you can reach out to nearly anyone!

» TWITTER SETUP BASICS

Twitter set up issues are not complex. Basically, you'll need to set up an *Internet You* account on Twitter by choosing a short Twitter handle. Next, create a profile picture and background image. Go to Settings > Design to modify your theme, background image, and color. Then, write your summary. To do this, start at your main Twitter page. On the far right, click on "Edit Profile." Next on the far left, you can change your summary, city, and Web link. Here's a screenshot:

As on LinkedIn, you want to write a summary of your "personal branding statement" that conveys your value to potential employers. Be sure to add a link to your personal website or blog.

Optimizing your account on Twitter is pretty straightforward. As indicated above, a good way to do this is to compare / contrast pages that you like and use your inventory list to identify todos. As indicated above, the main elements are:

- **Your Account / Your Username / Twitter Handle**. A username such as **@jasoneg3** becomes your Twitter URL (http://twitter.com/jasoneg3) and shows up in your tweets. Choose a short user name that reflects your personal brand identity. **Shorter names are better** because tweets are limited to 140 characters and your username or "handle" counts as characters. As with most social media, you need an email address to sign up, or you can use a mobile phone number; unlike Facebook pages, you can only have one email address / password / user – or you can use third party apps like Hootsuite to control your account.

- **Profile Photo**. This is essentially the same as a profile photo on Facebook. The recommend images size is 400x400 pixels. It shows on your Tweets when viewed in a follower's news feed.
- **Bio**. You have 160 characters to explain your personal brand and career goals. Be sure to include a URL link to your personal blog and/or website.
- **Header Image**. Similar to the Facebook cover photo, you get 1500x500 pixels to run as a banner across your account page.
- **Pinned Tweet**. You can "pin" a tweet to the top of the page, so that it shows first when users click up to your Twitter account page. For example, compose a tweet that promotes your email newsletter, and then "pin" this to the top of your Twitter account.

If you haven't already signed up for Twitter, simply go to http://jmlinks.com/1h.

For your second **TODO,** download the **Twitter Career Building Twitter Set Up Worksheet**. For the worksheet, go to https://www.jm-seo.org/workbooks (click on Job Search and Career-building, enter the code 'careers2016' to register if you have not already done so), and click on the link to the "Twitter Career Building Set Up Worksheet."

Fill out the section on set up issues.

>> BRAINSTORM AND EXECUTE A TWEETING STRATEGY

As you work on a tweeting strategy, you'll quickly realize you need a lot of content! Twitter serves primarily as a "headline service," wherein you share with your followers (including potential employers) off loads to blog posts, images, YouTube videos, infographics, SlideShares, and other elements of your content marketing strategy.

Remember, you need to create a **content marketing system** of:

- **Other people's content**. Relevant content in your industry. By curating out the garbage and identify the cool, fun, interesting stuff, you can use other people's content to help your tweets stay top of mind.

- **Your own content**. Twitter is all about off-loads to blog posts, infographics, images, photos, videos, Memes, and other types of your own content. Twitter and blogging go together like peas and carrots, while Twitter and video go together like scotch and soda.

To identify relevant content from other people, I recommend setting up a Feedly account (http://www.feedly.com/) and using tools like Buzzsumo (http://www.buzzsumo.com), and Google Alerts (https://www.google.com/alerts). Organize these tools into topic groups, and then as you find content useful to your target audience, "tweet out" that content. Use a tool like Hootsuite (http://www.hootsuite.com/) to schedule your tweets in advance.

IDENTIFY TWEETABLE CONTENT

As for your own content, Twitter is best used by staying on topic and sharing original useful content such as in-depth blog posts, free eBooks or webinars, infographics and instructographics, or videos on YouTube. Because Twitter is a headline service pointing to the "rest of the story" on your blog, video, or infographic, you need a lot of content to point your followers to.

For your third **TODO,** download the **Twitter Job Search and Career-building Marketing Worksheet**. Go to https://www.jm-seo.org/workbooks (click on Job Search and Career-building, enter the code 'careers2016' to register if you have not already done so), and click on the link to the "Twitter Job Search and Career-building Marketing" worksheet.

In the second section, you'll brainstorm a Tweeting strategy, one that builds on your content marketing plan.

» GROW YOUR TWITTER REACH

Once you've set up your Twitter account, and begun to populate it with tweets on a regular basis, you've essentially "set up" your party on Twitter. Now it's time to send out the invitations.

In and of itself, a Twitter Page will not be self-promoting! You've got to promote it!

Assuming your Twitter account shares lots of yummy, useful, fun, provocative content that when seen by someone relevant to your industry, will entice him or her to "follow" you on Twitter, here are some common ways to promote your Twitter account and Tweets:

- **Real World to Social.** Don't forget the real world! As you attend networking events, speak at conferences, interact with students and professors at your school or with coworkers if you are employed, mention that you are on Twitter. Twitter has a tradition of "follow for follow"- you follow them, and they'll follow you back. Connecting in the real world is one easy way to grow your follower base. Use the real world to promote your Twitter account, and be ready to explain "why" they should follow you on Twitter. What's in it for them?
- **Cross-Promotion**. Link your personal blog or website to your Twitter Page, your blog posts to your Twitter Page, your YouTube to your Twitter Page, etc. Notice how successful personal brands like Kevin VanDam, Zak George or Michelle Zaffino do this - one digital property promotes another digital property.
- **Email**. Email your contact list and ask them to follow you on Twitter. Again, you must explain what's in it for them.
- **Twitter Internal**. Interact with other accounts via the @ sign, share their content, comment on timely topics using #hashtags, and reach out to complementary pages to work with you on co-promotion. (See below).
- **Use Twitter Plugins**. Twitter has numerous plugins that allow you to "embed" your Twitter Page on your website, and thereby nurture cross promotion. To learn more about plugins, visit https://dev.twitter.com/web/overview. Among the better ones –
  - o **The Tweet Button**. Make it easy for people to tweet your content (e.g., blog posts).
  - o **The Follow Button**. Make it easy for Web visitors to follow you on Twitter.
- **Leverage your Followers**. People who like your Twitter Page are your best promoters. Do everything you can to get them to retweet you to their own followers. Remember, it's *social* (!) media, and encouraging your followers to share your content is the name of the game. You want to leverage your followers as much as possible to share your content.

DON'T FORGET THE REAL WORLD AS A TWITTER PROMOTION STRATEGY

Three Special Ways to Promote via Twitter.

Twitter has three very special ways to promote yourself and your personal brand that are much stronger than on other social media.

The first is the **hashtag**. Because Twitter is all about news, the use of hashtags (designated on Twitter by the "#" or "hash" sign) on trending or controversial topics is bigger on Twitter than on any other social media. Identify trending or important hashtags and include them in your tweets. Use http://hashtagify.me to identify hashtags in your industry, and don't forget about major trade shows which often have (and promote) their own hashtags. Then include these hashtags in your tweets, and make sure that your tweets are not only on topic but also off link to something useful, provocative or important. In that way, they'll discover you via a hashtag and then follow you permanently.

Industry Trade Shows and Hashtags

Here's a hashtag use you do not want to miss: industry trade shows. Nearly every industry has THE trade show, or a few KEY trade shows. Nowadays, these will have hashtags, such as *#CES2016* for the 2016 Consumer Electronics Show. Pre-identify the hashtags of your own industry trade show(s), as well as subordinate, session or topic hashtags, and start tweeting on those theme before, during and shortly after the show. Attendees know to look for the show hashtags to find out what's cool, exciting, and worth visiting.

For many job seekers and career builders, simply knowing the hashtag of "the" industry conference and tweeting during the yearly, or twice yearly, trade conference in and of itself, will justify using Twitter for marketing:

> *Hey #CES2016 attendees! Read my latest blog post on what's hot (and what's not) at CES 2016!*

Identify the Twitter account of the industry trade show(s), and they'll easily show you the relevant hashtags. Make sure you have a robust Twitter account set up before the big show, and then during the show, start tweeting on show-related hashtags. For many businesses, the trade show use of Twitter is the most important marketing use of Twitter.

The second promotion strategy is what I call **@someonefamous**. The idea here is to reach out and "have a conversation" with someone more famous (with more followers) than you. Think of it like Dr. Phil making it on the Oprah Winfrey show. Her audience saw this new "doctor," and some of *her* fans became *his* fans. The trick is to find business partners, companies in your industry and/or their key employees, or other people or companies on Twitter who are influencers and who have more and/or different fan bases than you.

Simply search on Twitter to identify people active in your target industry. For example, let's say you are looking to build your career in the "decision science" industry. Simply search Twitter for "decision science" and click on "accounts." Twitter will then identify the top accounts in your industry. Here's a screenshot:

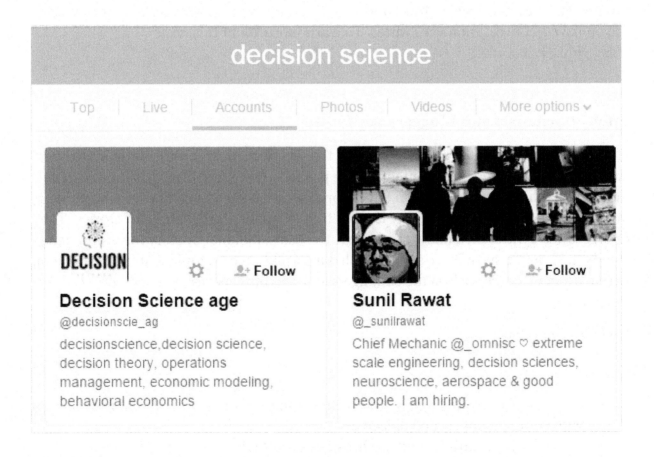

Here's a link to the search: http://jmlinks.com/8p. The idea here is to first identify important people in your industry and/or employees of target employers. Then, brainstorm content and things to tweet about that will pique their interest and possibly start a Twitter conversation.

One of the most useful third party tools is Buzzsumo (http://www.buzzsumo.com/). Search for your keywords and identify influencers tweeting about those topics. Make a list of the Twitter handles of key decision-makers you want to form relationships with; this is the easy part.

The hard part is getting them to engage in a Twitter conversation with you. You have to convince them to have a conversation with you on Twitter, and then once you're talking to their fans… convince their fans to follow you, too, or even pique the interest of their fans in having a career conversation with you. Twitter is all about being so interesting that key influencers want to talk to you, and their followers want to become your followers.

Once you are lucky enough to start a conversation with someone more famous than you, remember to use the "dot" in front of the "@" sign to correctly broadcast your messages as you have a conversation via Twitter. To learn more about this, visit http://jmlinks.com/2k.

Pitch Journalists and Bloggers via Twitter

Here's a key use of Twitter you do not want to miss: **pitching journalists** or bloggers via Twitter about interesting content you've produced as "story ideas." If you are in an industry that has a strong focus on educational content, such as computer programming or environmental issues, the reality is often that journalists are hungry for stories. They often browse Twitter on a daily, or even hourly, basis, looking for story ideas and news trends. Let's assume you have some detailed information on a topic that interests them, perhaps a new trends such as the endangerment of a bird species or a cybercrime safeguard.

Here are your steps:

- **Identify the topics** that matter to you, and to journalists, and that are in accord with your personal brand objectives.
- **Identify journalists and/or bloggers on Twitter** who cover these topics. Follow them, as well as make a list of journalist targets.

- When news strikes, or when you have something in-depth to share, **Tweet "to" these journalists**, thereby pitching them on your story idea and information.

This isn't necessarily easy, but in addition to a strong email list of journalists and bloggers, it's one tool in your toolbox to take content of yours such as a blog post or important photograph and get the attention of journalists, bloggers, and other influencers. I call this the @journalist strategy of using Twitter for publicity.

TWEET TO JOURNALISTS

You can even take it the next level by advertising to select lists of journalists by using username targeting on Twitter (see below).

Retweets as a Promotion Strategy

The third Twitter promotion strategy is the **retweet**. By posting items that are funny, scandalous, interesting, shocking, outrageous or otherwise highly contagious, you get people to retweet your tweets, thereby (again) allowing their followers to see you, and hopefully begin to follow you as well. To research what is retweeted in your industry, simply do a Twitter search with the words RT in front of your keywords. For an example, visit http://jmlinks.com/2l.

Advertise on Twitter

Besides these three promotion methods, you might consider paid advertising on Twitter. In a nutshell, you can pay your way into someone's news feed. You can promote your tweets as well as create custom advertising campaigns to promote your account and/or clicks to your website. To learn more about advertising on Twitter, visit https://biz.twitter.com/start-advertising or https://ads.twitter.com/. Because journalists and bloggers often follow Twitter intensely for breaking news, as mentioned above, one strategy is to make an "influencer list" of influencers on Twitter, and then advertise your tweets directly to those high-impact Twitterers. To learn more about username targeting on Twitter, visit http://jmlinks.com/1k.

In all cases, you want to first brainstorm and create interesting content (for your blog, your YouTube channel, or image / photograph portfolio), and then use promotion tactics to reach out to targets and influencers on Twitter.

Outline Your Outreach Strategy

For your fourth **TODO,** download the **Twitter Job Search and Career-building Marketing Worksheet**. Go to https://www.jm-seo.org/workbooks (click on Job Search and Career-building, enter the code 'careers2016' to register if you have not already done so), and click on the link to the "Twitter Job Search and Career-building Marketing" worksheet.

In the third section, you'll brainstorm how to use Twitter to reach out to key influencers as part of your job search / career-building plan.

» MEASURE YOUR RESULTS

Measuring the success or failure of your Twitter marketing can be a challenge. Let's look at it from the "bottom up" in terms of items a job searcher or career builders might want to know or measure vis-a-vis Twitter:

- **Job Interview Leads**. Have tweets or Twitter marketing resulted in actual conversations or even job interviews?
- **Branding / Awareness**. Has Twitter increased your personal brand awareness and/or improved your personal brand image?
- **Top of Mind / One Touch to Many**. Has Twitter helped us to stay "top of mind," by reminding potential hiring managers of your value as a potential employee?
- **Tweet Interactivity**. Have people read your tweets? Interacted with your tweets by designating them as "favorites," and/or retweeted your tweets?
- **Twitter Account**. Is your follower count increasing, and if so, by how much and how fast? Where are your followers physically located, and what are their demographic characteristics?

The last of these is the easiest to measure: simply record your Twitter follower count each month, and keep a record of it month-to-month. I generally do this on my *Keyword Worksheet*, where I also track inbound links to my website, and my review count on review media such as Google+ and Yelp. (Watch a video on a Keyword Worksheet at http://jmlinks.com/1l).

Analytics Inside of Twitter

Inside of Twitter, click on your profile picture on the top right of the screen, and then in the pull-down menu, click on Analytics. Here's a screenshot:

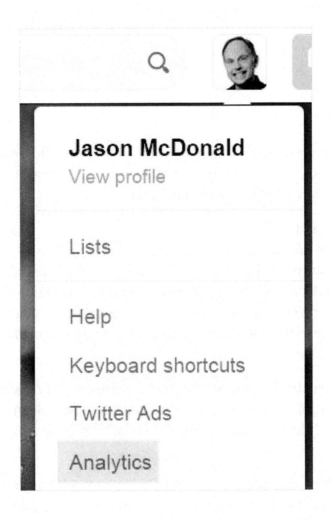

There, you can see which tweets gained the most impressions, as well as engagements by Tweet such as clicks, follows, and retweets. Twitter will also tell you whether links you are sharing are getting clicked on and so on and so forth. Twitter also has a feature called **Twitter cards**, which bridges your website to/from Twitter activity. According to Twitter:

With Twitter Cards, you can attach rich photos, videos and media experience to Tweets that drive traffic to your website. Simply add a few lines of HTML to your webpage, and users who Tweet links to your content will have a "Card" added to the Tweet that's visible to all of their followers. (https://dev.twitter.com/cards/overview, browsed 7/8/2015).

If you enabled Twitter cards on your personal blog or Website, you get attribution for your Web content plus more data on that inside of Twitter. Learn more at https://dev.twitter.com/cards/overview.

Google Analytics

If not a direct job interview lead, most of us want to drive traffic from Twitter to our personal blog or website. Google Analytics will measure how traffic flows from Twitter to your website, and then what happens upon arrival.

Sign up for Google Analytics (https://www.google.com/analytics) and install the required tracking code on your personal blog or website. Inside of your Google Analytics account on the left column, drill down by clicking on Acquisition > Social > Overview. Then on the right hand side of the screen, you'll see a list of Social Networks. Find Twitter on that list, and click on that. Google Analytics will tell you what URLs people clicked to from Twitter to your Website, giving you insights into what types of web content people find attractive.

You can also create a custom Advanced Segment to look at only Twitter traffic and its behavior. For information on how to create custom Advanced Segments in Google Analytics, go to http://jmlinks.com/1f. For the Google help files on Advanced Segments, go to http://jmlinks.com/1g.

In summary, on Twitter, you can see how people interact with your Twitter account and tweets. Inside of Google Analytics, you can see where they land on your website and what they do after they arrive.

≫≫ DELIVERABLE: A TWITTER JOB SEARCH AND CAREER BUILDING PLAN

Now that we've come to the end of our chapter on Twitter, your **DELIVERABLE** has arrived. Download the **Twitter Job Search and Career-building Marketing**

Worksheet. Go to https://www.jm-seo.org/workbooks (click on Job Search and Career-building, enter the code 'careers2016' to register if you have not already done so), and click on the link to the "Twitter Job Search and Career-building Marketing" worksheet.

Once you've completed the worksheet, you'll have an outline to a robust plan on how to use Twitter to support your job search and career-building objectives.

» APPENDIX: TOP TWITTER JOB SEARCH AND CAREER-BUILDING TOOLS AND RESOURCES

Here are the top tools and resources to help you with Twitter marketing. For an up-to-date and complete list, go to https://www.jm-seo.org/workbooks (click on Job Search and Career-building, enter the code 'careers2016' to register if you have not already done so). Then click on the *Job Search and Career-building Resource Book* link, and drill down to the Twitter chapter.

TWITTER ADVANCED SEARCH - https://twitter.com/search-advanced

Search to see what others are saying about topics relevant and your organization's interests, before, during, after you use Twitter. Here's a nifty trick: Use the 'Near this place' field to find people in a city near you tweeting on a topic like 'pizza.' Great for local brands.

Rating: 5 Stars | **Category:** tool

HASHTAGIFY.ME - http://hashtagify.me

Hashtagify.me allows you to search tens of millions of Twitter hashtags and quickly find the best ones for your needs based on popularity, relationships, languages, influencers and other metrics. Also useful for SEO link building and keyword discovery.

Rating: 5 Stars | **Category:** tool

HASHTAGS.ORG - http://hashtags.org

Tool which attempts to organize the world's hashtags. Provides hashtag analytics for your brand, business, product, service, event or blog. Input words that matter to you, and Hashtags looks to see the trends on Twitter.

Rating: 4 Stars | **Category:** engine

TWITONOMY - http://twitonomy.com

Twitonomy is a free online Twitter analytics tool which provides a wealth of information about all aspects of Twitter, including in-depth stats on any Twitter user, insights on your followers, mentions, favorites & retweets, and analytics on hashtags. It also lets you monitor tweets, manage your lists, download tweets & reports, and much more. Definitely worth checking out if Twitter is part of your social media strategy.

Rating: 4 Stars | **Category:** tool

TWITTER ANALYTICS - https://analytics.twitter.com

The official page for Twitter analytics and metrics. Sign up via Twitter, and learn how your tweets are doing!

Rating: 4 Stars | **Category:** tool

FOLLOWERWONK - https://moz.com/followerwonk/

Followerwonk helps you explore and grow your social graph. Dig deeper into Twitter analytics: Who are your followers? Where are they located? When do they tweet? Find and connect with new influencers in your niche. Use actionable visualizations to compare your social graph to others. Easily share your reports with the world. Brought to you by Moz.

Rating: 4 Stars | **Category:** tool

TWITTER HELP CENTER - https://support.twitter.com

Did you know Twitter has technical support? Yep, they do. It's relatively hidden, but here it is. It's more for users of Twitter, but it does have some juicy help for actual businesses on Twitter as well. Tweet, tweet, tweet.

Rating: 4 Stars | **Category:** resource

BITLY - https://bitly.com

Bitly is a URL shortening service that will track your click-throughs. Very useful for email marketing, blogging, and Twitter.

Rating: 4 Stars | **Category:** service

10

OTHER PARTIES

Although blogging, LinkedIn, Facebook, and Twitter are the four most important ways to use the Internet to advance your job-search and career-building goals, don't forget about the other "social media parties" happening on the likes of YouTube or Instagram, Pinterest or Google+, Snapchat or Tumblr, etc. These days, it seems as if a new social network pops up at least once a month, each with its own "hype factory" to terrorize you into thinking that if you're not on (*fill-in-the-blank-network*), you've missed the boat and you are oh-so-square. Remember when everyone "had" to be on Twitter, or everyone "had" to be doing Snapchat? The world didn't end, so don't panic. Blogging, LinkedIn, Facebook, and Twitter are usually more than sufficient to build a powerful personal brand on the Internet.

The other social media networks, however, are at least worth a look.

The way to succeed is to be systematic, looking for *pitfalls* and *opportunities* on each. Is YouTube, for example, for you? Well, a) is your **target audience** using YouTube (and if so, for what purposes), b) can you **create** YouTube-friendly **content**, and c) can you promote that content in an effective way? If so, great. If not, that can be OK too. YouTube (or Snapchat or Instagram or Pinterest...) can be used as a) a "**trust indicator**" showing you really do know your job-related stuff, and/or b) as a "**networking engine**" to get friends to share with friends, and your job or career-related message to be co-promoted via your friends as well.

On the *negative* side, a really inappropriate YouTube video with you in it can be discovered by a potential employer, thereby nixing your opportunity at a promotion. All of these same dynamics are at work on the other networks, be it Snapchat or Instagram.

These networks can help, they can hurt, or they can do nothing.

If you have an account on any or all of these networks, you must audit it to at least prevent any negative impact on your online personal brand image.

Even better, you should brainstorm a strategy to use each network as a "trust indicator" and/or "networking engine" to advance your personal brand.

In this Chapter, we will first overview the ways that each social network – no matter how seemingly new and innovative – shares similarities with Facebook, LinkedIn, and Twitter. We will calmly identify the potential **pitfalls** and **opportunities** that each can pose as you build out your personal brand online. Finally, we will review each social media network with pointers to information resources for how to get started and how to optimize each network to advance your job search or career.

Let's get started!

To Do List:

» Remember It's Always a Party

» Identify Pitfalls and Opportunities

» Instagram: A Picture is Worth a Thousand Words

» YouTube: A Video is Worth Ten Thousand Words

» Pinterest: Do You Shop or Do-it-Yourself?

» Party On: Amazon, Google+, Snapchat, Tumblr, and New Kids on the Block

»» Appendix: Top Other Network Job Search & Career-building Tools and Resources

» REMEMBER IT'S ALWAYS A PARTY

There's *always* a party going on somewhere, and that includes each social media network. Your party attendees want food / drink / entertainment, while you want to use that "party" to schmooze with potential employers, spread your message from friend to friend, and justify your job or career coolness by producing impressive content for everyone. It's *always a party*, whether it's on Twitter or YouTube, Facebook or Instagram.

Here are the universal points to remember:

- **Target Audience**. You have to determine whether your target audience (*potential employers, hiring managers, key decision-makers or influencer employees, and/or friends, family, and other contacts*) is actually on the social network in question, and if so, figure out what they are doing there / what they want. Can you influence any of them to advance your job search or career objectives?

- **Set Up**. Next, if your target audience is using the network, you have basic set up issues: creating an account, setting up appropriate profile pictures, cover photos, etc., and populating the text summaries appropriately. Don't forget to set your *privacy settings* to be open or closed in accord with your strategy!

- **Posting Strategy**. You have to figure out *what to post* (pictures, videos, text, etc.) on *which topics*, and a *posting rhythm* that's 80% fun and 20% "hire me – I'm in the market." On all networks, if they don't like your content, they'll ignore you. Your posts must satisfy a need that your target audience has (80% of the time), to get the 20% of the time in which you are posting something that specifically and directly promotes your job search and/or career-building goals. It's 80% for them, and 20% for you.
    - **Content Marketing**. In all cases, you'll have to take advantage of your content marketing system to generate the quality and quantity of content you need to "feed your party" on a regular basis. If the food (*content*) stops, the party (*social media marketing*) stops, too.

- **Objectives**. This is a *party with a purpose*. You're not going to be using YouTube (or Instagram, Snapchat, etc.) for fun only. You're going to be using each network a) as a **trust indicator** for potential employers to see, b) as a **means to alert** hiring managers, friends, family, and contacts that you're "in the market for a job." and/or c) as a **promotion engine** for you to reach, not just your own contacts, but *contacts of your contacts* or even *complete strangers*, in the hopes that they'll realize what a career genius you are and reach out to you with a job interview or promotion offer.

In summary, as you research each network, the **basic questions** are:

Is your audience of hiring managers, employers, and others who can advance your career on this social media network?

What are they doing? Why are they on this network?

How do you set up and optimize your own account?

What should you post, and how often?

What is your posting rhythm going to be? What will be fun (useful, interesting) and what will self-servingly promote your online personal brand image and career goals?

How are you going to promote your account and posts? How will you grow your network of contacts? How will you get contacts to spread the word to their contacts that you are an ideal job or promotion candidate?

How will you measure whether the results you see from each network justify the efforts?

» IDENTIFY PITFALLS AND OPPORTUNITIES

Let's start with a story from my own personal experience. One time, my Dad and I happened to be at the Eisenhower Presidential library in the small town of Abilene, Kansas. It was a pretty boring tour, as Eisenhower was a pretty boring president (his most famous achievement was the Interstate Highway system). As we were going exhibit by exhibit, my Dad kept humming "Ummmm" in a positive way. Pretty bored, I asked my Dad, "Dad why are so you so upbeat about Eisenhower? Why do you think he was such a great President?"

And my Dad replied, "Because he didn't screw anything up."

Eisenhower, in contrast to Lyndon Johnson, for example, is known for peace and prosperity. (Lyndon Johnson is known for both the *successful* Great Society and the *disastrous* Vietnam War). Lyndon Johnson was probably much more influential, but Eisenhower may have been the better President.

Be President Eisenhower not President Johnson

What's the point? As you go through the universe of social media, remember that your most important goal vis-à-vis your job search or career-building objectives is to "not screw anything up." If you never post to Tumblr, never upload a video to Snapchat, or refuse to have a YouTube channel, at least you won't hurt your job prospects. If there are any doubts, your best strategy is not to participate, or if you do participate, remember the Social Media "Golden Rule" of always staying positive and never posting anything that, if seen by a potential employer, you might regret.

In addition, for 99% of job seekers and career-builders, the main networks of blogging, LinkedIn, Facebook, and Twitter are more than sufficient to advance their personal brand image. Don't work strenuously on Snapchat, if your audience is on LinkedIn!

Pitfalls

Don't screw anything up is Rule #1.

If you're already on Instagram, Tumblr, Snapchat, YouTube, etc., audit what you've posted already and revise your posting strategy going forward, so that nothing exists that could hurt you. The pitfall of posting the crazy "Last Friday Night Video" to YouTube, is that it might be seen by your employer on Monday. Look for mistakes of that type as you audit your accounts on each social media, and remember that your own likes, comments, or shares may be construed as a type of endorsement of shady or unacceptable behavior.

Delete any and all posts that might hurt you; indeed, if an account such as your YouTube or Snapchat is really negative for your personal brand, don't hesitate to kill the entire account!

Going forward, if you have nothing positive to say about something, don't say it. If you are endorsing a topic that is pretty controversial and might be construed the wrong way by an employer, don't like / comment / share on this topic. (This goes both for life, and for social media, when you think about it: *don't make enemies*).

> *On some networks such as Instagram, the default settings are public. So you may not realize it, but everything you post is available for viewing by anyone including potential employers!*
>
> *Consider anything you post to any social media as potentially public despite your privacy settings. If you do not want an employer to see it, don't post it!*

Opportunities on Other Networks

With the pitfalls out of the way, brainstorm potential **opportunities** for each network. Find persons or companies you like who are using the social network, and "reverse engineer" what they're doing to advance their personal brand image. Research what your targets are doing on the network, and what type of content they might want. Generally, your opportunities will be all or one of:

Trust Indicators. By being on the social network (on YouTube or Tumblr, on Pinterest or Instagram, on Snapchat or the next new thing, etc.), your account and/or posts will bolster your personal brand image as a "helpful expert," someone an employer would want to hire and/or promote.

Staying Top of Mind. If your friends, family, and contacts are on the social network, by posting on it yourself, you can stay top of mind in their heads, and occasionally remind them that you are "in the market" for a better job or career promotion.

Social Spread. Some networks, like YouTube or Tumblr, can create massive social spread or even the proverbial "viral" piece of content. Or, at the least, encourage contacts of contacts to learn about you, to the extent that your content is "spreadable." You can use a social network as a promotional engine for your career goals.

As we turn to each social media network, remember that at a conceptual level they all share similar *pitfalls* and *opportunities*.

Let's now turn to each of the 2nd tier social media networks.

>> INSTAGRAM: A PICTURE IS WORTH A THOUSAND WORDS

Instagram (https://www.instagram.com), owned by Facebook and very popular with the Millennial generation, is probably the most important 2nd tier social network. It's entirely possible that, someday soon, it will replace Twitter as the "go to" place for news and trending content. It certainly doesn't hurt that Facebook and Instagram are working together to remain the #1 social network. Let's review the basic steps for Instagram vis-à-vis your online personal brand-building strategy.

Instagram Basics

Structurally, Instagram is very similar to Facebook: users have accounts, users can follow / friend each other, and when a person posts a picture, that picture shows up in the news feed of his followers / friends. Friends can like, comment on, or share the photos of others. (Sharing on Instagram is a bit one-to-one unlike on Facebook, and is called *Instagram Direct* (http://jmlinks.com/11r).

(If you don't already have an account, go to Instagram and set one up. For official Instagram set up instructions, go to http://jmlinks.com/11q.)

However, unlike Facebook, the default privacy settings are **open** *not private*; you do not actually have to "accept" friend requests on Instagram. It's more like Twitter in terms of privacy. Pretty much anyone can follow anyone, anyone can like / comment / share on anything, and all posts are public (unless you change your settings from the default). This is a very important difference between Instagram and Facebook.

Like Twitter, posts to Instagram are 100% open to public view!

Generally, therefore, consider anything posted to Instagram as easily available to a potential employer or hiring manager. (You can, however, change your privacy settings to 100% private if you like).

Find Your Target Audience

Once you have an Instagram account, your first task is to research whether your target audience of potential employers or hiring managers is using Instagram and in what way. You're also looking for people "like you" to emulate. Instagram is primarily used on the phone, but for purposes of systematic research, I recommend you use your computer or a tablet such as an iPad.

Sign up for a basic Instagram account, and do one of two things:

Search Instagram Directly. Identify persons and/or brands that are using Instagram for personal branding purposes. Instagram is all about photos and videos, so careers that are image-friendly are most likely to be represented (e.g., photographer jobs, user interface design jobs, architecture jobs, etc.). Simply login to Instagram, and type one of your keywords into the search box. Note: Instagram (like Twitter) uses #hashtags, so you can often find useful #hashtags such as #wedding, #photography, #webdesign, to browse potential accounts.

Here's a screenshot:

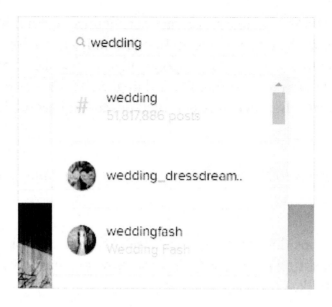

As you find accounts (people or brands) to emulate, simply "follow" them by clicking the "follow" button.

Search Instagram via Google. Google is the world's best search engine, so go to Google and type in *site:instagram.com {keyword}* as in *site:instagram.com web design*. Remember: no space between the site: and Instagram! Here's a screenshot:

Again, look for #hashtags relevant to your job search or career-building goals, and identify people to follow (and ultimately emulate).

At this point, you're building a list of people to follow. In addition, by looking at who follows and interacts with them, you're beginning to find out whether potential employers or hiring managers might be using Instagram, and if so, how they are using it. Most probably, you'll realize it's a lot like Facebook: employers and hiring managers are on Instagram, but in their capacity as "real people" not "employers."

Account Set Up & Privacy

It's time to optimize your Instagram account. First, click on the person icon on the top right of Instagram, and click "edit profile." Here's a screenshot:

Choose an account name, write your summary of yourself (*remember to be professional!*), and indicate your blog or personal website. Click on your photo to the top left, and upload an appropriate headshot or icon for your profile picture. (This shows in the news feed of others).

I am not trying to be a killjoy here. You can use Instagram primarily for fun. Just be aware that your "fun" (appropriate or not) will be visible for all to see.

Note that your account name becomes your public URL on Instagram. Just click on the person icon on the top right to see your account name, then look at the URL in the top of the browser. This is your public URL. Here's a screenshot of mine:

To see my public URL on the Internet and hence Instagram feed, go to http://jmlinks.com/11t. See how public it all is?

If you want your account to be private (meaning you have to approve friend requests, and only friends can see your posts), you have to change this setting on your phone, not on a desktop computer. Instructions are here: http://jmlinks.com/11s. Remember: the default setting (as on Twitter) is for everything to be *public*. To learn more about Instagram privacy, visit http://jmlinks.com/11u.

Content Marketing and Posting Rhythm

Instagram, like all social media, is hungry for content! Because Instagram is visual, you'll need a large feed of your own **photos** or **videos** to share frequently. Instagram is well-integrated with both iPhones and Android devices, so it's easy to take pictures or quick videos and share them to Instagram. Make a habit of taking pictures as you move throughout your daily life, and take two basic types:

Fun Photos. Photos of you having fun, doing things, going places, hanging out with friends BUT make sure that if seen by an employer that they are OK. You don't have to be fake, but you don't want to be offensive either.

Self-serving Pitches. Perhaps 20% of the time or less, post something that reminds your friends and contacts that you are "in the market" for a job / career advancement, or that your passion is your job (e.g., you are a wedding photographer and you love to take photos, or you are an architect, and you love to photograph and comment on buildings). The purpose here is to stay top of mind and remind your connections that you are "in the market" for a job. Even silly posts such as "selfies" of you before, during, and after a job interview can advance your objective of increasing awareness among friends and family that you are "in the market," so "be creative."

Alternatively, you can create photo images on your desktop computer, and share those as well. This could be useful if your desired career has something to do with design: web design, graphic design, even consumer design.

Whatever you post and why, just realize that you need a lot of images to use Instagram effectively to promote your online personal brand image.

And, remember, the 80/20 rule in terms of your posting rhythm: 80% fun stuff, and 20% stuff that promotes your job search or career-building needs.

Don't bore your audience!

Instagram Pitfalls

The main **pitfall** on Instagram is to not realize that every post you make is by default "public" and accessible to anyone. So, unless you set up a fully private account, that stupid picture of you with your shirt of next to the Donald Trump statue at the Wax Museum in Las Vegas – *yep, a potential employer can see it.* That strange addiction you have to Star Wars paraphernalia, and your hundreds of posts on that topic... *yep, a potential employer can see that, too.*

Instagram is not only public, it's easy to search. So the prying eyes of a potential employer can easily see what you're up to on the network.

Instagram Opportunities

For those seeking jobs or careers in visually oriented areas such as photography, web design, user interface design, architecture, any type of art, etc., Instagram is a fabulous opportunity to have an easy place to showcase your passion and your portfolio.

The first Instagram opportunity is as a "trust indicator." Create a vibrant, active, and engaging account on Instagram as "proof" of your talent.

In addition, because Instagram is truly open, you can gain new followers (not just friends and friends of friends but actual people out of the blue). New people can find you, get excited about you, perhaps become your real friends, and perhaps clue you in to job or career opportunities.

Since Instagram is open like Twitter, you can use it to grow your social reach by participating in the Instagram community via "hashtags" and "at signs" (@).

In a fashion similar to Twitter, you should:

- Identify **#hashtags** that matter to you and your career, and post to them. So the *#timelytopic strategy* of using hashtags works both on Twitter and on Instagram. To find hashtags on Instagram, search by keywords and write new hashtags down as you discover them. Upload photos or videos, use the appropriate hashtag and chime in on a discussion.
- Build a **portfolio of interesting photos / videos** on your stream, so that followers see how cool you are ("content marketing").
- **Use the @ sign** to reach out to people "more famous than you." By being mentioned in the posts of more famous people, their followers can see and follow you. So the *@someonefamous strategy* works both on Twitter and on Instagram. To find people, simply search Instagram by keyword and "follow" accounts of people or brands who can help you in terms of your career. The tough part is to identify a reason why they care enough to mention you in a post.
- **Post 80% fun stuff, and 20% shameless self-promotional stuff** (or, realistically, at least indicate you're open to job offers in some of your posts). In other words, use *content marketing* to promote yourself on Instagram.
- **Like, comment, and share the posts of others.** People pay attention to who's following them, so by following a person and being interactive with their

account, you can build a relationship, grow your network, and expand the reach of your job search and career contacts.

Instagram Deliverable: An Instagram Job Search & Career-building Plan

Your Instagram **DELIVERABLE** has arrived. Go to https://www.jm-seo.org/workbooks (click on Job Search and Career Building, enter the code 'careers2016' to register if you have not already done so), and click on the link to the "Instagram Worksheet." By filling it out, you'll determine if Instagram is for you, and if so, how to optimize Instagram to promote your career.

» YouTube: a Video is Worth 10,000 Words

If a picture is worth a thousand words, then does that mean a video can be worth 10,000? Perhaps. Certainly some videos that have "gone viral" on YouTube have helped their producers. YouTube (https://www.youtube.com/) offers the opportunity to upload videos of your own to your own channel. It gives you both a place to put any video content of yours, and a social network for liking, commenting on, and sharing (as well as being liked, being commented upon, and being shared).

Let's investigate!

YouTube Basics

Video and YouTube are among the most dramatic, most viral components of the Internet. Who doesn't know the "Harlem Shake" (http://jmlinks.com/1m) or the "Ice Bucket Challenge" (http://jmlinks.com/1n)? Who hasn't watched "Will it blend" (http://jmlinks.com/1o) or "Dear 16 Year Old Me" (http://jmlinks.com/1p)? And who hasn't fallen into the trap of assuming all YouTube is are silly cat videos, Rihanna videos, and inappropriate High School humor? It is, but YouTube is much more than that as a marketing opportunity (and as a social phenomenon).

As we shall see, there are three basic ways that YouTube videos can help you with social media marketing for your personal brand image online:

1. **Video as a supporting medium**: acting as the "content" that you "share" via other social media, including your blog or personal website.

2. **Video as a discovery mechanism via SEO** (Search Engine Optimization), helping you promote yourself via search.
3. **Video as a share / viral promotion tactic**, because people love and share provocative videos.

We'll dive into the details in a moment. But first, log on to YouTube and get your bearings. (For the official YouTube starter guide and to set up a new account, go to http://jmlinks.com/1q). If you're familiar with Facebook, you'll see many similarities right out of the gate:

- Individuals have an "account" or "**channel**" on YouTube, set up by registering with an email address and using Google+ to manage their account.
- Individuals can **upload videos** to their "channel," and when uploading give each video a TITLE, a DESCRIPTION, and KEYWORD TAGS as well as designate a VIDEO THUMBNAIL.
- Individuals "**subscribe**" to the channels of other individuals (or brands) on YouTube, and when someone you subscribe to uploads a new video, you get a notification on your YouTube logon, as well as via email that a new video has been posted.
- Individuals can **thumbs up / thumbs down videos** (akin to "like" on Facebook of a post), comment (via Google+ comments), and share the videos via other social media as well as create playlists of videos on YouTube.
- Companies can create **brand channels** on YouTube. Like Twitter, YouTube is very easy and open. Anyone can quickly create a channel, no serious user authentication is required.

For assistance on how to set up a personal or a company YouTube channel, visit http://jmlinks.com/1r. (Similar to the situation on Facebook, most of us will have a personal channel but if you have a good reason, you can have a "brand" channel as well).

Structurally, YouTube is thus very similar to Facebook. However, unlike Facebook, the default settings are very **open** and *not private*. You do not actually have to "accept" friend requests on YouTube; it's more like Twitter in terms of privacy. Pretty much anyone can follow anyone, anyone can like / comment / share on anything, and all videos are public (unless you change your settings from the default). This is important:

Like Twitter or Instagram, consider YouTube 100% open to public view!

As you audit your existing account, you should **delete** any videos (or make them private), as well as any comments that might hurt your career prospects.

Your Target Audience on YouTube

Once you have a YouTube account, your first task is to research whether your target audience of potential employers or hiring managers is on the network. You're also looking for people "like you" to emulate.

Sign up for a basic YouTube account, and do one of two things:

Search YouTube Directly. Identify persons and/or brands that are using YouTube for personal branding purposes. YouTube is all about videos, so careers that are video-friendly are most likely to be represented (e.g., photographer jobs, videographer jobs, jobs like sales or marketing that require customer promotions, etc.). Simply login to YouTube, and type one of your keywords into the search box.

Here's a screenshot:

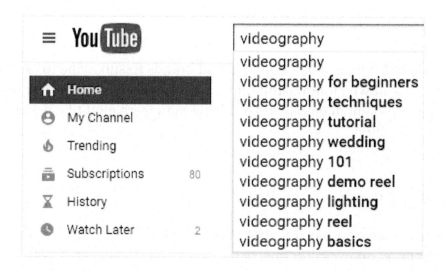

As you find accounts (people or brands) to emulate, simply "subscribe" to them by clicking the red "subscribe" button.

Search YouTube via Google. Google is the world's best search engine, so go to Google and type in *site:youtube.com {keyword}* as in *site:youtube.com wedding videos*.

Remember: no space between the *site:* and YouTube! Here's a screenshot:

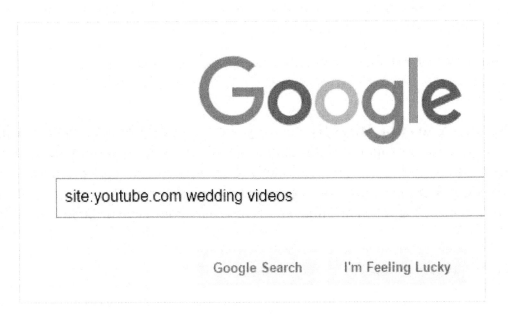

At this point, you're building a list of people and brands to subscribe to on YouTube. In addition, by looking at who follows and interacts with various videos, you're beginning to find out whether potential employers or hiring managers might be using video / YouTube in some fashion.

Account Set Up & Privacy

If you don't already have an account, go to YouTube and set one up. For official YouTube set up instructions, go to http://jmlinks.com/1r. Once you have an account, optimize it by clicking on the person icon on the top right of YouTube, and click "YouTube settings." Here's a screenshot:

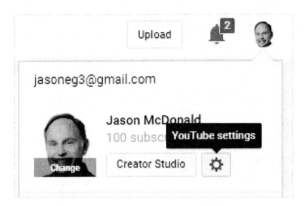

Click on "Connected Accounts," and de-connect Twitter if you have connected it. (The reason for disconnecting them is that, if they are connected, your YouTube activity will automatically be shared to Twitter, which is 100% public). Click on "Privacy" and review your privacy settings. *Unless you will be using YouTube for your own promotional efforts, I'd recommend keeping most of your YouTube activity private.* Hence:

Going to Use YouTube Only for Personal Use: Set it to Private.

Going to Use YouTube to Promote Your Online Personal Brand: Set it to Public

Next, click on "My Channel" at the top left. Fill out the information about your channel, especially the "about" section on the middle right. This information will become public.

Note that your account name may become your public URL on YouTube. If you've had your account for a while, you may not even know your public URL. YouTube doesn't make it easy to find it, as it is hidden under Account Settings > Overview > Advanced. Or just click on http://jmlinks.com/11v.

Video Privacy

You can't really keep your channel private; you can only change your privacy settings to hide your likes and subscriptions. If you upload a video to your channel, you can change the video to private, however. To do this, click on your name in the top right, then "Creator Studio," and then click on "Video Manager." Click "edit" under any videos you have uploaded, and then click the settings on the far right pull-down menu. Here's a screenshot:

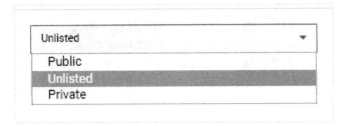

"Public" means anyone can see it, and it appears on your YouTube channel. "Unlisted" means anyone can see if they have the exact video URL. "Private" means that you must share it via emails.

Content Marketing and Posting Rhythm

YouTube, like all social media, is hungry for content! Because YouTube is visual, you'll need a large feed of your own videos to be constantly sharing. Remember, the 80/20 rule in terms of your posting rhythm: 80% fun / interesting / useful videos, and 20% videos that promote your job search or career-building needs. Don't bore your audience!

YouTube Pitfalls

The main **pitfall** on YouTube is to not realize that every video you upload is by default "public" and accessible to anyone. So is your channel, and so are your video likes, thumbs up / thumbs down, comments, and subscriptions. Basically if you've posted a video you'd rather not have an employer see, you should either **delete** it entirely or change the privacy settings to unlisted or private.

As for thumbs up / thumbs down on inappropriate videos as well as stupid comments, it goes without saying that you shouldn't do or say anything on YouTube, that you wouldn't want a potential employer or hiring manager to see.

Consider all YouTube activities public!

YouTube Opportunities

For those seeking jobs or careers in visually oriented areas such as photography, videography, or any profession that requires presentation skills (e.g., sales or marketing), YouTube is a great opportunity to have an easy place to showcase your passion and your portfolio.

> *The first YouTube opportunity is as a "supportive element" or a "trust indicator." Create a vibrant, active, and engaging account on YouTube as "proof" of your talent.*

In addition, because YouTube is truly open, you can gain new followers (not just friends and friends of friends but actual people out of the blue). New people can find your videos and your channel, get excited about you, perhaps become your real friends, and perhaps clue you in to job or career opportunities.

> *Since YouTube is open like Twitter, you can use it to grow your social reach by participating in the YouTube community*

YouTube also has an opportunity created by the potential for "how to" or "instructional" videos.

Let's review the opportunities on YouTube:

Opportunity #1: Supportive Use of Video. In this use of YouTube, you create a video that showcases your skills. For example, let's say you gave a class presentation to your engineering class on integrated circuit issues. You can record this, upload this video to your channel, and showcase your skills. By including a URL in your video description, you can also promote your website or blog. Here are examples: http://jmlinks.com/11w, http://jmlinks.com/11x, and http://jmlinks.com/11y. Your **TODO** here is to brainstorm something that you do that supports your claim to be a "helpful expert" (such as a class or work presentation), get it recorded, and upload it to your channel. These type of videos can be embedded on your blog, or shared on other social networks, but their primary purpose is to "support" your personal brand image.

Opportunity #2: SEO Use of Video. Among the most popular searches on YouTube are "how to" searches. If, for example, you are looking for a job in the culinary arts, you might create a video on "how to truss a turkey," or "how to make a soufflé." These videos might both support your claim to expertise and be found by potential employers or key employees who might search YouTube for "how to" videos. Here are examples: http://jmlinks.com/11z, http://jmlinks.com/12a, and http://jmlinks.com/12b. The basics of SEO'ing a video are:

- **Keywords in the video title**. Identify your keywords and make sure that you title the video accordingly.
- **Keywords in the video description**. Similarly, write complete sentences to describe your video and be sure to include your target keywords. If you include an *http://* format URL in the video description, it will become clickable (as for example to your website or blog). For example, if my video description says: "Get more free stuff at https://jmlinks.com/free," then that URL is clickable on YouTube.
- **Tag the Video**. Use YouTube "tags" that reflect the keywords you'd like to rank for. You set these in Video Manager.
- **Interactivity**. The more views, thumbs up / thumbs down, comments, and shares a video gets, the better it shows on YouTube search, including minutes watched. YouTube rewards quality, interactive videos!

Opportunity #3: Share / Viral Use of Video. Videos are among the most shared objects on the Internet. What gets shared? *Emotion, emotion, emotion. Humor* is a "safe" emotion, and sometimes, a *sentimentality* approach can work as well. I'd stay away from revolting, shocking, outrage, or other negative emotions, however. By creating a powerful emotional video, you can encourage sharing up to and including viral. Just be sure that what gets shared is something that is positive for you; as once sharing gets started, you can't necessarily stop it. An example is Rebecca Black's "Friday" video, which "went viral" and promoted her as a singer (although a lot of people reacted negatively to her). You can watch it at http://jmlinks.com/12c. Another famous example is the "Ice Bucket Challenge," of which you can watch an example at http://jmlinks.com/12d.

For each opportunity, you have to devise the content for your video, shoot the video, and then promote the video. The *bad news* is that videos are hard to create, much more difficult than a blog post or image. The *good news* is that videos are hard to create and so few people actually create them. If you go to the effort to create a vibrant YouTube channel that showcases your job / career skills, you will really stand out!

YouTube Deliverable: a YouTube Job Search & Career-building Plan

Your YouTube **DELIVERABLE** has arrived. Go to https://www.jm-seo.org/workbooks (click on Job Search and Career Building, enter the code 'careers2016' to register if you have not already done so), and click on the link to the "YouTube Worksheet." By filling it out, you'll determine if YouTube is for you, and if so, how to optimize YouTube to promote your career.

▶ PINTEREST: DO YOU SHOP OR DO-IT-YOURSELF?

Pinterest (https://www.pinterest.com) is strong in three inter-related segments: consumer retail, do-it-yourself, and women. Shoppers use Pinterest to browse the Internet and "pin" items they might want to buy to "boards." Do-it-yourselfers use Pinterest to share ideas on how to build this or that, knit this or that, or construct this or that. Women, always a heavy shopping demographic, have been the early adopters of Pinterest, both as a "buying / idea platform" and as a great platform for do-it-yourself crafting and recipe-sharing.

Along with Instagram and YouTube, Pinterest is a visual medium. It's heavy on photos and videos, and light on text and commentary. Thus it's great for people who have photogenic items to share for their personal brand image such as photographers, videographers, do-it-yourselfers with projects, those who "make" things, anyone involved in retail etc. It's not so great if you are into something abstract like accounting or chemical engineering; all the more so, if those abstract things are not "fun," as Pinterest has a heavy dose of fun and leisure in its culture.

Pinterest, in short, is *the* network for consumer retail, *the* network for craftsy do-it-yourself, and *the* network for women (especially in shopping mode).

Pinterest Basics

The best way to understand Pinterest and social bookmarking is to grasp the concept of an "idea board."

Let's use the example of someone planning out her ideal dorm room for freshman year at college. First, she signs up for Pinterest and creates a profile. Compared with Facebook, Pinterest is very basic. Not a lot of information is displayed in a Pinterest profile, pretty much just a profile picture and a very brief description. Next, she should download and install the Pinterest button (see http://jmlinks.com/2m) or Chrome Pinterest extension (see http://jmlinks.com/2n). Once installed, she can now surf the Web (or use the Pinterest app for iPhone or Android) and "pin" interesting items to "boards" that she sets up.

For example, she'd set up a board "my dream college room" or even more specific boards like "my dream bathroom supplies," or "my dream desk." Let's say she goes to Amazon and finds an amazing desk light. She can "pin" this desk light to her "dream desk" board. People who follow her (or this board) on Pinterest, thus see this desk light in their Pinterest news feed, whereupon they can comment on it and (gasp!) and even buy it for her. And of course, she would pin not just one desk light, but several possible desk lights, several pencil holders, several ink pads, a few art posters for above her desk, and so on and so forth. It's as if she's building a collage of desk possibilities, from which she can select the perfect accessories. As she creates idea boards for her dream desk, dream closet, dream dorm room, and dream bathroom supplies, she can invite her friends, her Mom, her sorority sisters to collaborate by commenting and pinning to the boards as well.

Pinterest, in short, is a **visual bookmarking** and **idea board system**, one that can be social as well, and one that makes online shopping as easy as discover, click, buy. People also use it before purchase in the real world, and as a social scrapbook to group together products and services they might want to buy at a brick and mortar store. Do-it-yourselfers use it to share ideas about how to build this or that, how to cook this or that.

THE ESSENCE OF PINTEREST IS

THE IDEA BOARD

The structure of Pinterest in a nutshell is:

Individual profile: me, Jason as a person.

Idea board: collections of items from the Web on topics like my "dream dorm room," "dog toys to possibly buy," "do-it-yourself Christmas decorations," or "recipes for summer parties."

Pins: I can "pin" things I find on the Web such as blog posts, videos, images, or products to buy, to my "boards" as a collection of ideas, things to buy. I can also upload items directly.

Search. I can browse Pinterest, search Pinterest, or search the Web for interesting things to "pin" to my boards.

Collaboration: I can invite others to comment on my board or pins, and to pin items to my boards directly. I can also pin things to their boards.

Social: I have a news feed, wherein Pinterest shows me the pins of people, brands, and boards I follow, as well as suggestions based on my (revealed) interests. People can also follow me and my boards, and like, comment, and re-share ("re-pin") -items that I am pinning. Through collaborative boards, we can pin and share ideas together.

To get the hang of Pinterest, create your personal profile, create some boards, download the "Pin it" button, and start playing with the site. Using Pinterest is the best way to begin to understand how to market on Pinterest. For example, to view a Pinterest search for "dream college dorm rooms," visit http://jmlinks.com/20. To visit some sample idea boards, visit http://jmlinks.com/2p. Notice how people use Pinterest as a visual bookmarking system of ideas (largely, but not exclusively, of stuff to buy or make), and how others can comment on, and even contribute to these boards in a collaborative fashion.

Once you understand the idea of **visual bookmarking** or "**idea boards**," then you've "got" Pinterest.

As on other social media, people can "follow" other people or brands (or just their boards) and when that person, brand, or board has a new pin, that new pin shows in their news feed. In addition, notifications are generated when someone likes, comments, or re-pins one of your pin (or boards, or account).

Find Your Target Audience

Your next step is to search Pinterest to determine if your target audience is on it, and/or to find people to emulate with similar career goals or personal brand images. People can search Pinterest directly, or by clicking on the categories button, one can browse Pinterest by categories. To do that, simply click on the categories button at the top right of the search screen. Here's a screenshot:

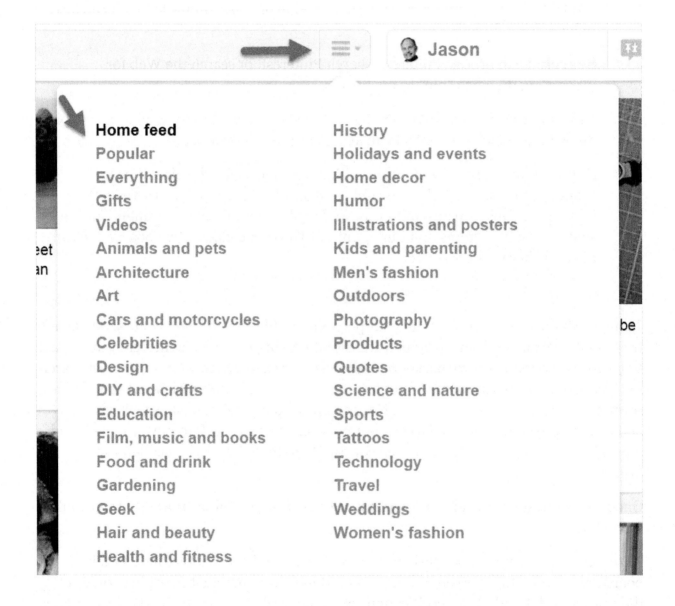

The "home feed," of course, is your news feed on Pinterest. Pins selected for you by the Pinterest algorithm based on your previous interests and engagements. The other categories are a way to browse Pinterest by topic, just as you might browse Amazon.

You can also use Google to search Pinterest by using the *site:pinterest* command as in *site:pinterest.com marketing presentations* or *site:pinterest.com corporate photography*.

While most of Pinterest is retail-oriented and most of that, female-oriented, if you're a man, don't despair. There are men to be found on Pinterest and topics of interest to men. For example, check out Men's fashion at http://jmlinks.com/2q or pet accessories at http://jmlinks.com/2r. Classic cars, sporting goods, and other shopping and/or do-it-yourself activities are popular with the male demographic and can be found on Pinterest. Anything connecting to do-it-yourself or recipes / cooking / home decor is also a good bet as a marketing opportunity.

Pinterest has an excellent guide on how to use the platform at http://jmlinks.com/2s, an in-depth help center at http://jmlinks.com/2t, and a *Pinterest for business center* at http://jmlinks.com/2u. Between using these official guides, and systematically researching what's happening on Pinterest, you'll easily see opportunities for your personal brand. (*Or, you'll quickly realize that Pinterest is not for you, and you can move on to a more promising social media.*)

Like Instagram, you'll quickly realize that if your target audience of employers and hiring managers (or friends, family, and contacts who can help your job search) is on Pinterest, they are probably in "fun" mode, not in "find employees" mode. So your best shot is to use Pinterest as a "trust indicator" showcasing your career-related passions in a visual way. (And, of course, you'll also realize that you don't want to share things on Pinterest that might be embarrassing).

Account Set Up & Privacy

Now that you've got the basics of Pinterest down, it's time to set up or optimize your Pinterest page. As on Facebook, people have "profiles" and businesses have "accounts" on Pinterest, often also called "Pages." You'll generally want a personal account. But if you want a business account, or Page, on Pinterest, you can do that, too. To set one up for the first time, go to *Pinterest for Business* at https://business.pinterest.com/. You can also convert a "profile" to a business "account," if you mistakenly joined as an individual at https://business.pinterest.com/.

Once you've joined, you have only a very basic set up – your profile picture, username (URL), "about you," location, and website. That's it. Once you've filled out this information, you're set up on Pinterest.

Next, set up some boards by clicking on the "Create a Board" on the left of the screen. Here's a screenshot:

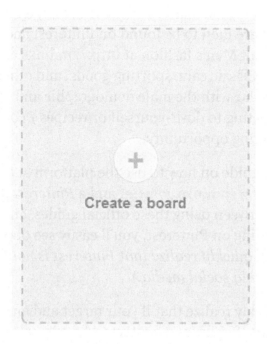

When you create a board, give it a name, a description, a category, a map or location (useful if you are a local business). If you're just building out the board, you can also temporarily make it *secret* and then change it to *public* at a later date. A **board** should reflect a **concept** such as "San Francisco Buildings I Like" for a prospective architect, or "Wedding Dresses that I admire" for a prospective dress designer or "My Favorite Soufflé Recipes" for a prospective chef.

If you want to make a board collaborative, you identify "collaborators" by typing in their names or email addresses. Pinterest will then invite them to start pinning items to your board. The easiest way to start pinning items to your board is to download the "Pinterest button" onto your browser. You can also manually copy URL's over to pin an item. With the concept that a board is an "idea board," start identifying and pinning items from the Web such as blog posts, images or photos, and yes, even products from your eCommerce store to your new board.

Board Strategy

Social media is a party, not a prison, and that's certainly true on Pinterest. Each board should attract people to follow it by providing something useful, something visual, something fun. Ask these questions. What is the board "about"? Who will want to "follow" it, Pin stuff from it (or to it), comment, share, and click from the board to your products. Take a board like "Gifts for Dog Lovers" at http://jmlinks.com/3a vs. the board "Dog Gifs" at http://jmlinks.com/3b. The purpose of the former, is to identify fun dog gifts to BUY, while the purpose of the latter is to share funny pictures of dogs and build the brand image of *BarkPost* (http://barkpost.com/), a New York-based blog on dogs that also sells dog-related products. Both are legitimate social media marketing users of Pinterest – the former is just a more direct plea to "buy our stuff," whereas the latter is more a "look at this cool stuff" (and by the way check out all the cool stuff we sell).

> *Hard sell* or *soft sell*. Both work on Pinterest.

In summary, your best strategy is to brainstorm the purpose behind each board. The questions are:

- **What is this board about?** What ideas does it collect, how does it function as a useful "idea-generator" on a particular topic?
- **Who will be interested in this board?** What value are you providing as the board-creator and board-curator by having this board? A board on dog toy ideas "saves time" for people who a) love dogs and want toys and/or b) need to buy a gift for a person who loves dogs and wants toys. Your value is curating "in" the cool stuff, and curating "out" the dumb stuff. A board that collects funny pictures of dogs is meant to give viewers a quick and easy way to get a few laughs during their busy day, and a board that collects do-it-yourself ideas for cheap dog toys helps dog lovers save money, and have fun, by building their own dog toys. Who will be interested is a function of what the board is about.
- **What will you pin to this board, and where does that content live?** Is it stuff from your eCommerce store? Stuff on Amazon? Blog posts, or how to articles? Items from your own blog? Images of your photographs? YouTube videos? Content is king, on Pinterest, as on all social media.

For job search, you will primarily use boards as a way to showcase your portfolio or interests. As on YouTube, that "supportive" use of Pinterest is most common. However, by optimizing your pins and boards, you can show up on Pinterest search and be "discovered" and "followed" by total strangers; so there is a "search" opportunity on Pinterest as well.

Content Marketing and Posting Rhythm

Content is king, queen, and jack. Now that you've set up your Pinterest Profile and/or Page, you need to think about posting (or rather pinning). Turn back to your Content Marketing plan, and remember you'll need both other people's content and your own content to pin:

- **Photographs and Images**. Pinterest is very visual. You'll need to systematically identify photographs and images that fit with your personal brand message, and ideally encourage likes, comments, and re-pins (re-shares).
- **Blog Post and Content Summaries**. When you have an active blog and are posting items that fit with the common uses of Pinterest, pin your blog posts to Pinterest.
  - Note that the first or "featured" image will become the shareable image. Choose striking, fun images for your pins, even if what you are pinning is just a blog post!
- **Quotes**. People love quotes, so taking memorable quotes and pasting them on graphics is a win/win.
- **Infographics and Instructographics**. Factoids, how to articles (especially ones that are fun, do-it-yourself articles, lists or collections of tips or products, are excellent for Pinterest. Anything that helps a person organize ideas about products or services to buy or make will work well on Pinterest.
- **Quizzes, Surveys, and Response-provoking posts**. Ask a question, and get an answer or more. This is great for encouraging interactivity. Use a board to actively ask for collaboration; a board on do-it-yourself dog toys is a natural way to ask your fans to participate. Also it will help you, if you want a job as a veterinarian or a veterinary technician. *In other words, brainstorm boards with quizzes, surveys, and responses that show a passion for the industry you want a job in.*
- **Items to Buy**. You can (and should) pin items to buy on your Pinterest boards. Unlike most other social media users, Pinterest users are "in" the shopping mode in many ways, so pinning cool items that can be bought is not just expected but encouraged. This is an excellent strategy if you want a job in retail or marketing!

Clearly, Pinterest will help you shamelessly promote, link to, and sell your stuff! In this sense, it is unique when compared with other social media in that it is clearly and unambiguously pro-shopping. In conclusion, if your target audience is in retail, do-it-yourself, or skews female, Pinterest can be an important addition to your online personal branding strategy. Anything visual is also a great fit for the network.

Remember, the 80/20 rule in terms of your posting (or pinning) rhythm: 80% fun stuff, and 20% stuff that promotes your job search or career-building needs. *Don't bore your audience!*

Pinterest Pitfalls

The main **pitfall** of Pinterest is when you do not realize that every pin or board you make is by default "public" and accessible to anyone. Unless you set up a fully private account, that stupid picture of you embarrassing yourself at last year's corporate New Year's Party – *yep, a potential employer can see it*. That strange addiction you have to Pez Candy collectibles, and your hundreds of pins and dedicated boards on that topic... *yep, a potential employer can see that, too*. Whatever your interests are and why you Pin, remember that they can be viewed by anyone on Pinterest. (Fortunately, Pinterest is the least crazy of the social media; there's not nearly as much insane stuff on Pinterest as on Instagram, for example).

Pinterest Opportunities

For those seeking jobs or careers in visually oriented areas such as photography, web design, user interface design, architecture, any type of art, etc., Pinterest is a great opportunity to have an easy place to showcase your passion and your portfolio.

> *The first Pinterest opportunity is as a "trust indicator." Create a vibrant, active, and engaging account and/or boards on Pinterest as "proof" of your talent.*

In addition, because Pinterest is truly open, you can gain new followers (not just friends and friends of friends but also people out of the blue). New people can find you, get excited about you, perhaps become your real friends, and probably clue you in to job or career opportunities.

Since Pinterest is open like Twitter, you can use it to grow your social reach by participating in the Pinterest community via "hashtags".

In a fashion similar to Twitter, you should:

- Identify **#hashtags** that matter to you and your career, and post to them. So, the *#timelytopic strategy* of using hashtags works both on Twitter and Pinterest. To find hashtags on Pinterest, search by keywords and write new hashtags down as you discover them. Upload photos or videos, use the appropriate hashtag and chime in on a discussion.
- Build a **portfolio of interesting photos or videos** on your stream, so that followers can see how cool you are ("content marketing").
- **Pin and/or Comment** to reach out to people "more famous than you." People are notified when you pin and/or comment on their pins or boards, so this is a way to "get some attention."
- **Post 80% fun stuff, and 20% shameless self-promotional stuff** (realistically, at least indicate you're open to job offers in some of your posts). In other words, use *content marketing* to promote yourself on Pinterest.
- **Like, comment, and re-pin the pins and boards of others.** People pay attention to those who follow them or their boards, so by following a person and being interactive with their boards, you can build a relationship, grow your network, and expand the reach of your job search and career contacts.

Pinterest Deliverable: A Pinterest Job Search & Career-building Plan

Your Pinterest **DELIVERABLE** has arrived. Go to https://www.jm-seo.org/workbooks (click on Job Search and Career Building, enter the code 'careers2016' to register if you have not already done so), and click on the link to the "Pinterest Worksheet." By filling it out, you'll determine if Pinterest is for you, and if so, how to optimize Pinterest to promote your career.

▶ PARTY ON: GOOGLE+, TUMBLR, SNAPCHAT, AMAZON, AND NEW KIDS ON THE BLOCK

While Blogging, LinkedIn, Facebook, and Twitter are the "big four" and a few other networks such as Instagram, YouTube, and Pinterest are the 2nd tier, there are other social media "parties" that might have a specific value for you. None rise to the level of the "big four," but if your target job or career goals match who's on the network and your content matches as well, they might be great for you. Your career isn't about what everyone else is doing, it's about what works for you.

Basic Strategies

Let's take a whirlwind tour of some other opportunities. For all potential social media networks, remember:

- **Don't do any damage**. It's better to not participate at all than to participate and do damage to your career. If you're already using a network, make sure to inventory what you've posted to date and delete any potentially damaging posts. Going forward, participate in an appropriate manner. Do a "privacy checkup" as well.
- **Research your target audience**. Is your industry, and especially the key employers and decision-makers using the social network? If so, that's a huge plus. If not, why bother?
- **Research Examples to Emulate**. Search each network and use the Google *site:* command (as in *site:tumblr.com technical writers*) to identify companies on the network, as well as persons with strong brands that you want to imitate. "Imitation is the highest form of flattery," and it's also the easiest way to conceptualize what you should be doing.
- **Brainstorm your content**. Different sorts of content work on different networks. What type of content "fits" the network, and can you produce it on a regular basis?
- Remember the two key **strategies**:
    - ○ **Trust indicators**: participate on a network if for no other reason than to look savvy and experienced.
    - ○ **Social spread**: participate to get friends / contacts to share with their friends / contacts.
- **Measure your results.** Try a network out. If it helps your career in a measurable way, keep doing it. If it doesn't, stop. There's no shame in experimenting and then terminating.

Google+: Google's Baby

Google+ started out with much fanfare, but has pretty much died at this point. To sign up, go to https://plus.google.com/. The easiest way to use Google+ is to connect a Gmail account (https://www.gmail.com/) to Google+. Outside of very techie, nerd communities like computer science, it is not used very much. The big bonus is that by using Google+, those people who follow you will see email alerts from Google about your latest posts, and you can influence what they see in Google searches if they are signed in to their Google+ account and you post something on that keyword / topic.

Photo-sharing and Google+ collections (which function like Pinterest) are probably the most successful features, and you need a Google+ account to comment on YouTube. For the official help files, visit http://jmlinks.com/12e.

Tumblr: Social Blogging

Tumblr, now owned by Yahoo, has a passionate following among bloggers and those who like a funny take on the world we inhabit. To get started, visit https://www.tumblr.com/. Tumblr is a blog platform in its own right, and could be used as an alternative to either WordPress or Blogger. To visit the help files, go to http://jmlinks.com/12f. What makes Tumblr unique is that it combines blogging with an easy-to-use "follow" system a la social media.

Snapchat

Snapchat (https://www.snapchat.com/) is accessible only via the phone. It rose to fame on the idea that "chats" could be instantly deleted, thereby solving the problem of an unwelcome digital footprint, until it didn't. With the new "stories" feature, Snapchat now does allow a digital footprint, and is used by big brands for their most passionate followers. You can access the Snapchat help files and FAQ's at http://jmlinks.com/12g.

Snapchat is having strong success with big consumer brands as well as (believe it or not) with politicians; those who have devoted fans that want to follow them in a pseudo-exclusive way. Whether it has much job or career-related value remains to be seen.

Amazon

Most people do not think of Amazon (http://www.amazon.com) as a social network, nor do they think of it as a way to promote a personal brand, but they're quite wrong. Here are a two incredible opportunities available on Amazon:

- **Read books, write reviews**. Most of us position ourselves as a "helpful expert" in a particular domain, and in most domains, there are books on the subject.

Read books in your topic area, and write thoughtful reviews on Amazon. These can be co-shared on your blog and other social networks (thus substantiating you as an intellectual), and many people actually read the reviews on Amazon. Just mention in your review that you have a blog and to Google you to find it, and set up your Amazon profile to make it easy to find you. Be thoughtful, not shameless, be positive, not negative, and you may find that writing reviews on Amazon can be a huge assist to your personal brand image online.

- **Write books**. Through both CreateSpace (http://www.createspace.com) for print books and KDP (https://kdp.amazon.com/) for Kindle (digital) books, Amazon has made it incredibly easy to self-publish a book. There is no better way to be an expert than to publish a non-fiction book on a relevant topic.

Writing a book is not something to be undertaken lightly (*believe you me!*), but if you are experienced in your career, sharing your own experience and knowledge will prove not only a good boost to your career prospects, but also a worthwhile effort in its own right. There is no better way to become a real expert on a topic, than to teach it or write a book about it! In addition to books, Amazon allows you to self-publish audible audio books or blogs as well as sell products online.

New Kids on the Block

The Internet changes rapidly, and there will certainly be new ways of brand-building online. (*Podcasting is, for example, one of the latest trending ideas on social media*). They probably won't replace blogging, Facebook, etc., nor even replace some of the 2nd tier social media networks like Instagram or Snapchat. However, stay tuned for new opportunities, and be the first to jump on them. Often, the first to embrace new technologies are the ones who become its most prominent masters!

»» DELIVERABLE: AN 'OTHER NETWORKS' JOB SEARCH AND CAREER BUILDING PLAN

Now that we've come to the end our chapter on other social media networks, your **DELIVERABLE** has arrived. Download the **'Other Networks' Job Search and Career-building Marketing Worksheet**. Go to https://www.jm-seo.org/workbooks (click on Job Search and Career-building, enter the code 'careers2016' to register if you have not already done so), and click on the link to the "Other Networks Job Search and Career-building Marketing" worksheet.

This worksheet will help you identify relevant social media networks, and once identified, help you conceptualize how to use them for your personal brand image online.

≫ APPENDIX: TOP OTHER NETWORK JOB SEARCH AND CAREER-BUILDING TOOLS AND RESOURCES

Here are the top tools and resources to help you with the other social media networks discussed in this Chapter. For an up-to-date and complete list, go to https://www.jm-seo.org/workbooks (click on Job Search and Career-building, enter the code 'careers2016' to register if you have not already done so). Then click on the *Job Search and Career-building Resource Book* link, and drill down to the Other Networks chapter.

AMAZON

CREATESPACE BY AMAZON - https://www.createspace.com/

CreateSpace, owned by Amazon, allows you to self-publish a book to both paperback and Kindle formats.

Rating: 5 Stars | **Category:** service

KDP ON AMAZON (KINDLE DIRECT PUBLISHING) - https://kdp.amazon.com/

One of the very best 'validations' that you are a 'helpful expert' is to publish a book. Amazon's Kindle platform makes this easier than ever. You can easily self-publish a book on Amazon. Here's where you get started.

Rating: 5 Stars | **Category:** service

INSTAGRAM

INSTAGRAM FOR BUSINESS - https://business.instagram.com

Hey you're a business! Here's how to get on Instagram as a business, and use it to your advantage.

Rating: 4 Stars | **Category:** resource

INSTAGRAM MARKETING GUIDE - http://socialmediaexaminer.com/instagram-marketing-guide

This guide from Social Media Examiner isn't (just) for Instagram newbies, as it includes links to SME articles on topics like integrating video and running contests. There's something for just about everyone here, from the marketing strategist to the social media practitioner. Check it and see.

Rating: 4 Stars | **Category:** resource

SNAPWIDGET - http://snapwidget.com

Use this widget to quickly and easily embed an Instagram photos on your website or blog.

Rating: 4 Stars | **Category:** tool

LATERGRAMME - https://www.latergram.me/

Hootsuite for Instagram: schedule posts into the future. In this way, you can make your Instagram account "look" like it's always active, but you can manage it on a scheduled basis. Go to the beach or go shopping.

Rating: 3 Stars | **Category:** service

POSTRIS - http://postris.com/

An advanced, web-based Instagram dashboard for tracking and organizing your Instagram account and daily updates from leading publications and social networks. Helps users keep up with what is trending on Instagram

Rating: 3 Stars | **Category:** tool

PINTEREST HELP TOPICS - https://help.pinterest.com/en/articles

Browse topic by topic through the Pinterest help pages. For example, learn the basics of what pins are and how to use them. Great for beginners.

Rating: 3 Stars | **Category:** resource

PINTEREST HELP CENTER - https://help.pinterest.com/en

Need help? Well, guess what, Pinterest has a robust help section, mainly for users but useful for you as a business marketer. You gotta know how they use it, to use it to market to them!

Rating: 3 Stars | **Category:** resource

PIN SEARCH - https://chrome.google.com/webstore/detail/pin-search-image-search-o/okiaciimfpgbpdhnfdllhdkicpmdoakm

An extension for Chrome browser that allows users to easily find related photos and information for photos posted on Pinterest.

Rating: 2 Stars | **Category:** service

CANVA - https://canva.com

This free image editing tool is optimized for Pinterest so all of your pins and boards look sleek. Also has an iPad app.

Rating: 3 Stars | **Category:** tool

PINTEREST GOODIES - https://about.pinterest.com/en/browser-button

Made more for the end user than the business user, this is a resource by Pinterest about Pinterest. For example, both the iOS and Android apps are available here. Don't miss the 'Pin It' button which makes it easy to pin content from your browser, as well as widgets for your website to encourage Pinterest.

Rating: 4 Stars | **Category:** tool

SNAPCHAT

SNAPCHAT - https://www.snapchat.com/

Snapchat is the new new thing, especially among the teenage set. It may or may not help you with your personal brand image online.

Rating: 5 Stars | **Category:** service

SNAPCHAT HELP CENTER - https://support.snapchat.com/en-US/

Yes, it exists! Despite what the teen set would have you to know, you can learn how to use Snapchat. Here are the 'secret' help files.

Rating: 4 Stars | **Category:** service

TUMBLR

TUMBLR - https://www.tumblr.com/

Look up in the sky! It's a blog, it's a social network, it's a subsidiary of Yahoo! Tumblr is all of the above, and especially if you're 'artsy,' it can be an excellent place for your blog content to live.

Rating: 5 Stars | **Category:** service

TUMBLR HELP - https://www.tumblr.com/help

Here are the help files on how to use Tumblr. Did you know you can have a primary and a secondary blog?

Rating: 4 Stars | **Category:** service

Tumblr Tutorials - http://unwrapping.tumblr.com/

Yes, of course, there's a Tumblr blog that collects tutorials on how to use Tumblr.

Rating: 4 Stars | **Category:** tutorial

YouTube

YouTube Tools - http://bitly.com/ytcreatecorner

YouTube has done more and more to make it easier to publish and promote videos. This page lists six tools: YouTube Capture, YouTube Editor, Captions, Audio Library, Slideshow and YouTube Analytics. All of them are fantastic, free tools about YouTube by YouTube.

Rating: 5 Stars | **Category:** resource

YouTube Creator Hub - http://youtube.com/yt/creators

Help center for those creating YouTube content. Learn how to better edit your videos, get them up on YouTube, etc. Has lessons on growing your audience, boot camp, and how to get viewers and even how to earn money via YouTube.

Rating: 5 Stars | **Category:** resource

iMovie for Mac - https://apple.com/mac/imovie

Apple's free, downloadable movie / video editor. Great for making YouTube videos!

Rating: 4 Stars | **Category:** tool

YOUTUBE CAPTURE - https://youtube.com/capture

YouTube Capture is an app for your mobile phone, which makes it easy to capture and edit videos right on your phone. Imagine you are a marketer / retailer and you want to use your phone to easily capture customer interactions, and upload (quickly / easily) to YouTube. Get the picture?

Rating: 4 Stars | **Category:** tool

WINDOWS MOVIE MAKER - http://bitly.com/windowsmov

For those on the Windows platform, Movie Maker is the goto free program to edit videos for YouTube and other platforms.

Rating: 3 Stars | **Category:** tool

WIDEO - http://wideo.co

An online video maker, similar to iMovie or Windows Movie Maker.

Rating: 3 Stars | **Category:** tool

YOUTUBE EDITOR - https://www.youtube.com/editor

While there is Microsoft Windows Movie Maker and Apple iMovie, there is also a free YouTube editor for your videos. Not incredibly powerful, but free and easy to use 'in the cloud.'

Rating: 3 Stars | **Category:** tool

11

YOUR PLAN

We've come to the end of our job search and career-building journey. Or at least, the end of our exploration together. Now, it's time for you to go "do it." It's not enough just to read this book, and to think about having a powerful online brand image. The *Real You* has to work to create the *Internet You* that can help you achieve your dream job or career in the *Real World*.

In this Chapter, let's review what we've learned at the "big picture" level, and outline a step-by-step plan of attack. We'll start by remembering the "real world" and the importance of your dreams and aspirations. We'll summarize the technical mechanics that this book has brought to your goal of projecting a powerful brand image online. We'll send you on your way by pointing you to the companion online materials of the *Dashboard* and *Resource Book*. We'll conclude by reminding you to reach out by email or even phone with questions, comments, and feedback.

Let's get started!

To Do List:

» Figure Out What Color the Internet is to You

» Remember the Big Picture

» Never Stop Learning

» FIGURE OUT WHAT COLOR THE INTERNET IS TO YOU

The classic book for job search and career building is undoubtedly *What Color is Your Parachute* by Richard N. Bolles. It's a book born of the 1960s and 1970s with a heavy emphasis on "Doing what you love" and a rather light emphasis on "Doing what's in demand." *What Color is Your Parachute?* was first published in 1970, when Bolles was forty-three. It was an era of incredible optimism even amidst great trauma: the end of the 1960s, the end of the Vietnam war, the beginning of a new era of Civil Rights and Women's Rights. That 1960s generation was what economist John Kenneth Galbraith called children of the "Affluent Society" in his book of 1958.

This book recommends that you buy at least one job or career book that is "inspirational" in nature such as *What Color is Your Parachute*, but this book is not in any way, shape or form associated with or endorsed by *What Color is Your Parachute* or any other book on careers or jobs. Dreamy-eyed books on doing what you love have their place; life is, after all, about more than money. However, as someone born in 1963, and a proud member of the embattled "X" generation, my perspective on the earlier generation of job and career book writers is that they were very fortunate to be born in a much kinder, easier American economy and society than the one I grew of age in.

My generation and those born after me, certainly did not confront the Vietnam War, nor the racism of America in 1960. But our economy has been neither kind nor gentle. I count myself among the fortunate. I graduated from Harvard in 1985, worked at a very difficult but rewarding job in the legal profession for a year, and went on to graduate school at U.C. Berkeley. While there, the US economy went into the most severe recession since the great Depression in 1992 (followed of course by the Great Recession of 2008). This caused me to abandon my dream of becoming a professor, and instead to seek work in the exciting world of Silicon Valley. It wasn't easy to make the transition, and I've experienced two formal company bankruptcies and one total meltdown in my professional life.

The times they were a changin' (Bob Dylan), and not in a good way.

My generation, and certainly those born after 1963, have experienced a much harsher, more difficult economic world. Dreams have their place, but I hope that this book helps those less fortunate than I, to make their career path easier in this harsher, more difficult economy, in which parachutes are more needed than ever and yet less likely to be found.

The color of our parachute has seemed less important, at times, than the color of our paycheck, if we have been lucky enough to have one.

I am not, however, a cynic. My hope for you, dear reader, has been to try to help you to split the baby, between the unrealistic optimism of *What Color is Your Parachute* and the total cynicism of Michael Douglass in the 1987 classic film *Wall Street*. "Greed," said Mr. Gekko, "is good." Greed may not be good, but your job search and career-building strategy needs to have at least one eye on the demands of the marketplace.

Your **TODO** here is to figure out what color the Internet is to you. Meaning, where on the continuum between complete optimism of "doing what you love" and complete cynicism of "doing what the market wants" is your comfort zone? The reality of projecting an *Internet You* is that, to some extent, it is an idealized You and like Cher or Lady Gaga, only you can decide the boundary, where the "real" you and the "Internet You" become separated, if at all.

As you finish this book and begin to make a plan, take a walk, sit down with a cup of tea or coffee, contemplate the world from your backyard or a park bench, and define your career goals at the boundary between *what your heart wants* and *what the world wants*. Do this before you dive into the technical details. Buy a copy of *What Color is Your Parachute*, and read it as an excellent way to address the question of what your heart wants. This book (I hope) has helped you to think about what the world wants, and how to make the world want you as an amazing employee.

» REMEMBER THE BIG PICTURE

There are at least four major social media platforms – blogging, LinkedIn, Facebook, and Twitter, many 2nd tier platforms, and a major search engine (Google) that all impact your personal brand image online. Employers, hiring managers, and recruiters, not only might find out about you online, but might also research you before, during, and after a hiring decision. The Big Picture is to project an Internet You that is in harmony with the Real You but also substantiates you as a "helpful expert."

After defining your **Personal Branding Statement** or PBS, identify your target audiences of employers, hiring managers, and/or recruiters. What do you "have," that they "want?" Look for connection points between your skills and desires and the skills required by the marketplace. These become your **keyword themes** to be hit on in your blog, your online resume postings, your social media posts, etc. Next, brainstorm the five **discovery paths** used by potential employers of search, review / recommend / trust, eWOM / share / viral, interrupt, and browse. Place your content, showcasing your personal brand image, in the most likely discovery paths being used by employers.

Turning to **content marketing**, create a machine for identifying other people's content, which you can share, to keep yourself top of mind and for creating your own content such as blog posts, images or photos, and videos that can showcase you as a "helpful expert." Use tools such as Feedly and Hootsuite to streamline this process, remembering that you are "throwing a party" and like any good party, it will have an element of illusion. Successful personal brands online make it "look easy" even if it is not.

Drill down to each **Internet opportunity** from SEO / search ("get to the top of Google") with your blog to the big four of Blogging, LinkedIn, Facebook, and Twitter to the 2nd tier networks. Identify the best opportunities for you and populate them with your content. **Promote your content** by reaching out to friends, colleagues, and friends of friends as well as via tactics such as SEO and trend-watching, to become as visible as possible. Consider advertising if necessary.

Don't forget the **Real World**. Ask everyone you know to connect with you on social media, and use the real world to promote the social media world and vice-versa. Don't forget email marketing, the "Rodney Dangerfield" of social media: use emails to reach out to friends, family, and colleagues in a polite manner, and use email to promote your social media efforts and then use your social media efforts to promote your email system.

Finally, measure your results. What promotes your online brand image? What detracts from it? Grow what works, and kill what doesn't.

▶▶ DELIVERABLE: A JOB SEARCH AND CAREER-BUILDING INTERNET PLAN

Your chapter **DELIVERABLE** has arrived. Go to https://www.jm-seo.org/workbooks (click on Job Search and Career-building, enter the code 'careers2016' to register if you have not already done so), and click on the link to the "Job Search and Career-building Big Picture" worksheet. This is your "Big Picture Plan" to be used in conjunction with the medium-by-medium plans outlined in the other Chapters.

▶ NEVER STOP LEARNING

As a passionate instructor, I learn as much from my students as I hope to give to them. I am "always learning," and I look to my readers and students to bring me questions, comments, and suggestions. Please email me at j.mcdonald@jm-seo.net or, if you're brave, give me a call at 800-298-4065. I hope to learn as much from you as hopefully, you will have learned from me.

Remember to write an honest review of this book on Amazon and receive one of my other books at no cost. Just contact me after you've posted your review online for details.

Never Stop Learning

Turn to the resources in the Appendix, utilizing the *Dashboard* and *Resource Book* to help you leverage the awesome power of the Internet. Spend some quality time perusing the amazing wealth of information available at the click of a mouse.

Good luck!

12
APPENDIX

Register your copy of this Workbook to receive access to the *Job Search and Career-building Dashboard* and complete *Resource Book*. I've worked hard to identify the best online resources to help you build your personal brand image online. (If you know of others, please send me an email at j.mcdonald@jm-seo.net!)

To access these supplementary materials, go to https://www.jm-seo.org/workbooks (click on Job Search and Career-building, enter the code 'careers2016' to register if you have not already done so). You'll see them clearly marked on the landing page.

Any questions? Don't hesitate to contact me.

CPSIA information can be obtained
at www.ICGtesting.com
Printed in the USA
LVOW03s0043160117
521004LV00017B/294/P

9 781533 265142